Each Breath a Gift:

A Story of Continuing Recovery

Thomas B.

Each Breath a gift: A Story of Continuing Recovery

Copyright © 2017 Thomas B.

All rights reserved. No part of this book may be used or reproduced by any means, graphic, electronic, or mechanical, including photocopying, recording, taping or by any information storage retrieval system without the written permission of the publisher except in the case of brief quotations embodied in critical articles and reviews.

Library and Archives Canada Cataloguing in Publication

B., Thomas, 1943-, author
  Each breath a gift: a story of continuing recovery / Thomas B.

Issued in print and electronic formats.
ISBN 978-0-9940162-7-0 (softcover).--ISBN 978-0-9940162-8-7 (ebook)

  1. B., Thomas, 1943-. 2. Recovering alcoholics--United States--Biography. 3. Recovering addicts--United States--Biography. 4. Alcoholics--United States--Biography. 5. Alcoholics Anonymous. 6. Twelve-step programs. 7. Alcoholics--Rehabilitation.

HV5293.B765A3 2017 362.292092 C2017-902173-7
                        C2017-902174-5

Published in Canada by AA Agnostica
Cover design by Rebecca Henigin
Interior layout and eBook version formatted by Chris G

Table of Contents

Foreword...1
Acknowledgements..3
Dedication..4
Introduction...5
Part One...13

   Chapter 1: Where I Come From..15

      Coiled Snake..16
      Sister Babs is Born..16
      Shanty Shacks...16
      Broken Collar Bone..17
      Lanced Ear...17
      Mother's Family Background...19
      Dad's Family Background..22

   Chapter 2 – Growing Up and High School...................................25

      Grandmother's House...33
      First Drinking Experiences and High School..........................35
      The Barbara Story..41

   Chapter 3—Xavier University..47

      The Masque Society and Roseanne..53
      The Story of Ruth...58
          there was this hill..59
          strollin'..61

   Chapter 4: Marriage to Kathy and Going to Vietnam...................65

      Active Duty in the US Army...66
      Kathy, My First Wife To Be..68
      Going to Vietnam..71

   Chapter 5—629th Supply & Service Company (Repair Parts)....75

      Daily Life In Vietnam...76
          Some Looks..77
          chief nurse..78

      Deranged Trooper...80
      Ammo Dump...81
      Almost Dying Getting Laid..82
      Trip to Phu Bai...83
      Dead MP..84

Lost Thai Sticks..85
Busted...86
Another Alert..87

Chapter 6—Gun Jeep..89
valentine's day, 1968..*90*
Christmas Eve and the Bob Hope Show................................91
Bob Hope Show, 1983...*93*
The An Nhon Orphanage and R & R......................................94
a love lament for Jackie Larn from January, 1968................*95*
Saigon French Meal..96
The Tet Offensive..100
stark memory...*103*
Coming Home..103

Chapter 7—Becoming A Civilian Again....................................107
I move in high circles...*110*
moontalk 1969...*112*
Debbie, My Second Wife To Be...116
Protests Against Vietnam...117
Institute of Modern Languages..120

Chapter 8: Marrying Debbie and Finally Becoming a New Yorker........123
Marriage and Honeymoon..124

Part Two...129

Chapter 9: First AA Meetings..131
First Identification and Meeting List....................................133
When I Decided To Stay Sober..134
My First Good Day Sober..136

Chapter 10: First Year Sober—Getting Involved in the AA Fellowship. 139
It's The Stories, Sweetheart..141
It's Never Too Late...142
You Can't Take Sobriety for Granted...................................142
compassion..*144*
Identification Is The Key...147
Neg-Fans..152
First Anniversary...153
The Power of Negative Thinking..155

Chapter 11: Unity and First Meditation Experience...................157

nightlight..*160*
Rock Roots..160
   Growing Light..*162*

Chapter 12: First and Only Sponsor, Peter 165
   More A Friend Than A Sponsor...167
   His Last Ten Years..168

Part Three..171

Chapter 13: The "R" Word – Relationships..173
   13th Stepping..173
   Gloria..177
      gloria...*178*
   Barbara...180
      afterglow..*180*
   Aneen..181
      connection..*182*
   Another Nancy...183
      sensations...*183*
   The Two Most Significant Relationships.......................................186

Chapter 14: Third Marriage – Sara...189
      Commitment..*191*
   The Albany Years..193
   Slumming in Gaardan Cityae...195
   Early Years in Islip...196
   It Was the Best of Times, It Was the Worse of Times................198
   The Beginning of the Long End..201
      Knick-Knacks..*204*
   Making the Best of a Bad Situation..205
      Hormones..*205*
   The Calm before the Final Perfect Storm....................................207
      voyeur..*208*
      Intrusive Recollection...*209*
      One Cluster of Precious Moments...*212*

Chapter 15: Relationships Redux..215
   Jane...215
      Hello GI..*215*
      burnings..*222*

    Bonnie..223
    Lynn..224
        Blond hair, Blond eyebrows, Blond eyelashes......................225

    Michele...227

Chapter 16: Jill, My Fourth and Final Wife............................229

    4th Marriage...231
    The Second Long Drive-About..232
    Our First Major Move..233
        For Jill at Christmastime, 2012..236

    Another Move Occurs...238
    Struggles with a Happy Ending...238
    One Final Move..242

Chapter 17: Sober Work...245

    The Theatre..245
    A career in Addiction Treatment...247
    September 11, 2001..262
        Sirens..266

Chapter 18: Activism for Peace with Justice............................269

        25th Anniversary..269

    Serving as an Unarmed Peacemaker in Sri Lanka................271
        entrenching tool...272
        The Bone..276
        Pleiku Jacket..279

    Veterans Stand for Standing Rock......................................280

Chapter 19: Challenges to Recovery..281

    Muggings..281
    Resentment and Rage...282
    Deaths...285
        Death Quartet...286
        Neirbo...288

Chapter 20: AA Service Work..293

Chapter 21: Deep Explorations of the Psyche..........................303

    The First Holotropic Breathing Experience.........................303
    The Second Holotropic Breathing Experience....................306
    The Third Holotropic Breathing Experience........................309
    Ayahuasca..311

Chapter 22: Why I am Mostly an Agnostic Nontheist—But Very Spiritual

313
  ee cummings..314
  Pierre Teilhard De Chardin...315
  Eric Butterworth..315
  Matthew Fox..316
  Thomas Merton..317
  Dan Berrigan..318
  Aldous Huxley & Ken Wilber..319
  Frank Schaeffer..319
  Buddhism and Hinduism..320
  Native American Spirituality..321
  Secular AA Literature..322
Conclusion..327

Foreword

Joe C, songwriter, broadcaster and author of
Beyond Belief: Agnostic Musings for 12 Step Life

Storytelling, vulnerable and sincere storytelling, unites us. More than just an ageless form of teaching and entertaining, storytelling is healing and nurturing for both the teller and the audience. Books, songs, movies, podcasts, chat-rooms, YouTube videos and meetings are places where gifts given are also gifts received. Each Breath is such a gift. Thomas may be new to authorship but he's a master storyteller.

To honor storytelling, let's borrow from a storytelling team—known as miners of story-gold to those who value storytelling—Katherine Ketcham and Ernie Kurtz, who gave us *The Spirituality of Imperfection* (1992) and *Experiencing Spirituality* (2014). *Experiencing Spirituality* reminds us,

> *The process of storytelling conveys certain experiences, even if these experiences are not talked about directly. These experiences, in fact, cannot be transmitted directly, by talking about them, but rather are conveyed only by means of "story," which invites identification. ... Bare words fail because the primary responsibility of words is to convey ideas. Words tell. Conveying experience requires more ... genuine sharing involves not merely communication but a kind of communion.*[1]

How to commune with Each Breath? It's written chronologically and it can be enjoyed that way. Or, you can treat it like a collection of stories. Let's say you want to understand the author's biases; you could start at Chapter One and explore an army-brat's beginning, born into the drama of World War II. Keep reading about formative southern gothic Mississippi family pride, sacrifice and dysfunction. On the other hand, you could fast-forward to authors and thinkers who impacted Thomas in Chapter 22. Learn about Holotropic Breathing Experiences (Chapter 21) and ponder if that's where the book title came from. Or, jump into the action: active duty in the Vietnam War starts in Chapter 4 on route to 629th S & S Company; the first drink in high school is in Chapter 2; open to Chapter 9 and share Thomas' first AA meeting experience on West 86th in New York City. If "Almost Dying Getting Laid" is too intriguing to pass by, start with Chapter 5. This is a gift that Thomas shares from his experience. Over hours, we get to explore years of the life of Thomas. We go from war abroad to domestic activism, romance and divorce, peacekeeping in Sri Lanka, 1970s AA recovery and 21st century service work that aided the first international gathering for agnostics, atheists and freethinkers in Alcoholics Anonymous in Santa Monica (2014).

Each Breath is mixed mediums. Stories of life are mixed with a lifetime of poetry. This book might only be possible in this era of publishing on demand. I referred to Thomas as a novice author but a seasoned storyteller and poet. Did you know that there are 85 new books being published every hour in America? I learned this from Forbes Magazine. That's hundreds of thousands of new titles every year. In total, planet Earth is home to 130,000,000 book titles. Old-school publishers are complaining about the expansion of titles; readers are not. Maybe a New York City acquisition editor of yesteryear wouldn't or couldn't take a chance on a rookie author but publishing houses aren't the gate-keepers and tastemakers that they once were. Storytellers control more of our destiny and we the readers decide what's compelling.

Thomas is not the hero of his autobiography; he's celebrating the people, places, awe and terror that life has gifted him. Each Breath is unabashed and authentic. Thomas lived in interesting times—be that a curse or a blessing. I am so pleased that these gripping stories are now recorded and preserved. Over the years, I have come to know Thomas. This book leaves me loving him more.

Maybe, as you're reading, you'll say to yourself, "I could do this; I should write my story." Maybe you're right and I know Thomas would laugh with pleasure that he had a small role in inspiring your dream. That's the thing with storytelling; you'll draw something out of this book and maybe, this book will draw something out of you.

Now, let the adventure of Each Breath begin…

---

[1] Ernest Kurtz, Ketcham, Katherine, *Experiencing Spirituality: Finding Meaning Through Storytelling* (New York: Random House, 2014) pp 30-21

Acknowledgements

I am most grateful to Roger C. and Chris G. for their encouragement and consistent support throughout the process of writing this memoir. Roger, I am especially grateful for the seminal work you've done since 2011 to foster the growth and evolution of the Secular AA movement. Chris, your magical manipulations of digital publishing software never cease to amaze me – they are well above my meager pay grade.

As well, I am especially grateful to Joe C., renown author and podcaster throughout the evolving secular AA community, who wrote the kind and most informative Foreword.

To my adult children, Rebecca, whose exemplary graphic skills designed the cover, second daughter Jennifer, and son Thomas, thank you for making me a most proud and contented parent.

Lastly, to Jill, my fourth (and final) wife, thank you for teaching me daily how better to live, to love, to serve.

Dedication

To anyone, anywhere who has a desire to get sober and who reaches out to AA for help, regardless of their belief or lack of belief.

Introduction

"What a long, strange trip it's been!"

The Grateful Dead, 1970

My version of this iconic lyric from some of the most memorable troubadours of my-my-my generation, Jerry Garcia and the Grateful Dead, is as follows: "What a long, strange trip it continues to be !~!~!"

Near the end of my 74th circuit around the sun, I've lived a considerably longer and a much more fantastically rewarding life than ever I could have possibly imagined, when I was an uptight, alienated, self-conscious, anxiety-ridden callow youth, ravaged by addiction to alcohol and other drugs, during the turbulent decade of my 20s. During this time, I was actively suicidal for at least five years, convinced there was no way that I could ever achieve any kind of satisfying, comfortable, fulfilling life. My distorted view of myself was that I was a loser to the nth degree, that everything I touched turned to shit, and that I was most unloveable. An even more pressing concern was that I was incapable of truly loving any partner, no matter how beautiful, how smart, and how appealing she might be—eventually the blush would fade from her rose, and I would become bored with her and our life together.

I am ever so grateful that contrary to my misguided fears, I have not only survived to live a long and most gratifying life, but in many ways I have also thrived to live a life beyond my wildest dreams and imagination, as is often touted around 12-step recovery rooms. The most consistent state of being I experience during these satisfying days of the final years of my long life is that I am so grateful my obsession to die young by living hard, fast and furious, so that I would look good in the coffin, did not come to be. I am perennially grateful, even when I have to "fake it until I make it," yes, even today sometimes through gritted teeth. These days I choose to *be* grateful, even when I don't feel it or believe it.

The deepest fear I had during senior year of high school was that my life would be boring. Hopefully, this book will demonstrate that my life has been anything but boring.

As a result of recovery, I've traveled extensively, both internationally, living and vacationing in Vietnam, France, the Caribbean, Thailand, England, Sri Lanka and Mexico, as well as visiting all 50 of the United

States. I've resided in eleven states, living in cosmopolitan cities, tiny farm towns and most everything in between. I've worked professionally in several captivating careers that include the theatre, Teaching English as a Second Language, publishing, advertising, and addiction treatment. I've pursued a wide variety of different endeavors that include running marathons, protesting for peace with justice, inline skating, advocating for civil rights, writing poetry, fiction and drama, painting and photography. Finally, I have been most fortunate to have loved, and been loved by, many vivacious and captivating women, four of whom I married and with two of whom I parented children, now adults with children of their own.

Most of my life I've been an inveterate journalist, recording the ups and downs, the various vicissitudes, of my often unpredictable and at times haphazard, chaotic life. I started journalling in earnest during the summer of 1966, after flunking out of my first graduate school, a consequence of excessive drinking. It was just before I entered the US Army as a Reserve Officer Training Corps 2nd Lieutenant, commissioned upon graduating from college the year before. Ever since, I've experienced journalling to be a most useful tool to explore some of what my life's journey has been about.

I still have the small 4" X 5" spiral notebook in which I first journaled. I carried it throughout Basic Officer's training and during my first active duty assignment in Vietnam. It's accompanied on a shelf in my office with 26 other handwritten journals of varying sizes and types, along with a stack of extensive 4th Step inventories I wrote out on legal pads. These journals and inventories, both general 4th Step inventories, as well as those dealing specifically with troubling areas I've experienced in recovery—resentments or relationships or jealousies or melancholia or despair or rage or what have you—are most useful to review from time to time.

I've only lost one of these journals, one written between late 2000 and early 2003. This notebook recorded one of the most difficult periods of my recovery. It related the 12-month period when a 22-year relationship painfully came to a crashing end, when my third wife and I sold our faux-Victorian cottage in a picturesque hamlet on the south shore of Long Island and divorced. Afterwards, I took my half of the proceeds from the sale and bought an upscale RV with all the trimmings, traveling alone for six-months throughout the US and Canada with Chutney, a trusted dog companion. For the next six months, I settled in Tucson, AZ to reinvent myself with a new lover. During this two-year period, my father died, I spent the first three weeks after 911 in downtown Manhattan as a Red

Cross Mental Health Volunteer for First Responders, and the new lover dumped me to return to her previous lover.

The journal was stolen out of the front seat of an unlocked car, while I was attending a Tuscon AA meeting. Though minimal compared to the total loss of houses and possessions through natural disasters or fire, the loss of this journal was another grave loss in a long season of devastating losses. I nearly lost another of these handwritten journals, one detailing the following two years of 2003 and 2004.

For most of this time period, I was on an assignment working for peace in Sri Lanka. I was there on December 26, 2004, when the devastating tsunami destroyed much of that country's shoreline. Fortunately, I went on a bike-ride inland to visit a 2,000 year-old temple complex shortly before the gigantic wave struck, destroying the guest house compound where I had been staying during a Christmas holiday. When I returned to see the destroyed building, where I had left my backpack, computer and journal, I was devastated again. However, I found the journal, water-soaked and sand-gritted, laying in a puddle about 30 feet down the driveway of the compound.

In addition to handwritten journals, I have on my computer some 1,500 pages of journals digitally composed, since I became computer-literate in the mid-1990s. These include additional inventories and various musings, including a 164-page—hmmmm, now that's a rather significant number for us recovering alcoholics, isn't it—"Missive to Peter," my sponsor for 33 years who died in August, 2006. In the mystery of the Kosmos, I believe somehow he perceives my musings to him; likewise, I also believe he still conveys to me his deep wisdom.

Further, I have written some 530 poems, three unpublished plays, a passel of short stories and three blogs online. I have also contributed to three other blogs, including some 22 articles written for *AA Agnostica* and *AA Beyond Belief*. In addition for years I was an active participant in the virtual communities founded by digerati Howard Rheingold, Electric Minds and Brainstorms. In these online forums, I've written reams of posts and commentary. Writing is obviously one of the chief means I use for self-examination and self-reflection.

In my experience writing, whether putting pen to paper or fingers to keyboard, has been an essential component of my on-going recovery process, which continues to this very day. Writing prevents me from falling prey to the oft-heard statement around the rooms, "We alcoholics are as sick as we are secret." For me, this includes especially being honest, authentic, and open with myself, delving into my psyche for hidden agendas and spurious rationales. Continuously taking inventory of myself through writing as suggested in AA's Step 10 has from early-on in the recovery process been an essential tool not only for staying sober, but for continuing to lead a productive, satisfying and useful life in recovery.

It strikes me that historically writing has always been one of AA's primary tools for staying sober a day at a time. It's an inferred crucial process of three of AA Twelve Steps, Step 4, Step 8 and Step 10. Certainly Bill Wilson is a primary model for this behavior in sobriety. Not only was he the primary author of AA's seminal literature, but he wrote numerous articles for the Grapevine and carried on extensive correspondence with both AA members and others from around the world. I'm certainly no Bill Wilson, but I am privileged and most grateful that I can emulate his positive example by copiously writing to help me clarify to myself and others how I maintain the gift of sobriety a day at a time. It is one of the primary techniques I use to give away what I have, so that I may continue to experience a daily reprieve.

Getting the often jumbled thoughts, which cascade haphazardly in different directions, organized in some semblance of order, whether on paper or computer screen, helps me sort out the cacophony of sometimes conflicting feelings and misperceptions that I experience even with longterm recovery. When I attempt to communicate what I am thinking, feeling, and experiencing, whether to myself or to others, it helps me to discern or clarify what actions I need to take to gain relief from my sometimes confused state of dis-ease and discord. Writing centers me. It is a primary means of achieving some semblance of balance in my life, at times in contentious disarray, even after years of recovery. It helps keep me grounded, here and now, to accept the things I cannot change, to change the things I can, and to have the wisdom to know the difference. I get not only to experience sobriety, I get to experience evolving serenity, even during times of distress and discord. It just doesn't get any better than this !~!~!

Each Breath A Gift is a natural culmination of my long life of writing poetry and journaling since 1966. My ability to recall and relate details from the various episodes of my now long life has been immeasurably enhanced by having my journals and poetry with which to refer. This book has been in concept for some 20 years. In the mid-90s, I envisioned someday publishing a book of poetry, including a form of prose poems reflecting upon my life that a poet friend of mine on Long Island termed "poemoirs". Then, I conceived the title, "Each Breath A Gift," which would depict incidents from my many adventures and experiences this time around. It has finally come to be.

Essentially, the memoir follows the schema of how we alcohol addicts share our stories at 12-step meetings. It is divided into three parts, the first describing "How It Was" while drinking, the second describing "What Happened" to get into recovery, and the third describing "How It's Been Since" throughout recovery. Interspersed throughout the 22 chapters are excerpts from my journals and a number of my poems, both free verse and prose poems. Another tripartite outline of my life story could be summarized by what I was called. During my youth through high school I was called, "Tommy." At college and throughout much of my middle age, I was known as "Tom." Throughout the latter third of my life, as I've become a senior citizen, my name has been "Thomas," hopefully indicating that I have achieved some modicum of maturity and dignity.

I am one of those alcohol addicts described in "How It Works" who belong to the following cohort of folks: "There are those, too, who suffer from grave emotional and mental disorders . . ." I have been diagnosed and treated for several mental health diagnoses. Besides addiction to alcohol, I have been labeled with Post Traumatic Stress Disorder, Bi-polar I Disorder, Attention Deficit Hyperactivity Disorder and Generalized Anxiety Disorder.

In addition, I recently became aware of the syndrome Developmental Trauma Disorder (DTD). Also, known as Complex PTSD, two psychiatrists instrumental in legitimizing PTSD during the 1980s, Judith Herman, MD and Bessel Van de Kolk, MD, strongly advocated for DTD to be included in DSM V, but it was not included as a separate diagnostic category. Elements of the syndrome, however, were incorporated as part of the revised PTSD diagnosis. They describe DTD as being relational, chronic and includes these clusters of symptoms:

- **Emotional Regulation:** May include persistent sadness, suicidal thoughts, explosive or inhibited anger, extreme fear or anxiety.

- **Consciousness:** Includes forgetting traumatic events, reliving traumatic events, or having episodes in which one feels detached from one's mental processes or body (dissociation).

• **Self-Perception:** May include self-loathing, helplessness, shame, guilt, stigma, and a sense of being completely different from other human beings.

• **Distorted Perceptions of the Perpetrator:** Examples include attributing total power to the perpetrator, becoming preoccupied with the relationship to the perpetrator, or preoccupied with revenge.

• **Relations with Others:** Examples include isolation, distrust, or a repeated search for a rescuer.

• **One's System of Meanings:** May include a loss of sustaining faith or a sense of hopelessness and despair.

Whew !~!~!

When I first read about DTD, I was struck by how it is a most cogent and precise description of what I have often felt and perceived since earliest memories. As my story shall relate, with the dysfunctional, as well as bizarre, family backgrounds of both my parents, and the circumstances of being born in the middle of World War II, it makes sense to me that perhaps I might also have DTD.

Even today, after years of 12-step recovery, lots of therapy, daily meditation and other self-help endeavors, and persistent spiritual pursuits, the above listing of DTD symptoms can still sometimes be experienced just as strongly alive within me as ever they may have been earlier in my life. Sometimes, I've self-deprecatingly quipped that I am "constitutionally incapable of pausing when agitated." Nevertheless, I continue to not use, to go to meetings, and whenever possible help others by doing service work.

During early recovery in the 1970s, long before John Bradshaw and others popularized the Adult Child syndrome, I would sometimes hear stories of alcoholics who had been brutally abused, either physically or sexually, sometimes both, during early childhood. I would deeply identify with how awful their memories were and how they felt, but I had no history of similar abuse that I could recall. After hearing their stories, I would sometimes feel crazier and sink deeper into despair, believing there was no hope for me.

However, in the New York City meetings I attended, I became well-grounded in the essentials of recovery: Don't pick up whether your ass falls off or turns to gold. Go to meetings. Whenever possible, help others. This, in essence, is what I have done throughout continued recovery since

October 14, 1972, when I had the last drink of my primary drug of addiction, Colt .45, preferably by the case lot.

So, here it is, my life's story. It's my story as I recall it. It's not necessarily gospel truth. After all, as Pontius Pilate allegedly queried, "What is truth?" Nevertheless, in truth (pun intended), I've been gifted with two major phases of recovery. The first occurred from 1972 through 2011, when I lived most of my life in or readily accessible to New York City, where I experienced AA meetings as open and inclusive to anyone who had a desire to stop drinking, the only requirement for AA membership per our Third Tradition.

However, when Jill, my fourth wife and I moved to the southern coast of Oregon in 2011, we experienced AA as an Alt-Right Fundamentalist Christian clique. As non-Christians, we were shunned and shamed for being non-believers. We despaired about how radically different this was from the AA with which we were familiar. Thank goodness, we found Roger C.'s *AA Agnostica* website which introduced us to the evolving and wide-ranging world of secular AA. Ever since, we have been most gratified to experience a second honeymoon with secular AA within traditional AA. We have been most privileged to be an instrumental part of our evolving special purpose cohort of AA members.

Another interesting dynamic has been that in writing this memoir, I've discovered the fickleness of memory. One example of this happened when I went back to read journal entries from early recovery during the 1970s. I discovered that I was much more "god-centered" than I recall I had been, especially during the last number of years since I've been so actively involved with the secular AA movement.

Finally, it's my sincere hope that you can relate and identify with some of the strangeness of my life story in recovery as it resonates with the strangeness of your life story in recovery. In any event, I hope you are as grateful for your recovery, as I am for the long, strange, life—sober—I continue to experience a day at a time, because I don't pick up, I go to meetings, and I help others, whenever possible.

In truth, each breath, indeed, continues to be a gift, most precious, most meaningful, most valuable …

Part One

What It Was Like

Chapter 1: Where I Come From

I entered the world this time around on April 24, 1943. My birth certificate notes that I arrived at 3:38 p.m. at the base hospital of the Squantum Naval Air Station, where my Father was an officer, teaching navigation to air cadets. He and Mother had been married in 1941, but initially decided they didn't want children during the difficult times at the end of the Depression, with war clouds gathering in both Europe and the Pacific. Mother was 19 and Dad, eight years her senior at 27.

It was in the middle of the Second World War, and though at the time Dad was safely assigned to stateside duty, he yearned to be transferred to a ship engaged in combat at sea. He wrote numerous letters to his commanding officers, requesting a transfer to combat duty aboard a ship. Mother showed me a stack of these letters after Dad died. She was terrified he might be killed on combat duty, so she pressured Dad to impregnate her. If he were to be killed in action, she would have a child to raise in his honor.

After Dad died, Mother related to me that she had been dating a young high school classmate from a very poor Jackson family, who sold shoes after classes. After they met at a music recital, Dad was utterly smitten by her, and they started dating. When he found out about Mother's other suitor, he confronted him. An imposing 6' 4" tall, he told the young lad in no uncertain terms to butt out, that "Bobbie," his nickname for Mother, was his and his only. Several years after Dad died, Mother exchanged correspondence with her former young beau. He had became a successful doctor in New York City and served as the staff physician for the Metropolitan Opera. I visited him in his apartment overlooking the Hudson River in Croton-on-Hudson in the summer of 2007. He said that he was still madly in love with Mother, that he had been all throughout his life. He asked me to intercede with her on his behalf. It was somewhat strange serving as a matchmaker between him and Mother. By this time, however, both of them were in declining health, so it was impossible for them to renew their relationship. I pondered what a different life I would have had were he to have been my father.

The first three years of my life I lived in college towns, where Dad taught navigation in Naval ROTC programs. From what I recall, we lived in Chapel Hill, NC, Pensacola, FL, St. Louis, MO, and Norman, OK. I have no memories of any of these cities. My earliest memories are from a tiny one-bedroom apartment in a duplex building at the top of Greymont Avenue in Jackson, MS. Here are several vivid memories from the time we lived in the duplex:

Coiled Snake

As a young child, three or four years-old at the most, Dad carried me one night out into the darkened garage. When he pulled the light cord on, there was a snake wrapped around it. Its head with beady eyes and forked tongue were eye level with mine. That's all I remember, just this snapshot of the snake's image.

Sister Babs is Born

I vividly remember as a four year-old being very excited when mother was pregnant, meaning, as she explained, that I would soon be a big brother to a younger brother or sister. Soon, Barbara Marie Brinson—nicknamed Babs, the eldest of my four younger sisters—came home from the hospital. Babs suffered from colic. Since the four of us shared the small single bedroom of the tiny duplex apartment, none of us got much sleep. I have a vague memory, after a week or so, asking Mother if she couldn't please take Babs back to the hospital. I was most disappointed when she brusquely replied, "No!"

Shanty Shacks

Down a steep gully in the woods behind the duplex, there were several shanty shacks. A number of black families lived in the shanties. An elderly black man also lived by himself in one of them. I remember visiting him several times. In his cabin, there were primitive shelves with scant tin-canned goods of hash and black-eyed peas, cereal, grits and such. His room with an attached outhouse had rough-hewn furniture, most well worn, in it.

One strong recollection I have is visiting him one late afternoon. For some unknown reason, I locked him in his shanty from the outside. I still recall his plaintive calls as I casually walked up the path out of the woods at dusk time back to our apartment.

Broken Collar Bone

There was a steep driveway, maybe ten feet long at the most, leading from our garage to Greymont Street. One afternoon, I got the bright idea to ride Babs' stroller down the driveway. I hopped in and down the driveway I went, squealing with delight! However, I had not factored in that we were the first house at the top of a large hill down Greymont Avenue. The stroller took a sharp right turn and sped down the hill, gathering speed. I crashed into the curb, feeling a sharp pain in my right shoulder. I had broken my collarbone.

I recall with clarity how upset Mother was. All dressed up to go to a Junior League function, she yelled at me and at Eva, our maid, about how stupid this was. Instead of going to her Junior League function, she had to take me to the emergency room to have the shoulder reset and my arm tightly wrapped to my side. There was another consequence of this event. A couple of weeks later, Mother and Dad, with Babs as a toddler and me with tightly wrapped arm to body, went to Allison Wells in nearby Canton, MS. Allison Wells was a resort and former art colony founded in 1879. I was most forlorn and disappointed that I could not go swimming in the large, inviting swimming pool. It was, most likely, the first swimming pool that I had seen.

Lanced Ear

As a child I was prone to severe earaches. One time, I remember sitting and thrashing around in the big back seat of the two-tone green Pontiac sedan we then had. Mother was driving me to the office of Dr. Gillespie, the kindly pediatrician we went to. I was screaming and writhing in pain. Mother tried to soothe me, assuring me that I would feel much better after we saw the doctor. Well, he lanced my infected ear to release the buildup of pus, and it was excruciating. I recall screaming all the way home. I don't think I ever fully trusted Mother again.

In 1948, we moved to the "New House" in a then new subdivision out in North Jackson on Hawthorne Drive. Mother and Dad built the house, utilizing Dad's GI benefits. It was our family home until Mother sold it in 2003, using the proceeds for her stay in a retirement village in Madison, MS, today the predominantly white suburbs north of Jackson.

I have a picture of me sitting on the front stoop of the new house with a very scrunched, worried look on my face, eyes deeply furrowed and with me scowling. To me, it is indicative of how I always felt growing up: befuddled, confused, perplexed about life and how to navigate it. Maybe, the sun was just in my eyes. My first memory of this new house is not a pleasant one. It occurred during the time when the house was being constructed. I was riding my tricycle out in the side yard, while Mother and Dad talked with the contractor. I looked down and a large black snake was writhing back and forth, stuck under the front wheel of my tricycle. I screamed, and Dad came running to pick me up. Isn't it weird that two of my earliest memories deal with somewhat frightening episodes with snakes? I also recall a time when as a teenager I was hiking in the swamps of the Pearl River behind my best friend's house. I stepped up on a log where lay a sleeping water moccasin in the sun. Luckily I saw it, struggling underneath my foot, and quickly jumped one way, as it—just as terrified, I believe, as I was—slithered rapidly away in the opposite direction instead of striking me.

It's a wonder that I don't suffer from ophidiophobia, an abnormal fear of snakes.

Both of my parents came from what is known in today's parlance as extremely dysfunctional families. Looking at my family background in retrospect, there are several episodes that would be appropriate on the pages of a William Faulkner novel or in a scene from a Tennessee Williams play. But, then again, I suppose every Mississippi family—or for that matter any family anywhere—has challenges and dark legacies to deal with and hopefully overcome.

Both sides of the family at one time had enjoyed considerable wealth and social standing in their Mississippi communities. However, by the time my parents' generation were young adults the wealth had largely been dissipated. Actually, I have no regrets about this—as I sometimes quip, had I been a scion of the wealth that formerly was on both sides of my parents' family, I might have ended up as a drunken frat boy at either Ole Miss or Mississippi State, belonging to *Sigma Alpha Epsilon*, the only national fraternity founded in the Antebellum South at the University of Alabama in 1856.

Mother's Family Background

Mother's grandfather, Col. Robert Hiram Henry, was the founding owner and publisher of the *Clarion Ledger*, Mississippi's largest newspaper and publishing enterprise. He never served in the military, but was awarded an honorary rank of Colonel by prominent Mississippi veterans of the Confederate Army. For years, he served as the official state printer in addition to publishing the newspaper. As well, he published two books, memoirs, one detailing his life in publishing and the other about his travels throughout Europe.

He built a Victorian mansion on the main street of Jackson at the end of the 19th Century. Unbeknownst to me at the time that it was once the family estate, I took dancing lessons from an Arthur Murray Dance Studio in what was once the large living room of the mansion. My first real girlfriend and I won a jitterbug contest there, when I was in the 6th grade. It was torn down sometime in the 1960s, when I was away at college. Today, a self-service gas station sits on the lot where it used to be. Two columns from the house, the only items still existing from the house, are on the campus of Belhaven University, "a top Christian College since 1883," to honor him for being a notable donor throughout his latter years.

He was prominent in both local Mississippi politics and national Democratic politics. As well, he was respected nationwide as a journalist and author. He declined serving in a foreign ministerial post during President Wilson's administration. However, he did join Henry Ford's peace expedition of 1915, traveling to Europe on "The Peace Ship," the ocean liner *Oscar II*, which sought an early peaceful solution to ending the First World War. I suppose my lifelong activism for peace with justice is in my gene pool.

Both of his sons, my great-uncle Thomas, and my grandfather, Robert, moved away from Jackson as young men, settling in Detroit, MI, where they pursued successful careers. Thomas was a founding Board member of the American Automobile Association, and Robert, my grandfather, became a prominent physician in Detroit. Neither of them wanted the family publishing business. When Col. Henry retired in 1921, he sold it to cousins, the Hederman family. The Hedermans built it into one of the largest publishing companies throughout the southeast, before they sold it to the Gannet Company in 1982 for $110 million dollars. None of this financial legacy is enjoyed by any of the progeny of "Daddy-Pops," as Col. Henry was affectionately called by his grandchildren.

My grandfather, Robert, and his first wife had two children, my Aunt Ida and Uncle Miller. When their mother prematurely died, Robert brought the two young children down to the Henry estate on the main street of Jackson to be raised by two old maid aunts, Aunt Gee and Aunt Mamie. Aunt Mamie had a birth defect, a shortened arm with a misshapen thumb and two fingers growing out of her elbow. Grandfather Robert returned to Detroit and married Gladys, who bore him two daughters, Barbara, my mother, and a younger sister, my Aunt Mary. Gladys was diagnosed as a dipsomaniac, a historical term from the 19th Century to describe the malady from which we addicts to the liquid, legal drug alcohol suffer. She spent much of her adult life in and out of state mental institutions in Michigan. Mother told me Gladys visited our family a couple of times during my early years, but I have no memory of her.

When mother was ten years old, she broke her leg and was in a body cast. Shortly thereafter, Gladys was committed again to a Michigan State Mental Hospital, so Grandfather Robert brought a second set of two children, my mother and Aunt Mary, to Jackson, again dumping them in the Henry mansion to be raised by the two maiden aunts. Mother, who passed at age 91 in 2013, remembered how uncomfortable she was on the long train ride from Detroit to Jackson in the body cast, but she always said she remembered very little else about her childhood. Aunt Mary, on the other hand, related that they were both mistreated by the two old maid aunts. Earlier when they lived in Detroit, Mary also related that when Dr. Henry made house calls at night, a housekeeper would lock them in the dark and dank basement of their house in Ferndale, then an upscale suburban neighborhood of Detroit.

After he brought Mother and Aunt Mary to Jackson, Grandfather Robert married his former nurse from Detroit, and they relocated to a small town in southern Mississippi. He never had much to do with Mother or Aunt Mary, or their half-sister, Aunt Ida, and half-brother, Uncle Miller. With his third wife, he had another child, Uncle Robert, whom I didn't even know about until I was in my mid-40s. One day, I got a letter from Mother, in which she related that she and Dad had spent a wonderful evening with my Uncle Robert. I immediately called her and queried, "Mother, who is Uncle Robert?"

"Oh," she responded, "I guess we never told you that your grandfather married a third time and had another child."

Mother was always most secretive and rarely talked about our family background. Perhaps, she was ashamed and embarrassed. Maybe, she repressed it due to childhood abuse. Our legacy was decidedly not anything like the *Donna Reed Show* or *Leave It to Beaver* variety of "normalcy." Quite the contrary!

Uncle Robert Henry became a well known motivational speaker, traveling nationwide, giving keynote addresses to educational, volunteer, and business organizations. One of the regrets I have is that I never met Uncle Robert. In 2007, on one of my visits to Mississippi, I contacted him where he and his family then lived in Auburn, Alabama. On my return trip to New York, I hoped to be able to visit him and his wife. Unfortunately, his wife informed me, when I called to arrange a meeting, that he was in critical condition in the hospital, that he was too sick to visit with me. He died before I got back to New York. After Aunt Mary died, his son, Patrick Henry, also a motivational speaker, and two of my sisters and two daughters of Uncle Miller met at her Memorial Service in Louisville, KY. It was the first time any of the Brinson cousins met with our cousin Patrick. Hopefully, we will soon plan a reunion, when all of us Henry cousins, wide flung as we may be, can connect and exchange stories of our family saga.

During the last eight years of Mother's life when she lived at St. Catherine's Continuing Care Retirement Community, I made it a point, no matter how far away I lived, to travel to Louisville, KY, at least once a year where Aunt Mary lived. I would then drive her to Jackson, renting a car if necessary, so that the two elderly sisters could spend some time together. This was part of my living amends to Mother. I last visited with Aunt Mary in her Louisville Assisted Living Apartment about six months before she died in August of 2015. She was a funny, vibrant lady, who never married, but devoted her life to helping others in her church and community. Quite liberated, in her youth she worked as a model and served passengers for several years as a railroad stewardess on the Southern Railway. During the last years of her working life, she worked for the headquarters of the Presbyterian Church in Louisville, KY.

Somewhere among the family photos there is a picture of Grandfather Robert in an Army Medical Corps uniform. From what I recall, he served as a doctor in a military hospital near the brutal trench warfare, during the First World War, or maybe I made that up. As a combat veteran from Vietnam with a PTSD disability myself, who is married for the fourth time, it strikes me as somewhat ironic if I also share this family legacy with my grandfather.

Dad's Family Background

Dad's background is somewhat different, but just as unusual. He was the only child of a turn-of-the-20th Century entrepreneur, Lonnie, as he was called, who owned the General Store and some 2,000 acres of prime farm land on the outskirts of the tiny, county-seat town of Monticello in Lawrence County, located in southern Mississippi. Lonnie was married to Mother Hazel, my grandmother, who taught piano lessons. She was also a Sunday school teacher and the organist for the First Baptist Church. As well, she wrote a town gossip column for the weekly Lawrence County Press. She never drove a car, but walked all over town at a brisk pace, carrying a brightly-colored parasol to shield her from the hot Mississippi sun.

Lonnie was a gambling addict, and perhaps a heavy drinker as well. Due to his gambling debts, he lost the General Store and his other business concerns before the First World War. Over the years, Mother Hazel sold off, parcel by parcel, portions of the some 2,000 acres of prime farmland to pay taxes on the house. Today, the Lawrence County Hospital and a housing development sits on land once owned by my family. Well into my young adult years, Mother and Dad would get a monthly check from a petroleum company for mineral rights that the family still retained for oil and gas extracted from underneath the land formerly owned by the family.

When Dad was a whopping six foot, four-inch tall adolescent in high school, his cousin, Eleanor, and her husband, Boyd Gurley, visited Monticello. While there, they proposed to Mother Hazel that Dad come back with them to finish high school in Indianapolis. Lonnie, who was mostly an absent father, didn't object. Dad, therefore, accompanied them back to Indianapolis, where he lived for several years. After graduating from high school with honors, he was awarded a scholarship to attend DePauw University, where he also graduated with honors and was both a talented artist and opera singer, a protégé of socialist Paul Robeson. One of my most prized possessions is a pen and ink drawing Dad drew of me from a one-year-old photograph entitled, "Tommy Lad."

After the First World War, this branch of our family in Indianapolis was part of the progressive, upper class of the thriving midwestern metropolis of Indianapolis. Eleanor's husband, Boyd Gurley, was Editor in Chief of the *Indianapolis Times*, which was awarded a Pulitzer Prize in 1928 for exposing the influence of the Ku Klux Klan in Indiana politics. I can only imagine what an incredible change this was for Dad to experience in adolescence, going from the small-town environs of Mississippi to a thriving metropolitan city.

Here's other information we know about Dad's family background. Mother Hazel, as a teenager, was graduated from Blue Mountain College, near Tupelo, MS, an evangelical Baptist college for women founded by a former Confederate General and his sons. Lonnie's older brother, John, married Mother Hazel's mother, Mary Lillie. So, in addition to being mother and daughter, they were also cousins! Most strange indeed.

Dad's maternal great-great grandmother, Mary Sophia Graves, traveled with her mother to Mississippi in the late 1840s to teach at Zion Seminary in Covington County, MS. Zion Seminary was founded in 1845 by her uncle, A. R. Graves, a Presbyterian minister, who was originally from Saratoga, NY. Zion Seminary was one of the earliest institutions for higher education in Mississippi. A co-ed school with a populaton of some 500 students, who studied law, medicine and religion, it was burned by Union sympathizers during the Civil War and again when it was struck by lightning in the 1890s.

I only knew one of my grandparents, Mother Hazel. Gladys, Mother's mother, was out of the picture up north in Michigan, mostly in mental institutions, and Lonnie had died in 1939 before I was born. Robert, my maternal grandfather, died in Mississippi, when I was a toddler. Mother told me that once when they were driving through Mississippi on the way to St. Louis that they visited him. Mother related that he broadly smiled, when he held me, and was very proud of me.

Mother Hazel lived in a large, rambling house near the eastern border of Monticello and a block away from the Pearl River. It had originally been the home of one of Mississippi's most prominent governors, Andrew Longino, who built it at the turn of the 20th Century. Within the past twenty or so years, the house has been restored to the original small cottage that it was when Governor Longino built it. Several additions of apartments and a large front porch with a swing on it were added over the years, when it was in our family. I would often read in the front porch swing on steamy, hot summer days when I couldn't play with my friends. The additions and front porch were torn down, so that today the house in no way resembles what it looked like during my youth.

When I was a young boy, I visited Grandmother every summer. I had a good friend, Vicky, who lived in a large house across old US Highway 84. He was exactly one year younger than me. We had several playmates, the two Riley girls, who lived down the street from Vicky, and the three Allen girls, several years younger than all of us, who lived in a large Victorian house across an empty lot next to Grandmother's house. The Riley girls, Vicky and I shared lots of adventures, playing in the woods by the Pearl River and going to Vacation Bible School at the First Baptist Church.

I recall getting "sanctified" in the church one summer, when I was baptized by total immersion in a large tub of water up on the altar in front of the congregation, who sang, "What A Friend We Have in Jesus." The pastor dramatically intoned "Buried with Christ in baptism, raised to walk in the fullness of life" as he dunked me under water. I remember sneezing violently afterwards, perhaps a premonition of how repugnant I would find such fundamentalist religiosity in AA during my elder years!

I remember one especially disturbing event as a young boy in Monticello. I had been playing outside one afternoon on a hot summer's day, running around playing army, or cowboys and Indians, or some other testosterone-driven boy's game. Since I was very sweaty and extremely thirsty, I asked one of the neighborhood kids, an older boy, where I could get a drink of water. With a smirky smile he pointed to a large tank in a nearby backyard that had a faucet on it. I went over, put my mouth to the faucet and turned on the spigot. I jumped back, spitting out the vile liquid, which tasted horrible. It was kerosene. I remember the shame and humiliation I felt as I ran, crying, back to Grandmother's house, while the boy chortled in glee, a young sociopath in the making.

In the next chapter I'll relate another tales about visiting Grandmother down in Monticello, while growing up in Jackson, MS.

Chapter 2 – Growing Up and High School

I have been primarily addicted to the liquid, legal drug, ethanol, preferably Colt .45 by the case lot, daily when I drink. Perhaps the more appropriate phrase is that *I am addicted*, instead of *have been*, since I fully believe were I to pick up that first drink again, I would in short order become totally addicted once again. I'm convinced I was a full-blown alcoholic the moment I left my mother's womb. Long before I took the first drink at 13 or 14, I was filled with feelings of inferiority and alienation. My earliest recollections are those of pervasive self-centered fear, of feeling like I did not belong to anyone or fit in anywhere. Looking at it some seven decades later, I can still recall how alienated I was as a child. My earliest drinking experiences did nothing to assuage these feelings of estrangement and self-doubt.

I grew up in a middle-class, white collar family in Jackson, MS, from prominent southern Scotch-Norman clans, one Presbyterian and one Baptist. Growing up in Jackson, MS, on the one hand was as "normal" as any young lad could hope to have in the halcyon days of the 1950s. In fact, in many ways, it was as exceptional and fortunate a childhood and adolescence as anyone could hope to have. Nevertheless, my earliest memories and feelings are that I was a misfit, an oddball, that I didn't belong. Both within the family and in my social activities with friends outside the family, I felt mostly alienated from, as well as inferior to, everyone.

Despite my longterm recovery, on occasion I can still feel this way.

Being the first born, Mother was very over-protective of me. When I was a child, she would often hover over me, literally taking my temperature every hour or so. I understand her concern. As an infant, I was diagnosed with rheumatic fever and had a heart murmur. Mother, also, never experienced any positive female or maternal role model. As a young, immature 21 year-old, no doubt she was overwhelmed and terrified with her role trying to care for this mewing, whimpering bundle of incessant neediness that I, like any infant, must have been. Her primary source of mothering skills came from magazine articles and newspaper columns. I wasn't breastfed. During the 1940s that was considered to be terribly archaic, the behavior of dullards, and rumored to be most unhealthy. I was a most modern baby, a formula-fed baby, in hard, sterilized bottles with cold rubber nipples. Big formula companies, such as Nestlé, mounted huge advertising and PR campaigns to normalize bottle-feeding of infants during WW II.

During the third grade, due to overcrowding in Jackson schools, there were two shifts of grammar school, and I was assigned to the afternoon shift. Mother wouldn't let me go out and play with other kids in the neighborhood in the morning, because she didn't want me to exert myself too arduously before school. Once, I recall that I was quarantined in my room with mumps for a number of days. One afternoon, while Eva, our maid, who mothered me and held me more than I ever remember Mother doing, was busy performing her endless housework duties, I climbed out my bedroom window, so I could play with some neighborhood kids I saw across the street. They all got the mumps. Mother was mortified to no end. I can still hear her screaming at Eva, as with head downcast, Eva murmured, "I'se so sorry, so very sorry, Misses. Dat chile, I just don't knowed how he do it!"

I started grade school at Boyd Elementary School, which was bursting at the seams due to the burgeoning baby boom. In the third grade, I had my first crush on Patricia, who had delightfully long, blond pigtails and sat in front of me. I used to love watching in awe the sensuality of her hands with exquisitely long fingers—I've been fascinated by watching women's hands ever since. On my first 4th Step resentment list, I included a resentment of my third-grade teacher for moving me to the other side of the room because I kept passing her notes.

In the fourth grade, my best friend, Bobby, and I were both quite advanced compared to the rest of our class. We were able to read at a senior high school level. As a result, we spent most of the time in the coat closet, reading novels and voluminous war histories. Both obsessed with war, we shared daydreams about being gallant war heroes. As well, we spent hours, drawing sailing ships, battle galleons and three masted schooners, with which we both were also obsessed.

In the fifth grade, due to overcrowding, I was transferred for the year to another school, Duling, where I had my first and only fight. I have no idea what it was about, but a classmate, Johnny, and I got into an argument about something or the other out in the school yard. We started screaming at each other. I did not handle this conflict very well. Instead of dealing with the conflict appropriately, I kicked him, hard, in the chest and ran sobbing away until the haunting shouts of our classmates disappeared. It is indicative of how even today I sometimes handle stressful and frustrating situations.

That winter on a cold, frigid morning, Jimmy, a friend in the neighborhood, and I were outside cooking our breakfast. It had been too cold for us to camp out, as we had planned, but his mother let us cook our breakfast in their large brick barbecue grill in the backyard. With the fire lit, we played a game of "Bombs over Tokyo" with soda glasses of gasoline. We made loud B-25 airplane noises, pretending we were one of Jimmy Doolittle's 16 planes that we had read about. We'd dive bomb the fire, pouring gasoline on it. The fire would flare up, and we would jump back giggling. On one pass, Jimmy poured too much on the fire and while jumping back poured gasoline all down his front. He burst into flames and started running around the back yard in agony, screaming. I had recently read about a similar situation in *Boy's Life,* the monthly magazine of the Boy Scouts. I took off after him, tackled him, and rolled him on the ground, which extinguished the flames. For this action, I was designated as "Child of the Week" on the nationally syndicated children's program, *The Pinky Lee Show.*

For this honor, I was given a Certificate of Achievement by the Mayor's Office and had a picture with my family, along with the Chief of Police and Chief of the Fire Department in Jackson's morning paper, the Clarion Ledger. Yup, the one founded by my great grandfather, "Daddy-Pops." It was one of the few "five seconds of fame and notoriety" I've achieved in my long life. Getting my "five seconds of fame and notoriety" was not the only thing I received as a result of this honor. *The Pinky Lee Show* also provided me and my family a set of Grolier's *Book of Knowledge* encyclopedia. This award may also have been the reason I got elected to my first leadership position the following school year. I was elected as Captain of the Boyd Elementary School crossing guards. Every morning with my special Captain's belt with the large, shiny gold buckle, I would walk around and inspect each station of crossing guards.

One of the few activities that Dad and I participated in together was a Boy Scout campout during the Suez Canal Crisis in the late fall of 1956. There, several of us huddled around a campfire, talking with disgust about how the hostilities in Egypt seemed to be quickly petering out without direct US military involvement. This meant there would not be a war in which we could gallantly fight. The irony here is that on the other side of the planet in Southeast Asia, Vietnam was beginning to smolder to burst into a roaring conflagration smack-dab right in the middle of our generation.

Later in the spring, I recall we all ran around, chasing each other, playing war games. A number of us brought water pistols to school, shooting them at each other, mostly during recess, but occasionally as well in the classroom. One afternoon, our teacher gathered them all up and put them in a pile on her desk. She sternly looked at us miscreants, huddled in front of her desk, telling us severely that no one was to touch any of these water pistols. Already developing the proclivity of being a royal smart-ass, I stared her down, slowly reaching out my right index-finger, and touched the water pistol closest to me.

"There," I said, "I touched one. What are you going to do?"

She promptly grabbed me by my arm and tugged me smartly down to the principle's office, where I was remanded to detention after school for a week. Mother was called, and, of course, she was mortified!

During the summer after the 6th grade, I experienced a most humiliating event. I had matured earlier than my friends, having profuse hair under my arms and on my chest. I used to be teased unmercifully by some of the boys for being "gorilla boy." One afternoon at the public swimming pool up in Riverside Park, there was a coed swimming pool party. Embarrassed about my hair, I took one of Dad's old razors and shaved my chest and arm pits before I went. The pool was heavily chlorinated. I jumped in, and hopped right back out like a Mexican jumping bean, screaming in pain from chlorine in the razor burn. I still hear the hoots and bellows of derision from my friends, both boys and girls. I was utterly aghast.

Every Friday night during that summer, there were also sock hops at the Riverside Park Community Center. There, I experienced my first woody, slow-dancing with a girl named Susan, if I recall correctly.

We took several vacations as a family during grade school, Mother and Dad, Babs and myself. The most memorable one was a trip we took to Tennessee and the Smokey Mountains, when I was 10 or 11. I remember the huge black and white signs for Rock City on barns all the way to Tennessee, during what seemed like an endless drive up from Mississippi. I recall, as well, that this was the first time that I had ever seen mountains in northeastern Mississippi. We stayed in a small cabin on the grounds of the Chanticleer Inn in Chattanooga, TN, on top of Lookout Mountain. I fell asleep each night we were there, listening for the first time to a nearby babbling brook.

Across the street was the famed Fairyland caverns of Rock City. We wound our way through the caverns with lit up scenes from fairy tales and ended up at Lover's Leap at the summit of the mountain. From there, we watched a hundred foot waterfall cascade down Lookout Mountain. I experienced my first vertigo walking over a deep gulch along the famous Swing A Long Bridge. We rode the Incline Railway, first down and then back up to the top of Lookout Mountain, most thrilling for me. I have on my bookshelf a black paper cutting of Babs and myself by eminent family silhouette artist, Otho Barden. During that trip we also visited Gatlinburg, TN, in the scenic Smoky Mountains, where we hiked too long on hot, humid mountain trails and visited the Cherokee Reservation in nearby North Carolina. I was fascinated with the beadwork and other crafts of the Cherokee Indians. There, I bought my first dream catcher, which I hung from the ceiling of my bedroom.

We made a number of visits down to Mississippi's Gulf Coast. where I waded in the tepid waters of the Gulf of Mexico and sunned on the hot, white sand with the family. I especially enjoyed eating at famed Angelo's Seafood Restaurant with the large oak tree growing in the middle of the dining room and staying in mission-style, stucco Buena Vista Hotel with palm trees and exotic flowers outside in the gardens. Onetime, we took a boat trip to visit historic Ships Island, where I played slot machines for the first time.

Mother and Dad also introduced me to my first gourmet meal on a trip to New Orleans. They took me to Tu Jacques, the famous restaurant in the French Quarter that has been operating since 1856, where I had their traditional five course meal. Every time I'm in New Orleans, I try to have one of their meals in honor of Mother and Dad.

During preadolescence, I became a rabid Brooklyn Dodgers fan, listening to games on the radio and cheering for such notables as Duke Snyder, Pee Wee Reese, Roy Campanella, Jackie Robinson, Gil Hodges, etc. I was ecstatic when they won the World Series in 1955 and crestfallen when they moved to Los Angeles in 1957. I yearned mightily to be star baseball player, but I had no talent at all. For four years I went out for Little League and two years for Babe Ruth. I never made a team. This was partially due to poor eyesight. I was near-sighted and couldn't see the ball, whether to catch it or to hit it. It was a very different time, where matters of inclusiveness and instilling self esteem were not nearly as prevalent as they are today. One had to have a modicum of actual talent to get on a team, and I had none. Even in neighborhood pick-up games, I was always one of the last persons, if not the very last, to be chosen on a team. This was humiliating for me. During grade school, I had one moment of a sports glory at the sixth-grade track and field day. I easily won first place among all the boys in a hundred-yard dash.

However, the following year in junior high school, I excelled in football. I played every football game from 7th grade through high school. My eyesight was not a problem. Coaches merely had to point to the fellas wearing the different colored jerseys and tell me to knock them to the ground. I was a vicious downfield blocker. Our team, the Rebels, was coached by the legendary coach Bill Raphael, a Mississippi Sports Hall of Fame member. He always matched us against teams that were considerably larger than we were and at least one division above us. In almost every game, we were outweighed some 25-30 pounds per man. Though considerably smaller, we were faster and more agile. As well, Coach had the coaching acumen and ability to teach us well the fundamentals of playing football. He also had an uncanny ability to inspire and motivate us to achieve our best. This resulted in us having winning seasons each of my years playing high school football.

I played junior varsity football in freshman year and lettered for the remaining three years as a two-way football starter at the small Catholic St. Joseph High School in downtown Jackson. Mississippi during this time was still mission country. There was one diocese for the entire state. A number of the priests and nuns we had in high school were of Irish descent, who volunteered to do missionary work in Mississippi. There were 49 students in my small senior class. During my sophomore year, I was one of the tallest boys in the class at 5 foot, 8 inches. My Dad was 6 foot, 4 inches tall, and mother was above-average height for women. When I ordered my high school letter jacket, I ordered it two sizes larger than my size, figuring I would grow into it. However, I got the recessive gene in my family for shortness—two of my four younger sisters push six feet tall, one is my height and the other is just a tad shorter. That jacket was two sizes larger for me in my senior year, and were I to still have it today, it would still be two sizes too large for me, perhaps even larger since I've shrunk somewhat in my elder years.

Football was critically important for me as I came of age. It provided for me a legitimate outlet for the pervasive anger and rage I felt. I've always had a hair-trigger temper and have a history of punching holes in walls and sometimes screaming in rage, whenever I'm in physical pain or my will is thwarted. In football practice and during games, I could channel my anger/rage at players opposite me or on the opposing team. One afternoon during practice when I was a freshman, Coach pitted me against an upperclassman, who outweighed me by some 30 pounds or more, in a blocking drill. We battled strenuously on four occasions. Each time, I bested him and Coach profusely praised me. It was one of my most memorable events from high school, about which to this day some 60 years later, I still smile in satisfaction.

The death of someone I knew first happened when I was ten years old. One afternoon after school, I was playing a pickup game of baseball with Lockhart Walker and several other friends. Lockhart was an excellent player, one of the first always chosen on a team. Suddenly, a late afternoon spring thunderstorm blew up. We dispersed as large raindrops began to fall, Lockhart riding his bicycle north, while I pedaled south. Later that evening Mother got a call informing us that Lockhart had been struck by lightening and killed. A few days later, I attended the funeral for Lockhart with a number of our classmates. Before the brief ceremony, I made my way slowly toward his open casket. I stepped up onto the dais and looked down into the open casket. His face was a pasty, grey-tinged white, eyes closed, lips slightly parted, showing the gap between his two front teeth. It was a shock for me to see how "dead" he looked. I couldn't believe that just a few days previously, he had been so vibrantly alive, hitting a home run, jubilantly whooping it up around the bases, laughing and taunting us on the other team.

Though Lockhart wasn't the first dead person I had seen, he was the first person that had died, whom I knew and for whom I loved and cared. A couple of years earlier, I had seen an aged great-aunt, whom I had never really known, lying in her coffin, wrinkled, lips-pursed, and grey, but she was old. It was not out of the ordinary that she died. Lockhart, on the other hand, was young and vibrant and popular and a good baseball player. It was a shock trying to comprehend why he was dead. I still recall the awe, the unfathomable mystery, the bewilderment I had when looking down upon his grey-tinged, smooth, unwrinkled young boy's face, lying so deadly and irrevocably still in his white satin-swaddled coffin.

The first church I vaguely remember attending was the old and musty First Presbyterian Church of Jackson near downtown. I remember more clearly attending Sunday School and the interminably long Sunday morning services, and the even more tortuous—if possible—Wednesday evening Prayer Meetings, at the new First Presbyterian Church near where the Henry mansion used to be. The new church was most plain and austere, lots of white, to remind us of the innocence we would need to acquire to enter heaven, contrasted with brilliant red tapestries to remind us of the blood of Jesus that was spilled for our sins. The symbolism of the stark white and bright red, as the pastor, Dr. Miller, explained in his Sunday morning and Wednesday evening exhortations, were to remind us about what miserable sinners we were.

This was what most I remembered about both the Presbyterian and Baptist churches I attended during grade school, the constant hellfire and brimstone sermons from the pulpit and at the tent revivals I attended. Once, I went with Mother and Dad to sit in a high school football stadium to hear the evangelist Billy Graham, who exhorted us to accept Jesus as our Savior, so we could all enjoy the fruits of heaven with him in glory.

Mother got religion and started taking Instructions to convert to Catholicism when I was in the early throes of puberty during the 6th grade. She had met a woman in the Junior League, Mary Alice, who was from a prominent New Orleans French family. She and Mother became fast friends, inseparable for several years. Mary Alice convinced Mother to convert to Catholicism. Mother related to me that one of the reasons she converted was because of the hypocrisy of Dr. Miller, who preached hellfire and brimstone on Sundays, but who during Saturday night parties would get drunk and pinch the ladies' behinds. I remember going with Mother to the closed casket funeral of Mary Alice's brother-in-law, who had been killed in the French Indochina War. I had no clue, then, about Vietnam, much less that some twelve years later I would be in the bloodbath of the American Indochina War in Vietnam.

I tagged along with Mother and converted to Catholicism, because my best friend since the fourth grade, Bobby, was Catholic. I was fascinated by the pictures of bleeding hearts, the rosaries and colored statutes in his Irish Catholic home. Besides, I wanted to drink, smoke, gamble and dance without fear of going to everlasting hell forever and forever as the Baptist and Presbyterian ministers ranted about. My very first steady girlfriend, Judy, with whom I had won a jitterbug contest, promptly ditched me, because I worshiped an idol of the Virgin Mary. I didn't realize before I converted that as a Catholic to even think about masturbation, much less to do it, would damn me to hell forever and ever and endlessly forever, were I to be struck dead, like Lockhart Walker was, before I could confess and get absolution from a priest.

After Mother and I converted, in short order the younger cohort of my siblings arrived. Kate, Meg and Beth were born about a year-and-a-half apart from each other, while I was in junior and senior high school. Obviously, the rhythm method of family planning espoused then by the Catholic church—and the only one allowed—was most ineffective.

During adolescence, I developed a most idealized conception of women and marriage. I came to believe that the primary purpose of my life was to find *THE* one and only true love. We would then get married and live forever till death did us part. Not so much to propagate and have children, but to live out all of the romanticized fantasies I had about what true love was all about. Yup, I bought all the hype of 1950s popular culture about romanticized love, as portrayed in movies and on TV shows, but especially in popular music. I became obsessed to find the-one-and-only true love, so I could dutifully love her fiercely for the rest of my life.

I had a number of potential true-loves in high school. With each of them, the scenario was essentially the same—we would finish high school, get our college degrees, so we could get good jobs, and then get married. Then, it would be okay for us to fuck. With each of these girlfriends, I was more concerned about their morality than I was about my own. When I accidentally brushed the heavily-corseted boobs of my junior high school prom date, Dora Louise, lingering momentarily to caress them, I was practically catatonic with guilt and terror. Why? Because I was afraid that I would go to hell? Nope! Because I was aghast that I had perhaps caused *her* to be damned to hell forever and ever and ever. My response was to get royally drunk. I ended the miserable evening by puking all down her dress. From early on, I experienced that drinking not only made my life most unmanageable, it often made my life unbearable!

Grandmother's House

Every summer before I started high school, I visited my grandmother in Monticello, MS. My best friend there, Vicky, the two Riley girls, Myrna, a year older than me, and her sister, Gail, two years older than me, and the

Allen girls, several years younger than us, would play from dawn to dusk. A couple of summers, we all went to the Baptist Church Vacation Bible School together. One summer, I made a wooden corner shelf for Mother.

The Riley girls, Vicky and I had a special place we called Pine Straw Hill in the shade of a thick grove of pine trees, several hundred yards behind the girl's house. We hung out playing for hours in the cool shade during the long, hot and languid summer days. There was also a large flower-filled meadow, through which we sometimes rode horses together to an ancient Choctaw Indian burial mound, where we would dig, sometimes finding arrow heads and shards of pottery.

I nearly died the summer after my fifth grade. The Riley's had a lethal Doberman Pinscher dog tied up on a long chain in their huge backyard. The girl's father was proud to boast that the dog had killed a "nigger," who had trespassed on their property. One time there was a family argument going on in the front of the house, when I needed to leave. I looked out the kitchen back door and saw the dog way on the far side of the yard. I thought I would be able to easily get around to the side yard before the dog could catch me. I was wrong. As soon as I opened the door, he took off after me like a shot. I heard his pounding feet on the ground and heard his slobbering, low-throated growl. I turned to see where he was and threw up my arm just as he lunged for my throat. Instead of having my neck and carotid artery torn apart, I received some twenty stitches to close the gashes in my armpit.

On nights during my last summer in Monticello, when I was 12 and Gail was 14, I would stand on a ladder outside of her house. We would passionately neck through her open bedroom window. One day in the late afternoon, as dusk was falling, Gail and I were by ourselves at Pine Straw Hill. Sloe-eyed, she leaned over, staring down at my lips, and asked, "Tommy, do you want to fuck?"

"Okay," I replied, "How do you play that game?"

She drew back with a pinched scowl, quickly getting up and began to rapidly walk away toward her house.

"Gail," I called after her, "Why are you leaving?"

With an emphatic toss of her head, swirling her dirty-blond curls, she curtly replied, "Never mind."

Back home the following week, a friend, Buddy, informed me what "fuck" meant. He also taught me how to masturbate. In the throes of puberty, I became typically lustful and obsessed with sex. I was an inveterate masturbator, sometimes several times a day all throughout my teens. One of the most embarrassing times I had was when Mother found my stash of Playboys and a pack of cigarettes. She was dutifully mortified. This resulted in one of the few times I recall that I was physically punished. She demanded that Dad lash me with his belt. As I leaned over, clasping my ankles, I could see her watching with a smirk on her face and a gleam in her eye. In retrospect, I discern that adolescent Protestant girls, though they sometimes balked at drinking, dancing, gambling or swearing, didn't seem to be nearly as uptight about sexual behavior as the Catholic girls I later knew and dated in high school.

I have many fond memories of Grandmother's House. Late at night, I would lie in a sweaty back bedroom and listen to the doppler effects of speeding traffic along US Highway 84 next to the house. I remember listening to Top 40 love songs on a small radio, especially one in particular, "Tears On My Pillow," sung by Little Anthony and the Imperials. Maybe it was after the sad scene with Gail on Pine Straw Hill!

First Drinking Experiences and High School

I started drinking sometime around age 13 or 14. I clearly remember the first time I got drunk. Bobby, my Catholic friend from grammar school, who was a year older than me, had his driver's license. One night, we went cruising in his father's black, '57 Cadillac coupe with electric windows. I remember being fascinated by the electric windows, pushing them up and then down, again and again. We had procured from a bootlegger in North Jackson a six-pack of Champale Ale, a strong malt liquor.

Mississippi, one of the last states to legalize the sale of liquor after the repeal of prohibition in 1933, was a "dry" state at the time, where the sales of all liquor and wine, along with beer and ale, were prohibited. Most counties were totally "dry" with no provisions for the sale of any alcoholic beverages. Some counties, however, mostly in metropolitan areas such as Jackson or along the touristy Gulf Coast, were allowed through local referendums to legally sell 3.2 beer, or "near beer", as it is derisively referred to by some hardy drinkers. The state law read something to the effect, "There will be absolutely no alcoholic beverages sold within the sovereign state of Mississippi." In small print, however, was an addendum, "If such prohibited alcoholic beverages are sold, the state shall collect a 32.5% *Black Market tax!*" This resulted in there being very few sanctions to monitor and control the sales of alcoholic beverages to anyone, including minors. Literally, I could ride my bicycle several blocks north of where I lived to a white fence out on US Highway 51. There, I could buy whatever I wanted, hard liquor, wine, beer, from the local bootlegger. As long, that is, if I had the cash to pay for the exorbitantly high prices caused by the Black Market tax!

Anyway, with our cold six-pack of Champale, Bobby and I drove to the Shamrock Inn, one of the local hangouts for Jackson teenagers. It had a large asphalt parking lot, jam-packed most nights. On Sundays and Wednesdays, church-going nights, it was closed due to Blue Laws. On other nights, the parking lot would be filled, mostly with cars full of teenagers. Waitresses on roller skates would bring out hamburgers, hot dogs and French fries. These were most often accompanied with frosty mugs of 3.2 beer on trays that could be affixed to the open front windows on the driver's side. No one was ever carded. We didn't have a church key, or beer opener, so when the waitress came to serve us, we asked if she could open the six-pack of Champale.

"Sure," she said, with a pert toss of her long pony tail, as she skated away. After a couple of minutes, she skated back with all six cans fully opened. A straw was stuck in two of the cans.

"Here you go," she said. "We didn't have a church key either, so we opened all of the cans with our electric can opener."

Since it was a hot, humid, late-summers night, we were both quite thirsty. We sucked down the three cans each in short order. Bobby drove us over to Pat, a friend's, house. She was having a party out on her back patio, where 45 rpm records of popular early rock 'n roll dance hits were being played. Some couples were dancing. Others necked in the shadows. When I stepped out of the car, the world whirled and twirled. I fell down giggling like crazy, feeling utterly exhilarated. It was the first time I recall being drunk. As well, it was one of the few times I can recall that I actually experienced the euphoric "high" of being drunk. I soon became aware, however, that I had difficulty talking. My speech was slurred and sloppy. As, well, I couldn't think coherently. I don't remember much else about the party or getting home. Maybe I blacked out.

Later that night, Mother found me pissing in my closet, where I had also vomited, thinking it was the bathroom. Needless, to say Mother was mortified. Dad was also quite upset, because his best friend from

Monticello had committed suicide, while drunk from drinking moonshine corn liquor, white lightening. I *do* remember the shame and humiliation I felt, when Mother and Dad discovered the results of my first drunk.

Another of my first horrid drunks was camping with a couple of buddies and getting royally hammered on six bottles of altar wine we heisted from our parish sacristy. We took the wine and camped out in the swamps alongside of the Pearl River behind a friend's house. The late summer afternoon started out well. We skinny-dipped in the Pearl River, built some sand castles on the sandy river banks, and had a grand old time for an hour or so, while we chug-a-lugged the bottles of altar wine. We clumsily made a fire and sloppily cooked some cheap steaks we had brought along with a couple of cans of chili. Since we were starving, we quickly gulped down the mostly raw steaks with mostly cold chili. We shortly all passed out, but later in the night, after the fire had died down, the three of us woke up and were terribly sick, puking all over ourselves.

I got my driver's license shortly after my fifteenth birthday. One night in early summer of 1959, I got drunk with a couple of buddies at the Shamrock Inn, drinking gulps from a whiskey bottle we passed around, chased by cold, frosted mugs of beer. After my friends left, I decided to drive downtown to visit my girlfriend at the time, Phyllis.

On the way, I stopped at a stoplight on the main street, and promptly passed out, my head slumped upon the steering wheel. I was awakened by a cop roughly shaking me. He reached through the open window and turned off the ignition of Dad's car, a yellow and black 1956 Chevy Belair —my, how I loved that most cool car, today just as much as then! He ordered me out of the car to go sit on the curb. He parked the car on the side of the road. Steadying me, as we walked to his police car, he not too gently put me in the back seat. Then, he drove me to my house, rang the doorbell and deposited me with Mother, who was mortified again. Lastly, he drove Dad back to retrieve his car.

Drinking wasn't always related to getting into trouble as a teenager. All through high school, I had a morning paper route in one of Jackson's most upscale neighborhoods. The papers were dropped off at Walker's Drive-In, where I would fold them in an entrance doorway on most mornings and in the foyer of a nearby office building on cold winter mornings.

Walking papers up to the front porch of my customers, I discovered that some left the keys in the ignition of their cars overnight. Sometimes, I would get up very early, say 3:00 a.m. in the morning. After finishing the paper route, I would take one of the cars out for a joyride. One morning, I took the car of the Family Court Judge, who lived down the street from us, for a spin. It was a wonderful car, a 1954 orange and white, two-door Mercury Monterey coupe. After a torrential rainstorm I lost control turning a corner, and drove it into the swampy front yard of a high school classmate. All four wheels were stuck in mud up to their hubcaps. Luckily, I just missed smashing into a couple of trees. I had to walk home and tell my parents what had happened, so they could get a tow truck to pull the judge's car out of the muck. Mother was, of course, mortified; he was amused. Chuckling, he said that this was just of kind of a stunt he would have likely pulled as a teenager. My parents were not mollified, and for several months half of my take from the paper route went to pay them back for the tow truck. As well, I spent a hot, late spring afternoon, washing the judge's car.

During my sophomore year in high school, two carloads of my high school friends and I spent a couple of afternoons one weekend, riding around town and throwing water filled balloons at passersby. We also would pull up beside a car with an open window and toss one in the front seat. It was great fun, we thought. Except someone turned in the license plate numbers of the two cars to the police, and they came looking for us. Nine of us were herded into the Jackson police station late one Sunday afternoon. Two of us were detained at a CYO, Catholic Youth Organization, dance on our parish grounds. We were taken downtown to the police station to join and be booked with the others. As we were riding up the elevator, the cop was tossing one of the water-filled balloons that had rolled out from underneath the front seat of my car, up and down, up and down. Splash, he dropped it, wetting both trouser legs of his uniform. The two of us couldn't help but guffaw!

Both this incident and the earlier incident when I passed out on the main street of downtown and was driven home by a cop, illustrate what a very different time it was back in the 1950s—today, either of these incidents would have likely resulted in serious legal consequences, which would have been most costly for me and my family.

On a spring weekend of the my senior year in high school, three friends and I drove down to New Orleans with the intention of getting laid. We guffawed and teased each other as two of us successfully procured condoms in a drugstore. We had no idea how to find a house of ill-repute, a House of the Rising Sun, and we were too shy and self-conscious to inquire, so we went to one of many strip clubs in the French Quarter. It strikes me now how easy it would have been to ask one of the barkers cajoling passersby inside the numerous strip clubs on Bourbon Street, but it didn't occur to us then. Since we were catnapping in the car, not having funds for a hotel or motel, we were all quite tired. We sat in the front row, right next to the gangway, where the strippers pranced, drinking stubbies, small 7 oz bottles of beer, exorbitantly expensive. John Albert, my best friend through high school was dozing, head slumped over his chest. The stripper noticed him and strutted over to him. Leaning down so that her ample breasts were level with his drooped face, she tapped him on top of the head. He looked up, startled, with the naked boobs an inch from his face, and jumped back with a shout, knocking his almost-full stubby of beer all over the counter. He was quite chagrined about losing his expensive brew, and mightily embarrassed, since we bellowed in glee, including the stripper.

We never did find a House of the Rising Sun, or come close to getting laid, though two of us flirted for awhile with a couple of girls out at the Lake Pontchartrain Amusement Park. Nothing, however, led to nothing. On the way back we guffawed, when we pulled along side a young couple, sitting close together in the front seat of a pickup truck. I threw the unopened package of condoms through their open window, like a couple of years previously we had done with water-filled balloons.

On another late spring weekend before we graduated from St. Joseph High School, a number of us went down to the Gulf Coast to participate in the Statewide Convention for the Catholic Youth Organization. As soon as we were settled in our rooms in the famed Buena Vista Hotel, suitcases were opened and out sprang bottles and bottles of various kinds of booze, which we had easily procured from bootleggers the week before. I don't remember anything about the convention, only the consequences of our drunken behavior. There were significant damages to a number of hotel rooms, as well a large mirror wall in the lobby that was shattered. The diocesan offices were most disturbed about the bad press we members of the Catholic Youth Organization received from our carousing in one of the Gulf Coasts most cherished and respected hotels.

The following weekend, the St. Joe Glee Club had two concerts scheduled down on the coast at Catholic high schools. The diocese considered canceling our trip, concerned that it would be a repeat of what happened at the CYO convention. As president of the Glee Club, as well as of the senior class, I had to assure the principle and diocesan officials that the members of the Glee Club would behave themselves and not repeat the shenanigans of the previous weekend. All Glee Club members had to sign a pledge that they would bring no alcohol to the hotel where we stayed. As far as I know, no one brought any booze to the coast. However, the father of one of my classmates was down on the coast for business. He took four of us out to a nightclub for an evening of heavy drinking and good-ole-boy-carousing conversation. Drunk and reeling, we somehow were able to sneak back into our hotel rooms undetected, so we escaped any negative consequences.

I was never a social drinker. I never become the cool, slick, debonair-chick-magnet, life-of-the-party kind of guy. Whenever I drank even a couple of beers, my speech became slurred. Much of the time, I got sloppily drunk, such as the time I threw up on my date, a decided impediment to getting a walk to first base, much less hitting a grand slammer! Whenever I drank, what early-on I judged to be an extremely unmanageable life, ended up becoming utterly unbearable. An example of this was when, at the raucous party after our graduation ceremony, one of my classmates cold-cocked me, almost knocking me out, when I tried to drunkenly open-mouth kiss her. I still recall the shame and humiliation as classmates guffawed in glee, teasing me. My natural response was to take a couple of long swigs of Rebel Yell whiskey and to gulp down several more Colt. 45s before I passed out in the large backseat of the 1950 DeSoto sedan I drove during my last two years of high school.

Now, mind you, externally my life was peachy keen. Good grades, lots of friends, starting football player, a star even sometimes, leading man in thespian productions, a number of one-and-one-only-forever sweethearts, president of the Glee Club and my senior class. I even won two academic scholarships for college. Didn't matter. Internally I was a fearful, nervous, isolated, alienated, teenybopper – no pimples or acme, but with a huge inferiority complex not soothed by any ego-enhancing achievements. I looked in the mirror and saw a gawky, gangly, geeky misfit. I was convinced that I was only capable of faking it, making it, somehow barely getting by. I was convinced that if my classmates knew the real me, the one that I negatively perceived, I would be forever spurned and shunned.

Early on, I developed a meme that I was a "maker of memories." Due to the insecurity and a raging inferiority complex, I was so anxiety-ridden in most social situations, especially with girls present, that my focus was to rush through the experience and escape into where I felt considerably safer, reading or daydreaming. Reading, I could experience life vicariously through characters in a book. When daydreaming, I could ideally write the script, so that I would be the gallant hero, rescuing the fair damsel, without dire consequences or having to face the prospect of failure. It was ever so much a safer, and surer, way after the fact, to nostalgically remember incidents from my life, usually while drinking by myself, and bask in those memories, than to relate to friends, especially girlfriends, as I was living life—the memories became more important to me than having to deal with the actual living of my life. That's a very sad and truncated way of living. Early on, I became addicted to experiencing nostalgia, remembering unrequited young love, especially listening to "oldies, but goodies" on long drives by myself in the car or drinking by myself in a shit-kicking bar listening to the jukebox.

Here's a story from the summer after I graduated from St. Joseph's high school.

The Barbara Story

Barbara was a precocious member of the freshman class. With her, I experienced my first non-masturbatory orgasm, dry-humping on her dirty, laundry-room floor at the back of her garage, while her Mother was cooking supper in the adjacent kitchen.

Our relationship resulted in me taking a disastrous trip to New Orleans to visit her, which resulted in both of us getting into a heap of trouble. Barbara was the first girlfriend that my good friend Jo-Jo, ever had. They were both classical music aficionados and Jo-Jo, a flaming boy-queen, even during high school, decided to experiment on the tame side of heterosexuality with her. Jo-Jo was one of my two best friends during high school. One day, shortly after we were graduated, I dropped by to visit him at his house, which had a large swimming pool in the backyard. Barbara was also there, but I hadn't known or noticed her before this afternoon. On this hot, sunny, Mississippi, early summer afternoon, however, she in her tiny bikini was *extremely* noticeable. We couldn't keep our eyes off of each other. Never was there more poignantly a case of fatal attraction. As if pre-arranged, we improvised a story where she had to be home for some errand with her little brother, and I offered to give her a ride in my DeSoto. We drove off, parked a few blocks away, and tore into each other. She was deliciously sweet. For a couple of weeks, we became an inseparable item, in the throes of teenage hormonal bliss. Jo-Jo was noble, but rightly pissed.

Her Mom was most concerned about our relationship. She disapproved of Barbara going out with someone several years older than she was. It turned out that she and Barbara's father, recently divorced, had met in high school with about the same age difference. She had gotten pregnant with Barbara and had to drop out of high school for a shotgun wedding. Late one night, Barbara called me in a tearful panic. She told me that her Mom had forbidden us to see each other again. The very next day she was being forced to go to New Orleans to spend the rest of the summer with an aunt. We were heart-stricken. This could not be! I could hear her Mom screaming in the background for her to "Get off the goddamned phone. NOW!!!"

Hastily, I got the telephone number of a close friend in New Orleans. Over the next couple of weeks, through hurried, breathless phone calls when she visited her friend and letters posted to her best friend's address, we made arrangements for me to come down to New Orleans to visit her the second weekend in August. On a Friday afternoon, I left my job early, first driving home to pick up Sister Babs, to begin a weekend trek to New Orleans. My cover was I was spending the weekend at Grandmother's house, taking Babs with me. My plan was to tell Grandmother that I was going to visit a friend, Ted, who lived in Brookhaven, a nearby town on the then main road to New Orleans, US Highway 51. It was a glorious late afternoon. I was blissful, anticipating our time together in New Orleans. There I was, driving down a country road with the wind wailing in the open window, my left elbow on the window sill, a cigarette dangling out of my mouth, pompadour slicked back, the radio blasting the best of 50's rock 'n roll songs. I cut the perfect picture of a James Dean wannabe.

Bam—a loud crash startled me. The green hood covered the windshield. Babs screamed. Somehow, I was able to pull over and stop the car on the side of the rode, a couple of feet away from a steep embankment.

I got out and discerned that the hood latch had come unfastened. The long hood had crashed into the windshield, crumpling irreparably. I was able to bang it down enough, so that I could nurse the car into a service station several miles away. There, I tied it down with a rope, so we could continue on to Monticello, traveling no more than 20 miles an hour. It took us about two-and-a-half hours to travel the 45-50 miles to Monticello. No way could I take the DeSoto to New Orleans. I was in a panicked rage, when I got to Monticello, but I was hell-bent determined to get to New Orleans anyway. I told Grandmother what was up, making her promise secrecy. After quickly talking to Barbara's girlfriend, letting her know about the change in plans. I lay awake in the dark, listening to the crickets and frogs and the long Doppler sound of cars on US Highway 84 until I slipped into a toss-turning sleep. I didn't have a radio playing "Tears on My Pillow," but it would have been most appropriate!

Early the next morning I limped the Desoto over to Brookhaven and caught a Greyhound bus to New Orleans. Eternal hope sprung deep again in my heart, as once more I was embarked upon what turned out to be a doomed adventure. We pulled into the Greyhound Bus Station near Canal Street, about 11:00 o'clock in the morning of an absolutely gorgeous summer day. I checked into a cheap hotel on Canal Street, a couple of blocks from the French Quarter, and called Barbara's friend. No answer. I was hungry, so I went out, and ate a tasty lunch in a cheap café, swished down with a couple of Jax beers.

Back in my room, I once more called her friend. Again, no answer. It seemed like forever for ten minutes to pass, so I could call again. Still no answer. I was frustrated, pent up with incredible anxious energy, so I decided to go out for a walk and see some of the City. I easily became distracted by the hustle and bustle of the New Orleans scene, so much more vibrant than my sleepy, small hometown of Jackson. After an hour or so, I hurried back to the hotel and eagerly dialed the number again. Still no answer.

I was beginning to panic, to really get worried. What if she had been in an accident? What if she was laid up in an ICU? What if she was dead?!?!? The only way I had to contact her was through her friend's number. I didn't even know where her aunt lived in New Orleans, a large metropolitan area of a million or so souls. I waited and called, went out, walked around some more, had several more beers, waited and kept calling. The afternoon slowly passed away, but there was nothing but no answers from her friend's phone number. Downtrodden, forsaken, about six o'clock I went downstairs and into a sleazy strip joint next door to try and figure out what to do. I was drinking an expensive beer, minding my own business, not even distracted by the undulating strippers on the mirrored runway, when one of the off-duty ladies, sidled up to me, and began rubbing her hand along my thigh.

"Hi, Big Boy. Want some company?" she sexily asked. "Buy me a drink, how 'bout it, Big Boy?"

"No, thank you, Ma'am. I just want to drink my beer and be left alone."

"Oh come on, Honey, a young man like you." She leaned in closer and moved her hand all the way up my leg, fondling my crouch. "Surely a big boy like you wants some company, some action."

Why hadn't something like this happened when my friends and I were down in the French Quarter earlier in the spring, I wondered to myself? Looking at her, first down into her swelling cleavage, pushing against a skimpy bikini top, then up into her face, I replied, "No Ma'am, I don't. Please. Leave me. Alone."

She purred, "Come on, baby … "

"Look, I got a girlfriend. I just want to drink my beer and think about her." She didn't move. Kept staring at me with tasty big eyes and fondling me. My cock began to respond.

"Okay then," I said, "What's good for the gander is good for the goose." With that, I reached down and grabbed both of her boobs, squeezing them, hard.

She yelled, and in a New Orleans' micro-second, two hefty bouncers were on either side of me, not too gently escorting me hastily towards the door. I was yelling at them to let me go, that she had been harassing me. I landed not too softly on the sidewalk, got up, brushed myself off, and aimlessly walked around the French Quarter, just beginning to get ready for another Saturday night on the town. I went back to my room and called one more time. The result was typical—no answer, so I went back to walking the streets, trying to figure out what to do.

After a while it came to me. In our preparations for the visit, we had planned to go to a symphony concert at the Municipal Auditorium in Louis Armstrong Park, right next to Congo Square. It was a short walk away. Walking to each entrance, I watched and desperately sought Barbara—to no avail. The concert started, and I was able to sneak in, hoping somehow to find her. I cautiously slinked around the main floor, I looked around at the cavernous, now darkened hall of some 7,000 people. How could I find her?

The intermission started, and I was desperate. What could I do? I glanced at the emptying stage, "Well, if I can't see her, I'll go to a place where she can see me!" Steadfastly, I headed straight for and hopped up onto the front of the stage. I peered out into the vast auditorium and up at the two tiers of balconies, peering, seeking, searching, strutting across the front of the stage, motioning to a center rear exit. The musicians started coming back on stage. A security guard was motioning for me to get off the stage. I started walking to the opposite end of the stage. Two more security guards were hastening towards me from that end. Again, I was in the firm grips of larger men, being roughly escorted out and dumped onto the sidewalk.

I suppose today one would get arrested and taken to a lock-up for such behavior, but this was still in the lazy, hazy days of an innocent summer of 1961, before race riots, burning inner cities, Vietnam, sex, drugs, and rock 'n roll. I waited expectantly for about a half hour, but no one came rushing out to encircle me with a swooning hug. Still alone, still so god dammed alone! I went to a dive bar, sparsely filled mostly with old men, a young man on his way to becoming one of them. I drank draft beers and shots of bar whiskey until about midnight. Then, I bought a six-pack and staggered back to the hotel. I slumped into bed and quickly chug-a-lugged the six-pack down. Finally, I passed out!

"RRRRRingggg. RRRRingggg," I jumped up, startled. I grabbed the phone. "Barbara, oh sweet Barbara. You found me. How did … MOTHER?????

It was worse than any nightmare. Mother was quite stern on the phone, her voice ice water. She was, of course, mortified. Plus, she was pissed, really pissed. She told me not to leave the hotel, that she and Dad would drive down and pick me up no later than 10:00 o'clock the next morning. This Sunday, decidedly would not be a day of rest for them nor for me. She said if I left the hotel, she would alert the New Orleans police to have me arrested for statutory rape. That's what Barbara's Mom wanted to have happen. Mother agreed that it was what I deserved.

"But, Mother, I just wanted to see …"

"But nothing, young man. I can't believe how you've shamed us. This is costing us money we don't have. I'm going to hang up now. I will see you in the morning." CLICK !!!

As I found out later, Barbara's friend betrayed her, told her aunt about our plans. Her aunt called her Mom. Her Mom called my Mother. My Mother called Grandmother, who spilled all the beans about what she knew. Mother methodically called each and every New Orleans hotel listed in the yellow pages until she found me registered under my name. A most determined woman, my Mother, and she was on a mission! I don't remember the next day, but I presume it had to have been a dreadfully long ride back up to Jackson. Nor, do I remember much of the two, maybe three, weeks left of that summer vacation, my last summer home before going off to college to be launched into young adulthood. I do remember that I was beyond grounded, that I was miserable, that I was lovesick and most forlorn. Barbara wasn't allowed to come back to Jackson until I had left for college, so I didn't see her again that summer. I had no way to contact her.

Chapter 3—Xavier University

I have hazy memories of Mother and Dad, driving me up to Xavier University in Cincinnati in early September. We packed my stuff, a couple of suitcases and an Army surplus foot locker, in our Chevrolet station wagon and hit the road. Besides being lovesick, missing Barbara, I thought a lot about the predominant fear I had leaving high school, that my life would turn out to be boring. After spending much of that day retracing the route we had taken to Lookout Mountain for vacation, we spent the night somewhere in southern Kentucky and the next day drove into the wondrous skyline of Cincinnati, coming up over a Northern Kentucky hill and around the big curve to have the whole of downtown Cincinnati with its several bridges connecting Ohio across the Ohio River to Kentucky all spread out before us. To this day, it is still one of my favorite sights to experience.

In short order, we found the Clef Club House near the Xavier campus, which provided lodging for members of the Xavier men's chorus. This is where I lived during my freshman year. We unloaded my belongings, and after brief hugs and goodbyes, Mother and Dad drove off to return to Jackson. I remember how tasty the cold Hudepohl beers were, as I bullshitted for a couple of hours with Dave, a sophomore from Michigan and Hank, a junior from Indiana. It was an excellent first night of freedom as an adult in a nearby tavern on Reading Road.

And what happened with Barbara? Well, as undying as our love surely seemed to be earlier that summer, by mid-October we had exchanged a couple of tepid letters. By Thanksgiving, our correspondence had petered out. She was smitten with a jerk who was a junior, and I was a big man on campus in a large city far, far away. By the time I took the long Greyhound bus ride home for Christmas break, I had been elected to student council; cast in two supporting roles in Masque Society productions, the Xavier theatre group; become a member of the Pershing Rifles, the drill team for the Reserve Officers Training Corps (ROTC) unit; and was rehearsing with the Clef Club for a concert with the world-renown Cincinnati symphony orchestra in Cincinnati's famed Music Hall early in the new year. At Christmas, I saw her briefly at the traditional home-for-the-holidays-reunion-sock-hop for members of the past graduating class at the St. Joe gym. We slow-danced once, rather awkwardly. I wondered whatever in the world I had seen in her. I think she thought the same about me.

As a Freshman, I was the only one from Mississippi at Xavier University. In fact, I was one of only a few students from the whole Southeastern region of the US, the Deep South, Dixie. There were fairly large contingents of students from Chicago, Indianapolis, Cleveland and Detroit, but the largest contingent of students was from Cincinnati, the many, many, many day hops, students who lived at their homes and commuted to Xavier for classes.

One of the upperclassmen, Tyler, a roomie in the Clef Club house, was super involved in Xavier student politics. He urged me to throw my hat into the ring and enter elections for one of the four officers of the freshman class the third week of October. I decided why not, what the hay? A friend, also a freshman in the Cleft Club, Larry, a day hopper, served as my campaign manager. The core of our campaign was to plaster the campus with signs reading, "Vote for Tom Brinson!" Large banners, sheets spray-painted with the simple slogan, were hung across each sidewalk and thoroughfare on campus. We also put flyers with the slogan on every desk of every classroom on campus every day during the week before the election. On the day of the elections, I walked around with a large sign around my neck that read, "I'm Tom Brinson!"

The instructor of my first-year German class, Dr. Wentersdorf, had a PhD in English from Oxford University and spoke in a very-clipped, aristocratic manner with a combination German and British accent. Of course, I wore my sign in his class. After we students had all settled in our seats, he took off his spectacles, pointing them at me, and curtly addressed me, "Mr. Brinson, do you really have that much difficulty remembering your name?" The class broke out in a chorus of guffaws and bellows. It was one of the most embarrassing incidents I had experienced so far in my fairly young life.

The day of student elections began with all of candidates giving their speeches at class convocations. I have no idea what I said and figured that since I had no large contingent of people with whom I had attended high school that it would be highly unlikely for me to be elected to student council. When the votes were tallied, I had the second highest plurality and so became Vice President of the Freshman Class.

Shortly after elections, I attended a wonderful Dave Brubeck concert in the cavernous Xavier Fieldhouse. It was the first concert of a major celebrity that I had ever experienced. I was thrilled to hear the iconic "Take Five" jazz song, which had been a favorite of mine for a couple of years, since it's release in 1959, but I was also wowed by other songs they played from the *Time Out* album. I was so enthralled by the concert that I went out and bought an LP album of *Time Out*—it's the only album that I have owned in LP, cassette—never 8-track—CD, and now iTunes on my MacBook Air.

One thing for which I'm most grateful is that I did not grow up with the usual southern stance towards African Americans. Both of my parents were very progressive by Mississippi standards, perhaps because both of them had spent time in the North. They were pro-integration and against segregation as it existed in Mississippi during the 1950s and 1960s. Both Mother and Dad worked within the community to liberalize positions on relations with African Americans. They volunteered as tutors for students at Tugaloo College, an African American school, just north of the then Jackson city limits. In addition, they both did public relations work for the Jackson Interfaith Interracial Council, an organization advocating for civil rights in Mississippi for African Americans, especially for voting rights.

African Americans throughout Mississippi and the rest of the deep south had been virtually disenfranchised since the late 19th Century. Such practices as poll taxes, literacy tests, and outright intimidation prevented African Americans from registering to vote. A common practice was to fire, or reduce the working hours, of African Americans who attempted to register to vote. Lynchings were not unusual for the first half of the 20th Century. In fact, Mississippi had the highest number of lynchings, 581, from 1882-1968. One of the first headline news stories I was aware of was the "lynching," the brutal beating and killing, of Emmett Till, a teenager from Chicago, who was visiting his family, when he allegedly flirted with a white woman proprietor of a store in Money, MS.

During the summer vacation of 1962, after working days at a summer job with the city, Mother and I would attend organizational meetings in the evening of the Students Nonviolent Coordinating Committee, SNCC. SNCC began organizing voter registration drives throughout Mississippi and the south in 1961. While working with SNCC, I met one of its founders, Julian Bond. Later that summer, I attended the annual convention of the National Student Association. I was one of three representatives from Xavier's student government to access whether we would join NSA. There, I was introduced to Students for a Democratic Society, SDS, which had just published the Port Huron Statement. This 27,500 word manifesto, primarily authored by Tom Hayden, directly appealed to my youthful idealism and resonated with my naive understanding of what JFK, and his brother, RFK, advocated in their administration. It was also quite compatible with the work I had done with the SNCC voter registration drives in Mississippi.

SDS at the time was radically—pun intended—different from what it devolved to become seven years later when members of the Weatherman Underground faction literally blew themselves to kingdom come making bombs in Greenwich Village. In 1962, we all wore suits with button-down shirt collars and narrow ties. Nevertheless, I became a life-long member of the values and aspirations of what was then called the New Left. During the Freedom Summer of 1964, busloads of students would come to Mississippi to register voters, while I was working in the evenings with SNCC. Right before I left Jackson to go to ROTC Summer camp up in Pennsylvania, three young voting registration workers, Chaney, Goodman and Schwerner, were killed near Philadelphia, MS. The White Citizens Council was a widespread organization of prominent Mississippi leaders and businessmen. They were characterized by many of the racially bigoted prejudices of the infamous Ku Klux Klan. This resulted in civil rights work being somewhat dangerous. Because of our activism with Tugaloo College, the Interfaith Interracial Council and SNCC, Mother and Dad were warned to cease and desist our civil rights work, or a cross might be burned in our yard.

During the fall of my sophomore year, for several weeks I dated a lovely, light-skinned African American actress and dancer with piercing green eyes, whose name is lost in the caverns of time. Neither of us had the maturity, however, to overcome the social prejudices of being an interracial young couple in the Cincinnati of the early 1960s, a conservative metropolitan area just across the Ohio River from Kentucky, beholden to the Confederacy for much of its cultural identity. I sometimes wonder whatever became of her, and hope she found the happiness she so richly deserved.

In my sophomore year I started working part-time for Nolan, Keelor and Stites, an advertising agency, which owned a brownstone building near downtown Cincinnati. I was a jack-of-all trades gofer for the managers and account executives. The ad agency specialized in producing magazine advertisements for the milling machine industry, the makers of the machines that make the machines and products we consume and use. As well, there was a huge General Electric plant in Cincinnati, which made jet aircraft engines for Air Force fighters and bombers. It was therefore a very scary time during the week of the Cuban Missile Crisis in 1962, especially since rumors were rife that due to the GE plant and the milling machine industry that Cincinnati was among the top five targets for missiles of the Soviet Union.

Since I was the president of the Masque Society, the theatre group at Xavier, I moved from the Clef Club house into the third floor of the home of theatre director, Otto Kvapil, and his wife Diane. For three years I lived in their home with a couple of other Masque Society members. Though paying rent, we became an integral part of their extended family and helped raise their four daughters. For the next several days, following October 22, 1962, when Kennedy informed the American public of the dire standoff with Khrushchev, Otto, Diane, my roommates and I gathered around the living room TV set to anxiously watch the late evening news. We and the rest of the country were greatly relieved when on October 28th, the news was announced that a resolution to the crisis was being peacefully implemented. We would not, after all, become pulverized particles of radioactive dust.

A bit more than a year later, on November 23rd, JFK was assassinated in Dallas. I was in an ROTC class at the time, when it was announced by our instructor, Captain Mitchell, that Kennedy had been killed and that classes were dismissed. It was a cloudy, cold, blustery walk back to the Kvapil's house, where once again we clustered around the television set to watch the sad proceedings following this tragic event. With deep sadness, I recalled one of the highlights of my then young life. On October 5th of the previous year, a couple of weeks before the Cuban Missile Crisis began, I was part of a rousing crowd of several thousand in Cincinnati's Fountain Square, who rabidly cheered a speech Kennedy delivered in support of Democratic candidates in the upcoming November election.

The large crowd that JFK gathered in Cincinnati that sunny October day is somewhat surprising due to the strong conservative influence of the prominent Taft family in Cincinnati. William Howard Taft was a most conservative president and Supreme Court Justice, while his son, Robert

A. Taft, was the conservative Senate Majority Leader, who resisted Franklin D. Roosevelt's New Deal legislation, especially regarding labor unions. I just found on YouTube a brief excerpt of JFK's speech that day in which with typical rhetorical aplomb, Kennedy states, "They (Republican congresspersons) have made 'No' a political platform. I believe in 'Yes!'" Not much has changed ...

Throughout my time at Xavier, I continued doing well in studies, graduating with honors. As well, I was heavily involved in a number of extra-curricular activities, which included the Masque Society and student government. I was also executive editor of the newspaper for a semester, when the editor and his staff were dismissed by the university administration for violations of the University Student code.

However, my most consistent extra-curricula activity was the two to four hours I spent daily drinking. Many late nights, I would sit in a darkened corner of a shit-kicking bar across from a Chevrolet plant in nearby Norwood that was within easy walking distance from Xavier. There, I would drink pitcher after pitcher of beer, mostly by myself. I would watch the old geezers come in and carefully lift that first crucial shot to their lips, quickly downing it, followed by a glass or two of beer, so as to quell their shakes. At age 19, I identified with them. I knew, and fully accepted then, they were what I was destined to become. Thus, that state of "incomprehensible demoralization" I experienced while drinking in high school continued to plague me throughout the years I was at Xavier. Actually, it got worse, because I was able to drink on a daily basis, whereas in high school I'd drink mostly only on the weekends, maybe one or two other nights at the most.

So why did I drink? Because I was addicted; because it was the only thing I could do to get a few moments of relief or, better yet, so I would pass out. Because I could literally cry in my beer and feel something, even if it was awful. I was more terrified of feeling nothing, of being a numb automaton, a no man, so to speak, than I was concerned about what happened when I got drunk. I preferred to be a bad drunk rather than a no man. Drinking did little to resolve my self-consciousness or insecurities, as I somewhat progressed into adulthood. Quite the opposite. I was often consumed with the usual feelings of inadequacy and self-consciousness that I had experienced all throughout high school. Early on, I became convinced that everything I touched turned to shit. Drinking offered me little relief or release. In fact, like in high school, many times it made my at times unmanageable life seem almost unbearable. When drunk, I also puked down the blouse of my fiancée, Roseanne, just like I had done with my junior high school prom date—decidedly not cool.

Under the tutelage of the Jesuits I became an avowed agnostic. They taught me well to doubt and to question everything. Like many of my fellow students, this is how I described myself when asked about my religion:

"Catholic?" *"Yes."* "Practicing?" *"No!"*

I became very dark and morose. I slithered around in a deep slough of despond, having a caustic, cynical and sarcastic view of the world, especially my place in it, especially after JFK was blown away.

The Masque Society and Roseanne

As indicated previously, I became very active in the Masque Society, the student theatre organization. I appeared in all four productions during my freshman year, and for the three subsequent years, since I was elected as its president each year, I functioned as Executive Producer for all productions. I had a number of leading roles. I also directed two plays in South Hall, the wooden World War II barracks building that was converted into the student snack bar and that had a primitive proscenium theatre in the rear wing of the building. My favorite role was that of the raging, young warrior prince, Harry Hotspur, in Shakespeare's *Henry VI —Part One*.

The first two years of study, I was a political science major with the career goal to become a diplomat with the US Foreign Service. I had been very smitten with the idealism of JFK's Camelot White House years. However, after Kennedy's assassination, I switched to a major in English with a minor in Communication Arts due to my involvement with theatre in the Masque Society. My career goals, thus, radically changed from joining the Foreign Service to wanting to pursue a career in the theatre, either acting or directing. Most likely, I figured, I'd end up as the chairman of the theatre department at a small liberal arts college somewhere in the midwest, just like my theatre mentors at Xavier, Otto and Diane.

During my junior and senior years, I volunteered for Advanced ROTC (Reserve Officer Training Corps) at Xavier. This meant that I would be commissioned as a US Army Second Lieutenant in the Artillery Branch upon graduation. As a Masque Society member, I did not have to wear my hair short or be clean shaven. I was given a dispensation, since often I was acting in Shakespearean or other plays. As a platoon or battery officer, I derived considerable masochistic delight in awarding demerits to freshmen and sophomores, who had not properly shaved or had their hair too long for military standards.

I attended ROTC summer camp at Fort Indian Town Gap, PA, during the late summer of 1964, after my Junior year. Summer camp was Army Basic Training for those of us who volunteered to become advanced ROTC students. It was a grueling experience, but also rewarding in that though it challenged me physically, mentally and emotionally, I was able to successfully pass all of the strenuous requirements. During our basic training field exercises, a battalion from the 502nd Infantry Brigade, part of the infamous "Screaming Eagles" 101st Airborne Division, were assigned to be the aggressors in our war games. I was extremely impressed by them and lusted to join their storied ranks. 5-0-Deuce members were short, slight of build, and tough as nails. They consisted of a large number of Blacks and Hispanics from metropolitan ghettos and white farm boys from rural America or the coal mines of Appalachia. I was short, slight of build and known to be tough as nails, especially when downfield blocking as a high school football player.

During the spring of my senior year, despite being a member of advanced Army ROTC, I helped organize a Teach In at Xavier to discuss and oppose the escalation of war in Vietnam and throughout Southeast Asia. Bombing of North Vietnam had been initiated by President Lyndon Johnson in March and the 9th Marine Expeditionary Brigade landed in Danang. This initiated the massive buildup of US combat forces in Vietnam. By the end of 1965, the majority of combat was done by the US along with an infantry division from the Republic of Korea as well as units from Australia and New Zealand. Xavier's Teach In was held on a weekend in April. Since I had met him in Mississippi during voter registration drives a couple of years earlier, I suggested inviting Julian Bond to be the featured speaker. Julian was a dynamic speaker and a most committed peace and civil rights activist. He was well-known both as a founder of SNCC and as a co-founder of the Southern Poverty Law Center in Montgomery, AL. He ended his professional career from 1998 to 2010 as chairman of the NAACP. I remember little of the Teach In except that Julian was most moving in passionately advocating that we students resist the draft and build a strong protest movement against President Johnson's escalation of US military forces in Vietnam.

During my sophomore year, I started dating the Masque Society secretary, Roseanne. The Masque Society theatre crowd was a heavy drinking group of folks. Most every night after rehearsals, a number of us would go out to a local dark and dingy bar out on Reading Road for a couple of hours. Sometimes I would join them; most often, however, I would ride the Honda motorcycle Roseanne and I had bought with her credit to a bar in Norwood to drink by myself. I often preferred this, since it was more comfortable than having to relate with others, especially when my speech became slurred and sloppy. There was another bar that we sometimes used to go to, the Greenwich Tavern, which served imported German brews on tap. I especially recall the wonderful, dark Dopplebock beer that was served during the spring. Since Roseanne worked full time at Proctor and Gamble corporate headquarters as a marketing assistant, she rarely went out drinking with us. When she did, she could certainly hammer down the beers brewed in her German tradition.

After each production there would be a raucous cast party, sometimes at Otto and Diane's home, other times in student apartments. We had a three-week party after the last production of my freshman year, a musical about the legend of Rip Van Winkle, entitled *Forty Winks*. The Party was centered in the apartment of two of the cast members near Reading Road, a major artery in pre-Interstate Cincinnati. The week before, during the week of final exams and the week after exams, members of the cast and friends would gather every late afternoon with cases of Pfeiffer's Ale imperial quarts, which were larger 40 ounce bottles of ale instead of regular 32 ounce bottles. We would drink and carouse into the wee hours of the morning. Some of us would just pass out, scattered about the living room of the apartment. We'd get up and go to take final exams the next morning. Amazingly, all of us students passed our exams.

One night, a number of us went to Eden park with its spectacular view overlooking the Ohio River, the hills of Kentucky and a portion of downtown Cincinnati. There we had a kissing contest. I was voted by the three women who took part as the sexiest kisser. I was also voted as the male cast member whose legs were most appealing when dressed in tights. Did these votes bolster my ego? Not really, I still remained anxiety ridden, full of estranged shyness and self-consciousness. On another late night, we had a game of chicken on Reading Road. Drunk, we proposed to lie down in the middle of this major thoroughfare and wait for vehicles to pass over us. Thankfully, we got bored, since there was little traffic, and went back to the apartment before one of us got killed.

Upon graduation, I was supposed to get married to Roseanne, who was a wonderful girl. We had been engaged for two years. Roseanne was most likable, a personality+plus kind of a gal, but she was not my type. I prefer willowy, thin, small-breasted women, and she was a full-bosomed, German gal with thighs larger than many NFL fullbacks. Nevertheless, we set a wedding date in August after I graduated in 1965. During the spring and summer, we finalized all the requisite arrangements to be married in her home parish, St. Monica's in Cincinnati. All throughout our relationship, we engaged in libidinous carnal activities except, of course, for the old "in out, in out"—actual intercourse. That, we were saving for our wedding night. Every week during my senior year we would meet with Fr. Von Kanal, SJ for required Pre-Cana counseling sessions, and every week we would be absolved in confession for our carnal endeavors.

However, as the wedding day came closer and closer, my feet got colder and colder. I finally determined that I could not go through with the wedding. Though I had a deep fondness for Roseanne, I doubted that I really loved her enough to stay married to her forever and forever and endlessly forever. The relationship didn't really resonate with my romanticized idealizations about what a true one and one-only real love relationship should be like. Though I enjoyed the sex and despite the reality that she was a delightful woman with a wonderful sense of humor, she remained far from my romanticized ideal of a woman to whom I could devote my life. I could not conceive that I could love her for a lifetime. Consequently, three-weeks before the wedding date, I cancelled the wedding. I spent the next couple of weeks, calling all of the family friends and relatives, telling them of the radical change of plans. I was most grateful when she and her family volunteered to inform the persons they had invited to the wedding. I felt terrible, but was greatly relieved. Besides, I was able to drink with impunity throughout both the day and the night. I easily drowned my guilty feelings in imperial quarts of Pfeiffer's ale, or cases of 16-oz cans of Colt .45 that I had discovered got me drunker quicker.

Since my parents and four younger sisters had taken time off to attend the wedding, they changed their plans to make a trip to New York City instead of Cincinnati. I decided to join them in Washington, DC and make my first trip to New York City, which I had been fascinated by since a preadolescent from watching B&W TV shows about "The City." I rode a Greyhound bus all day and met them in a downtown hotel. On the night that would have been our wedding night, I lay in agony. I was not nearly enough drunk, restlessly tossing and turning. I mercilessly berated myself, castigating and cursing myself, deeply regretting that I had broken the engagement with Roseanne. Had I not, I—finally—would have been getting laid for the first time that very night.

The next day we drove into Manhattan past all the refineries in New Jersey and stayed in a hotel in Times Square at 7th Avenue and 51st Street for the next couple of days. I was miserable, missing Roseanne and deeply regretting my decision earlier in the summer to cancel our wedding. After a couple of days, I decided I had to get back to Cincinnati and try to reunite with Roseanne. I concocted a story that I had to return to Xavier for urgent Masque Society business and took a bus back to Cincinnati. I made it just in time to meet with Roseanne, who about to leave for a trip to Chicago. I drove with her in her Cutlass convertible. While in Chicago, we walked around Grant Park, discussing our relationship, but we stayed in separate hotel rooms. In the ensuing days I bought another engagement ring, but she was most reluctant to become engaged again. For several weeks we tried to restart our relationship, but after awhile we realized it was done. A year later, I ended up losing the engagement ring, when I forgot about it and left it in a drawer in the furnished apartment I lived in during 1966 before I entered the Army—perhaps this was karmic payback.

The academic year following graduation in 1965, I was hired by Xavier as the salaried Executive Director of the Masque Society, along with one of my roommates, Tommy, who was hired as the Technical Director. We had a new, modern theatre with elevator stages and a huge roundtable stage with the latest in lighting and sound equipment to play with in the newly built Student Union building. It was quite a change from primitive South Hall. I also received a fellowship to pursue a masters degree in English, which entailed teaching two sections of Freshman English.

The most exciting theatre project in which I was involved, not only at Xavier, but in all of my later theatrical endeavors, was the two productions the Masque Society produced of *an evening with ee cummings*. Conceived and scripted by Diane Kvapil, it was the last production we did in the South Hall theatre and the initial production in the new theatre. *an evening with ee cummings* was a theatrical presentation of the poetry of renown 20th Century poet, ee cummings. It consisted of all elements of dramatic art—music, dance, chorus, dramatization, etc.—to portray his poetry to a contemporary audience. Only the words of cummings, as he published them, were spoken. In general, it traces his evolution as an artist *and* as a human being from an idealistic youth through a dark period as an adult—experiencing the despair of WW I and a callous world during the Great Depression—to a somewhat peaceful acceptance of life simply as it is, sometimes beautiful, sometimes brutal, but ultimately most worthwhile through the wisdom one experiences by surviving to become an elder. I was type-cast as the "dark" cummings archetype, rageful, sarcastic, demeaning of politics, culture and society. It was a natural sequel to my role of Harry Hotspur, the raging warrior prince. In some significant ways these "dark" personality traits are what I have continued to be challenged to overcome, not only before but throughout the decades of my recovery.

Towards the end of the first semester of graduate school, I experienced the reality that the work required to pursue a graduate degree in English was considerably more difficult, as compared with undergraduate courses. The extra time required for reading and study to merely pass courses interfered with my several-hours, nightly drinking ritual. My solution was to drop out of the Masters program, rather than flunking out or curtailing my drinking. This made perfect sense to me. My drinking time was very important to me! During the spring of 1966 before I left Xavier and Cincinnati for the Army, I started writing poetry. Of course, it was very much influenced by the poetry of ee cummings. It was also influenced by the sappy, maudlin poetry of Rod McKuen, at the time the "unofficial poet laureate" of America. Often, drunk, by myself I would scribble nonsensical musings, which seemed so poignantly brilliant at the time, but in the morning's light were mostly indecipherable.

The Story of Ruth

Before I left Xavier and Cincinnati, I had one other most significant relationship with a woman named Ruth. Ruth, a woman ten or so years my senior, was married to a successful child psychiatrist at the University of Cincinnati Medical School. They had two adorable children, a boy about 5 and his younger sister about 3. Our relationship altered considerably my idealized conception of women and my ambition to find

THE one and one-only woman to marry and faithfully to love forever and ever, etc.

We were cast opposite each other as Orestes and Electra, brother and sister, in an adaptation by Leo Brady of the Greek trilogy, *The Orestia*. Brady's adaptation condensed each of the three plays into an act of a three-act play. From the first night at auditions, our first encounter, we were immensely attracted to each other. Our director, theatre mentor Otto, picked up on the sexual energy between us and built into our relationship on stage a strong theme of incest between us. In short order, responding to the sexual energy between us, we began seeing each other outside of rehearsals. We started having an affair. She was exactly my ideal type of woman, thin and small breasted. As well, she was most sophisticated, witty and knowledgeable. I had never been with so captivating a mature woman. It was comparable to the relationship portrayed by Dustin Hoffman and Anne Bancroft in the Mike Nichols film, *The Graduate*. I was smitten, head-over-proverbial-heels, in obsessive love with her.

Here is one of the first poems I wrote in March of 1966, about our relationship:

there was this hill

and we sat atop it
your long, goldened hair nestled
within my arm and your face
against my warmly beating heart
below us spread out into the distance
was our mid-twentieth century city
the hill was smoothly green with new growth
early leaves like minted dreams blossomed from gnarled trees
on the wide horizon birds, three, four, maybe five,
who needs to count, spun threads of quiet motions
against the light blue sky just beginning to tinge orange

we talked occasionally, softly
of small and important matters,
private, known but to us
mostly we sat, just sat,
warm, still and at peace
with each other and all else,
fingering fingers, smiling smiles

once or twice we softly kissed
but without passion, no need,
only tenderness, eyes deep and soul touched,
as joined breaths breathed satisfied signs
you murmured something forgotten
while with one hand i toyed with a broken twig.

the sun slowly set and light glinted from your wedding band,
but it did not bother me, not even once, all that wondrous afternoon.

After a week or so, Ruth suggested we consummate the relationship. Her husband had a four-hour seminar class with medical students on Thursday evenings. We decided that this would be an ideal time for our tryst. Now mind you, I was still technically a virgin, having done everything else with Roseanne, but engage in actual intercourse, so I was extremely nervous when I arrived at her house a half-hour after the start of her husband's class. Ruth met me at the front door and took me into the darkened living room, where she had lit several candles. We talked for awhile, seated closely next to each other on a sofa. Eventually we started slowly making out. I had her blouse off and was nuzzling her small, soft breasts, when we heard a car pull into the driveway. Ruth looked out the window, seeing it was her husband returning home three hours early. I literally stumbled out the kitchen back door as he entered the front door.

During the run of the play, since we were not in the first act, we would make out backstage in our skimpy Greek costumes. We rationalized it being a necessary part of our preparations for acting on stage. One night her husband and a friend, bored since she wasn't on stage, came backstage looking for Ruth. Instead, they found us together, making out. Her husband shot me a killing look and curtly said to Ruth something to the effect that he wished she would stop having these sordid affairs with younger men.

I was shocked and most hurt that there had been others, that I wasn't the only one. She really didn't love me after all, that I was just another boy-toy, like others with whom she had spent time. My concept of a lifelong one-and-only love relationship with THE one and only one was shot to hell and back. It baffled me that she was messing around with me, ten years her junior, when she had such an ideal life with a successful and attractive psychiatrist with whom she had two lovely children. Several days later, we met in Burnet Woods, a park near her house. There she told me she was pregnant again and that her husband had accepted a faculty position in California. She told me she was moving there with him and their now three children. She hoped she had learned her lesson about having extra-marital affairs, especially with younger men like I was. This was the last time I saw her.

I was quite devastated by the sudden ending of the relationship with Ruth. I spent many hours drinking and literally crying in my beer about the breakup. The ending of the relationship had shattered my idealized, and certainly naive, illusions about what constituted a committed love relationship. It was a most painful lesson of growing up, and I felt horribly bereft for several weeks, very much like I felt after the ending of the relationship with Barbara, some five years earlier. But, I was young, somewhat resilient. Shortly thereafter, I was cast as the lead, Grandpa Martin Vanderhof, in the last production I produced and took part in at Xavier, *You Can't Take It With You*. Life trudged miserably on, fueled by lots of excessive drinking. My time at Xavier was ending. As well, my time in Cincinnati was winding down.

The summer of 1966, my last in Cincinnati, passed with me being employed as the Company Stage Manager for a summer outdoor theatre in Cincinnati that produced two plays, *Twelfth Night* and *Brigadoon*. One night, I had another opportunity to finally lose my cherry with another married actress, Shelia. However, we were both too drunk. We eventually passed out in a heap together, naked arms and legs entangled. I thought I was ready, and so did she, but instead we experienced the truth of the Porter's speech from *MacBeth* about lechery, i.e. drinking, "It provokes the desire, but it takes away the performance." After the summer theatre season was over, I prepared to go into the Army to fulfill my two-year active duty requirement as an ROTC-commissioned 2nd Lieutenant. I was most chagrined to have been assigned to the Ordnance Branch, due to my poor eyesight, which required glasses, instead of to the combat branch of artillery, in which I had been trained at Xavier. I spent several weeks back home in Jackson, MS, drinking daily, before I reported to Aberdeen Proving Ground, MD, for the basic ordnance officer course. Drunk one night, per usual, in a Jackson bar, I wrote this bitter, unrequited love poem to Ruth:

strollin'

through noises of small-city traffic,
i chance to see somebody,
hips wagging, boobs quivering
i sneak a glance casual over sunglasses
being red-blooded and straight though not tall,

and stop still rocked roots of me
seeping into cracked concrete,
heartbeat captured between teeth open wide
swishing by she reminds me so of you,
whom i have not quite at all forgotten
a moment longer than most passes,
the spade of your smile seems suddenly sharply near
and just when i think i can touch
a loud bird flies by
a horn or something honks
some guy guffaws at my closed gape
and deep within me glass shatters.

jerked out of memory, i realize a bit too abruptly
how distant are your hills, your golden bay long far away,
but most of all your children
precious and naive with their happy father
and probably someone else with whom you toy.

In early October, I left Jackson on a Greyhound Bus bound for Baltimore, nearby the large Aberdeen Proving Ground, MD army base. We student officers used to quip that if you consider Chesapeake Bay as the asshole of the world, APG was forty miles up it! After two days on the road, sweaty, suit rumpled from sitting for hours on a bus, or in grimy bus stations, I checked into a downtown hotel, at 9:00 p.m. or so, near the notorious "Block" in Baltimore, the red-light district near the waterfront docks.

Being quite thirsty, perhaps even craving a drink, like the old men I had encountered in Cincinnati bars, I immediately went out to cruise the Block. I didn't think to shower or shave, I just went out, wearing the same clothes in which I had spent the previous two days on the road. Thinking about it, I probably desperately needed a drink. I went into the first strip club I encountered and quickly downed a double shot of Drambuie—yes I loved that sweet, scotch liqueur—and then switched to much cheaper mugs of beer. I casually watched the non-sensual gyrations of the bored stripper on the gangway, when one of the off-duty dancers sidled up to me, "Wanna buy me a drink, Mister?"

At first, I gruffly said, "No way." In an instant, however, I had another thought,

"Hey Lady," I called after her. She turned and walked back to me, "Yes?"

"I won't buy you a drink," I said, "But how much would it cost for me to be with you?"

She paused, scornfully giving me, slowly up and down, the once over and pulled away with a pinched scowl on her face. Slowly she said to me, "Be with you? Mister, I wouldn't BE with you, if you were the last swinging dick on the planet!" In the parlance of strip clubs, to her I was obviously a PL—a Pathetic Loser. It ranked among the most humiliating incidents I'd ever experienced drinking, or not.

However, perhaps "the most unkindest cut of all" had been made by close high school buddy, Jo-Jo, a couple of weeks earlier. We used to love to pretend we were lovers in front of all the faux-macho men and faux-sophisticated ladies in Jackson, whenever we met for lunch in Poets, an upscale restaurant, during college vacations. He would dress up in a fedora with a large cape, swirling it around him, as he made a grand entrance, and we would run across the dining area, embracing each other, and kiss each other full on the lips.

One night before I left for the Army, I was with him in his apartment. Of course, we got royally drunk together, while listening to opera. I made the following proposition:

"Okay, Jo-Jo, let's do it."

"Do it? What do you mean, Tommy?"

"You know, whatever you do with your lovers."

Jo-Jo paused for a moment, staring at me, mouth agape. Then, he burst out laughing: "Lordy, Tommy, you're straight as an arrow." Making an appropriate queenly gesture, he continued, "Besides, you're not my type!"

"Sweet Jesus", I despaired, "I can't even get laid with a man. I'll never get laid."

Chapter 4: Marriage to Kathy and Going to Vietnam

After the relationships with Roseanne and Ruth had ended, along with my impotency with Sheila and the debacle of the stripper on the Block in Baltimore, I was convinced there was no way I could ever "get any satisfaction," the iconic lyric the Stones famously wailed about in 1965, much less achieve love and happiness. Since I was such a PL, a pathetic loser. I became increasingly suicidal in thought, just wanting IT, my life, to end, to be over. I was terrified, however, of putting a bullet in my head or driving my Honda Dream motorcycle into a telephone pole or concrete abutment at high speed out of terror that some god, despite doubting one even existed, would manifest itself out of the Kosmos to send me to hell forever. In retrospect, I can discern that subconsciously during my last year in Cincinnati, I had been trying to kill myself by driving most recklessly around Cincinnati without a helmet. Cincinnati, like Rome, is built on seven hills. Many late nights, I would drive drunk throughout the city up and down and around the hilly landscape at excessive speeds.

Late one night, drunk per usual, I was driving from Xavier to downtown Cincinnati through Eden Park on Victory Parkway, for whatever reason I today haven't the foggiest clue. Just before Eden Park, there is a large S-curve connecting two hills with a long bridge in between. I hit the first curve at an excessive speed, misjudging the curve. The front tire struck the curb, propelling me headfirst into the concrete railing. I hit the railing about 6 inches from the top and skidded to a road-rash halt. Though covered with abrasions from head to toe, I was not seriously hurt. I stood up, cursing, and saw that had I gone headfirst over the railing, I would have fallen about a hundred feet to my certain death. Luckily, the motorcycle was not severely damaged, and I putted off into the dark night.

I had another potentially fatal accident, just before I left Cincinnati in the late summer of 1966. I was driving at dusk in a light rain on a major highway. I saw just ahead of me that a car had pulled out from the right and was stopped in my lane, waiting for oncoming traffic so the driver could finish making a left-hand turn. Apparently the smaller headlight of my motorcycle was lost among the headlights of oncoming traffic behind me. I tried unsuccessfully to maneuver around the rear of the vehicle, but the motorcycle skidded on the wet pavement, propelling me headfirst towards the side of the vehicle. In that split second before I hit the car with my bare head, I did not jovially say to myself, "Well, Brinson, this is it. Your death wish has surely come true!" Nope, instead, the survival instinct kicked in, and the thought flashed through my mind, "Brinson, you have to downfield block this motherfucker out of the way." I was able to somehow in midair twist my body around so that my right hip and lower back took the brunt of smashing into the side of the car.

The pain was excruciating all down my back, as I lay spread-eagled on the ground underneath the open window on the driver's side. I let loose a stream of obscenities about how some son-of-a-bitch had broken my back. The ambulance came, and I was taken to an emergency room, where I was diagnosed with massive hematoma from the middle of my back down through the buttocks of my right leg. My back was not broken. I was even ambulatory with crutches for several days until the hematoma dissipated. When I met with the driver's insurance agents to settle my case for injuries sustained and to repair the motorcycle, I was told that the driver was an 18 year-old girl who had just gotten her driver's license the morning of the accident and was somewhat traumatized by the stream of invectives I screamed at her. I suppose she qualifies to be on my 4th Step Resentment List.

Active Duty in the US Army

Though formerly a rabid Peacenik, once I entered the Army, I became extremely gung-ho, enthusiastically dedicated to the warrior mythos. This is an example of how I sometimes am a chameleon, radically changing my beliefs, attitudes and characteristics, so as to adapt to whatever environment in which I find myself. While in college, I was an activist Peacenik—now that I was in the army I wanted to become an elite soldier.

First, I wanted to be reassigned to a combat branch, preferably the artillery, in which I had been trained at Xavier. Secondly, I wanted to go airborne, to jump out of perfectly good airplanes and glide down to earth in a parachute, like the gung-ho members of the 5-0-Deuce Brigade I experienced during ROTC Summer Camp at Fort Indiantown Gap. Third, I was most determined to volunteer for wartime duty in Vietnam, where I hoped Charlie would do to me what I was too chicken-shit to do—kill me stone-cold dead.

But first I had to attend the basic course for Ordnance Corps officers at Aberdeen Proving Ground. I did quite well there, graduating second out of a class of some 75 student-officers. Toward the end of the course we discussed our assignment desires with a personnel officer. I strenuously advocated for being transferred to a combat branch and going airborne, but for nought. The personnel officer informed me that my eyesight rendered me unqualified for the combat branch of artillery, and I could go airborne only if I were willing to go on a status of "voluntary indefinite". This would entail me serving a minimum of three years on active duty, instead of two years as a reserve officer. In addition, at the end of the my first three-year tour, *if* Uncle Sam wanted me to stay on active duty, he could remand me to do so—indefinitely. Thus, this is what the term "voluntary indefinite" meant. The personnel officer told me that six months previously anyone who volunteered to go airborne would be sent to Ft. Benning, GA for airborne training and receive jump pay. However, the Congressional Budget Office had recently mandated that only those actually assigned to airborne units, could receive airborne training, and only those who were willing to go voluntary indefinite would get assigned to an airborne unit. Nope, young officer, choose once again.

I regretfully had to accept that I could only serve as an Ordnance Officer, and also that I would not receive extra pay to jump out of airplanes. To add insult to hopeful heroic dreams of fatal injury, I was further assigned specialty training as an Ordnance *supply officer* and was ordered to report to the Quartermaster School at Fort Lee, Virginia. This prompted me to request if I could be trained in EOD, explosive ordnance disposal. Alas, with a smirk, the personnel officer, a Major who appeared most adept at leading desks and filling out paperwork, told me that this too was unavailable, unless, of course, I was willing to go voluntary indefinite.

With a broad smile, however, the Major did tell me that he would be most pleased to grant me my third wish. He informed me that my first active duty assignment would be as an Ordnance Supply Officer in sunny South Vietnam upon successful completion of supply officer training. Since I had been away from ROTC the year following graduation, I barely remembered how to march a platoon, much less know what the ef to do with one in a hostile, combat environment! Although I graduated from the Basic Ordnance Officer's Course with the second highest grade in my class, I finished the Supply Officers course in the last quartile, barely passing, so bummed was I about being an effing supply officer. No way was this anything close to my ideal of a dashing heroic role in the war of my generation, where I hoped I would die, gallantly, of course, if possible.

Kathy, My First Wife To Be

Halfway through the 16 week Basic Ordnance Officer's course, I started dating Kathy, whom I met on a modified blind date. One of my classmates, Ed, who had a car, drove down to Goucher College in a Baltimore suburb and met a student at a sock hop. She had three friends who were interested in meeting young officers, so the next Friday night, four of us, Ed and George, and Pete and myself, drove down to Goucher. Pete and I went in his Ford, and Ed and George were in Ed's car for an evening out with the four ladies. So Ed knew his date, Mary, from the week before, but how to match up George, Pete and myself with her three friends? Well, we decided to cut cards in the foyer of the girls dorm, and I ended up with Kathy. Kathy was a girl from a blue collar family in Connecticut. She was also a Republican and had worked on the campaign to elect Spiro Agnew as governor of Maryland. We couldn't have possibly been more mis-matched. I never was lucky at cards.

Pete with Susie, Kathy and myself followed Ed and Mary with George and Carol to a local college bar, where we spent the night drinking pitchers of beer and yelling at each other, while the juke box pounded out rock 'n roll intermixed with twangy country music. As I recall, Kathy drank me under the table, but at least I didn't throw up on her later, when we clouded up the car windows making out in the large back seat, while Pete and Susie did the same up front.

I really wasn't much interested in pursuing a relationship with Kathy, but I let peer pressure compel me to see her again a couple of times. This included taking her to a big Basic Officers Course dinner dance in November at the APG Officer's club. The four couples arranged amongst ourselves to rent two adjoining rooms in a nearby motel, where the afternoon of the dance and the evening afterwards, we got exceedingly drunk. It was here, drunk, in the bathroom on the hard porcelain of the bathtub that I finally lost my virginity. All the short while I was fully intimate with Kathy, George was pounding on the locked bathroom door, yelling that he had to take a huge dump! No pun necessarily intended, getting laid was really quite anti-climatic. I heard no angelic choirs, I wasn't covered with confetti nor flower blossoms bursting out all over. I felt very little except a crick in my neck, and as I climbed out of the tub, I slipped and banged my knee on the faucet. Kathy and I had become a full-time item. She was much more enthusiastic about our relationship than was I.

Over the Christmas break Pete and I drove to Cincinnati. He had an aunt he wanted to visit, and I could see old Masque Society friends. I rented a VW bug, and Mike, another friend, let me crash in his apartment while he went home to Chicago. On a whim, I called an old girlfriend, Carole, from freshman year before Roseanne and I met. Carole's family was having a Christmas Eve dinner party to which I was invited. It was a pleasant evening and wonderful food in their Walnut Hills home. After the meal, Carol and I went to the Blind Lemon, a noted upscale college hangout up on Mt. Adams. There we renewed our friendship, rekindling the attraction we had once experienced for each other. We then went to Mike's apartment, where we passionately made out for a couple of hours. We couldn't consummate our relationship, however, because we had no birth control protection. I wasn't particularly concerned, but she was, since she was at the most fertile part of her monthly cycle.

An MFA graduate student in theatre at Ohio University, she was in an off-and-on-again relationship with a fellow actor. I didn't tell her about Kathy, because I had swiftly swooned back in love with Carole, who was definitely prime one-and-one-only material. We had a bittersweet, tearful breakfast the next morning, since Pete and I had to drive back to Maryland. We agreed we would stay in contact since we had so sweetly rekindled our relationship. However, after a couple of weeks, Carole wrote me, relating that she had re-committed to her relationship at Ohio University. That was that, so I took up with Kathy again, mostly double-dating on weekends with Pete and Susie. One weekend, Kathy and Susie were able to join us in our BOQ, Batchelor's Officers Quarters. Somewhere, I have a picture of Kathy and Susie dressed in our fatigues and wearing our steel pot helmets.

In February, I went to Supply Officer School at Ft. Lee, Virginia. Another lieutenant and I rented a small, furnished two-bedroom apartment for the month. Every weekend, either Kathy would take the bus down to Ft. Lee, or I would take the bus up to Baltimore, where we would spend the night in a BOQ room at Fort Holabird, then the Army Intelligence School. During these visits we copulated like bunnies, neither of us having the presence of mind that Carole had. We blithely played the game of reproductive roulette, despite us having quite a scare when she was late for her period one month.

I got my orders to report to Vietnam, following a 30-day leave. Kathy and I decided to spend the first several days of my leave in Cincinnati, which coincided with her spring break from college. I got a Jesuit friend of mine, who had been the faculty moderator of the Masque Society, to get us a reduced rate at a hotel, which was affiliated with Xavier. I just told him that I was traveling to Cincinnati with a friend. He was quite flustered, when he met us at the train station and discovered that my friend was a young woman! During the time Kathy and I were in Cincinnati, she was again late with her period, which caused us both considerable consternation. We had a tense, but thankfully short, goodbye at the train station, when she boarded a train east for Baltimore. A couple of hours later I boarded a train south for Jackson to spend the rest of my leave before I traveled to Vietnam in early April. One night, I got a panicky call from Kathy, telling me the rabbit had died, that she was pregnant. I was not really surprised. It was typical of my fate to knock up a woman with whom I enjoyed being carnal, but with whom I had very little else in common. Of course, I got drunk that night by myself as usual, drinking pitchers of beer and downing shots of Drambuie at the Cherokee Inn, one of my favorite haunts. Early the next afternoon, I bought a bottle of Inver House Scotch and went over to my friend, Jo-Jo's house. There I got royally hammered by the pool, where several years earlier I had been smitten by Barbara. Drunk, I made the decision to marry Kathy before I went to Vietnam. So, I did the "right" thing. I called her, changing my plans to visit some college friends in Chicago and then going to California to try to connect with Ruth before I left to go to Vietnam.

Instead of going north to Chicago and then west to California, I got off at Cincinnati, then I took the train east to Baltimore. Ironically, I sat at the same table where several weeks before I had sat after putting Kathy on her train to Baltimore, the same train I was now taking to Baltimore. There, Kathy and I were married in a civil ceremony at Baltimore City Hall, the day before l was scheduled to start my journey for Vietnam. My best friend, John Albert from high school, studying in nearby Washington, DC, was the best man. Somewhere, probably long lost, is a faded color-Polaroid picture John Albert took of Kathy and me on the steps of the Baltimore City Hall, after we were married by a Justice of the Peace.

Kathy and I spent our honeymoon night cramped together on a single bed in a Fort Holabird BOQ room. Noble? Not really, I merely wanted to save her honor and legitimize the kid. A more pressing concern, however, was that I was terrified she would slap me with a paternity suit. This would have been most unpleasant for me to experience, an Officer and Gentleman, by act of effing Congress for god's sake, especially during my first duty assignment in the combat zone of Vietnam. In retrospect, it's amazing how clouded my mind was from the daily drinking I did, or maybe it's just the typical oblivion experienced by callow youth.

Nevertheless, it was still my firm intention for Charlie to kill me cold-stone dead in Vietnam. What difference would it make if she slapped me with a paternity suit? I had no intentions of coming home.

Going to Vietnam

It was a drizzly, grey morning when I flew on a Northwest Airlines Boeing 707 from Baltimore-Washington International Airport to Seattle-Tacoma International Airport, which is about 35 miles from McChord Air Force Base. This is where my orders instructed me to report to no later than 05:00, April 8, 1967, for transport to South Vietnam. I recall it was raining when we landed in the mid afternoon, after the eight-hour flight across the US. After taking a shuttle bus to downtown Tacoma, I checked in to the Hotel Winthrop. I remember sitting in the hotel bar, the Sabre Room, looking outside a window at a steady rain falling upon a profusion of daffodils. I happened to be there during the annual Daffodil Festival in Tacoma. It was a somewhat daunting reality, amid all the celebratory activities of the springtime festival, to realize that I was on my way to the war in Vietnam. Of course, I drank throughout the afternoon and evening, ruminating about Kathy and the strangeness of being married to her.

While at Ft. Lee, I continued writing poems as journal-type entries in a small, black notebook that I had bought at the Post Exchange. It was the first of numerous written journals I've kept throughout my life. In the black notebook, I made the following journal entry :

> *Time has passed. Here one month, lack two days, since the start of this my first journal, I sit. Much, so much even a great part of the more, has happened. I mean, like, oh shit, I've been drinking.*
>
> *Much has happened. A JET, fast, smooth, in a moment's time brought me here. And the journey was miraculous.*
>
> *A band of cheap silver has passed between. A promise, hopefully golden, not cheap, of (of course) roses & sunshine, has been made. I am indeed now married and the one, Kathy, is full of our child.*
>
> *The month has passed. Time has passed. In this particular place, I thank whatever there is, or not, above for all that has passed and hope, while enjoying too much booze, for all time all when with her, Kathy, my wife, Realness really is.*

Reading it today almost fifty years later, I am struck not only by how drunk I obviously was, but also by how naive and indeed callow a youth I was. Had I forgotten about my intention to die in Vietnam? Despite being somewhat hungover, I got up on time and reported to nearby McChord Air Force base. There, my orders were processed, and I got on an American Airlines Boeing 707, packed full with other soldiers flying to Vietnam. We took off and after several hours landed in Alaska where we refueled for the long trans-Pacific trip. We were not allowed to deplane. It was probably the longest time in a long while since I had been without a cigarette. It was surreal being served non-alcoholic beverages and sandwiches by young, attractive stewardesses on the way to the war zone of my generation. This was quite different from World War II or in Korea, when soldiers spent days on troop ships going to war, as I had read about as a kid. Our trip would take mere hours.

We were scheduled to fly straight into Cam Ranh Bay, Vietnam, where we would be processed by the 90th Replacement Battalion for our unit assignments in country. However, due to engine trouble, we had to land in the Philippines, where we sat on the tarmac for several hours while an engine was replaced. Again, we were not allowed to deplane, nor to smoke, so the anxiety of being in route to Vietnam was especially onerous. The trip to Vietnam was interminably long, but eventually we got there.

My first impression, walking down the gangway and onto an Army bus, was how oppressively hot it was in Vietnam. Mississippi had been hot and humid, so was APG and Fort Lee, but Vietnam was several levels more uncomfortable. Someone asked the sergeant herding us onto to the bus why the windows were covered with wire mesh.

"So Charlie doesn't throw a grenade in the bus and blow our asses the fuck off to kingdom come," he gruffly replied.

It was my first visceral realization that yes, I really could get killed and die here in Vietnam. A shiver raced down my spine deep into my gonads. I was undaunted, however, reminding myself that despite having married Kathy, this is what I wanted. Before it had been mostly an abstract ideation, but as the shiver coursed through me, I realized it was indeed possible, perhaps likely even, that I could, indeed, die here. It took several days for the slow wheels of Army bureaucracy to grind out my assignment. I had nothing to do but walk from my BOQ, where I read until late-morning, to the Officer's Club on the wooden sidewalks between the buildings. The pristine white sand reflected the sun's heat as blisteringly as a mirror. In the O-club, I would drink a late breakfast and continue drinking through the long, hot afternoons and into the late evening, while I waited for my unit assignment orders. The one meal I would eat was dinner. Some of the time I made small talk with other officers awaiting their orders. Other times I read. Sometimes I wrote:

A bar, one other place of drink. Here and there are people mostly alone, sitting and drinking, deep in thought, worry and frustration. One, a woman, a nurse, has perhaps seen blood today, one or several die. Another sits, legs out-spread, keeping time, passing time, with his downcast, dark head, swaying in time to the taped music from far, far away. Another stares at the ceiling. The bartender talks shop with one at the bar.

Yup, a bar like any other dimly lit, uncrowded bar with swinging music. A bar, one other bar, except it's in Vietnam and all the people are American. Something can't be right.

So, I write. And this is it. It really happened. I finally got to Vietnam. And you know the thing that's really strange is that it's no different than any other place. All is as unsettled as ever, but also BEAUTIFUL like the leering full MOON, which taunts me. Will I survive my year here? I hope not.

Finally, an orderly woke me up early one morning telling me to report at 0900 to the Orderly Room of the 90th Replacement Battalion with all my stuff packed and ready to be transported to my assigned unit. Later that morning, I boarded an Army C-123 transport plane with some 25 other soldiers bound for Qui Nhon. For the first 55 or so minutes the plane ride was most uneventful. Then, the pilot announced we were making our final landing approach into the Qui Nhon airfield. The plane started swaying radically from side to side in narrowing arcs as we descended. It frightened the bejesus out of those of us on the plane for which this was our first landing in Qui Nhon. On the ground, I asked a Sergeant about the swaying back and forth. He informed me that the Army airstrip was in a valley between two mountain ranges, which always had high winds. Pilots would have to swing back and forth between the two ranges of mountains, shortening the arc of their swings, timing it so that they could land on the runway. In November of 1967, two of the seven Army nurses killed in Vietnam died in a plane that crashed into one of the mountains during severe weather.

A couple of months later, when I was working on the night shift, I would go to Red Beach in the mornings after my shift. Red Beach was the local Army R & R, Rest and Relaxation, center, which was a short walk from my hootch, what we called our BOQ rooms. There, I would hang out for several hours, drinking beers and watching planes yaw back and forth, as they landed. After a couple of hours, when it got too hot, I'd go back to my hootch to continue drinking until I passed out before I had to report for duty.

Chapter 5—629th Supply & Service Company (Repair Parts)

As it turned out, it was quite easy for me to survive much of my one-year tour of duty in South Vietnam. I was assigned as the leader of the 1st platoon of the 629th Supply and Service Battalion (Repair Parts). The 1st platoon operated 03 Bin Storage within the large logistical complex of the Qui Nhon Army Depot, located on the seacoast of South Vietnam's verdant Central Highlands. 03 Bin Storage had scillions of repair parts for the vast array of army equipment—vehicles, radios, generators, weaponry, office equipment, etc. etc. etc. It also had the security area for sensitive items stocked in the depot. Sensitive items included cryptographic equipment, special weaponry, such as sniper rifles and their scopes, including some of the first starlight scope, instruments to provide troops with green-tinted night vision. There were, also, very expensive Leica cameras used by Army photojournalists, and other items which could be pilfered.

During November and December, 03 Bin Storage received some 20,000 M16s, designated as the standard weapon to be used by US Army troops in 1967. They were to be stored in a special security warehouse that had just been built. From this warehouse, the weapons would be distributed to Army units throughout II Corps, the twelve provinces in the Central Highlands. This mission turned out to be an example of what I often experienced in the Army, that the right hand at times has no clue regarding what the left hand is doing. The command element of the Qui Nhon Depot was extremely concerned about security measures for the temporary storage of these M-16s. For several weeks, I took part in a number of meetings at Depot Headquarters, discussing and planning tight security measures for their arrival and storage. One day, I took a helicopter trip down to Cam Ranh Bay for a two hour meeting to discuss the security plans with representatives of the SeaLand Corporation, who had been contracted to ship the M-16s to Vietnam. A major concern was that while the weapons were stored temporarily in the warehouse, they might become a temping target of opportunity for Viet Cong sapper squads, enemy suicide-mission cadre that might infiltrate the depot and blow up the weapons.

One of the security provisions we implemented was that the SeaLand containers would only be unloaded at night, when no Vietnamese nationals would be in the depot. About 1100 hours one night in early November, the first SeaLand container was offloaded into the empty new warehouse. On hand to take part in this auspicious occasion was the Depot Commander, members of his staff, the battalion commander and his staff, my company commander and myself with the night shift of 03 Bin Storage. A forklift went into the container and carefully brought down the first stack of crates holding the precious new weapons. When the crates were unloaded in their aisle, there was much consternation among the command element. Each of the boxes had been prominently stamped with a large silhouette of the M16 rifle—it was fairly evident what was inside the boxes.

The irony struck me as extremely hilarious. Obviously, the manufacturers and DOD procurement officers back in the states didn't have the same concern about security measures that my superior officers had. The solution? After a harried consultation among the members of the command element, I was ordered to instruct my men to cover the M16 silhouette with black spray paint. To my mind, this was a fairly obvious tell that the crates contained something of critical value, which any Vietnamese who saw them would, no doubt, eventually figure out. But like a good soldier, my men and I did what we were ordered to do. In any event, all of the weapons were safely distributed from our warehouse without incident.

Daily Life In Vietnam

My assignment to 03 Bin Storage was not much different from what I would have experienced had I been assigned to stateside duty. Nevertheless, it was most grueling work, since we worked around the clock in two 12-hour shifts seven days every week. The Qui Nhon Depot was under severe command pressure to try and organize the mountains of materials and supplies that had literally been dumped onto the beaches of Qui Nhon to avoid paying exorbitant penalties to shipping corporations, who had transported them from depots in the US to Vietnam during the rapid build-up of US involvement in Vietnam the previous two years.

I didn't get any time off for the first several weeks, working every day, learning the job and trying to meet unrealistic command goals. I was finally ordered by my Company Commander to take a Sunday afternoon off. I hitched a ride down into the city of Qui Nhon and walked around. I was fascinated by the different culture and way of life of the Vietnamese.

An older lady, still quite attractive, caught my eye. She beckoned me into her small apartment, where in broken English, after she served me tea and a sandwich, she offered herself to me for a $5.00 Military Payment Certificate (MPC). Of course, I obliged, though it was not nearly as exciting as I had imagined it would be. Generally, most Vietnamese women I experienced were very subdued during carnal relations. After we were done, she told me that her husband had been a soldier in the Vietnamese Army, that he had been killed the year before. This meant she had to be a prostitute in order to support herself. She related she was very fortunate not to have any children. As I was leaving, she shyly asked if I wanted her to be my full-time lover. I didn't know what to say, so I said nothing and just left.

It was my first understanding of how the US presence in Vietnam was much more harmful than just the vast destructiveness caused by our powerful military firepower. We were drastically impacting the whole culture in many damaging ways, I suppose as the French colonial rulers had done before us.

Throughout the cities and in small countryside villages of Vietnam, there were numerous "Boom Boom Shacks," places where GIs, and sometimes their officers, could relieve their carnal desires by way of intercourse or massages or what have you. Here is a poem I wrote relaying one of my experiences of carnal relief:

Some Looks

There are some looks which never fade
though a million memories pass
Looks that sharply cut into marrow
of a fragile soul seeking some solace

Such a keening glance the papa san shot me
It passed clean through shaking me asunder
soul-shocked making mush all my grunt lustful desires
He just simply sat looking at me
long wispy-bearded, silver-haired
in carefully laundered peasant pajamas
with thin-curved long pipe wafting home-grown herb
about his wizened stoic face

*He didn't miss a methodical thatch of conical basket
while his granddaughter I suppose and I
strolled arm-linked through the dappled courtyard
into a dark bead-curtained cubbyhole
where in tight sequined mini-skirt
so alien from long-flowing demure ao-dai
of Vietnamese gentlewomen
she would allow herself to be raped
for a $5.00 MPC-note by me
one other white devil
of another foreign army
exploiting pillaging destroying
their hallowed ancestor-spirited land
in the hollow name of freedom*

In the military, heavy drinking is as natural as breathing. Our BOQ had a small Officer's Club, where we could get simple meals, hamburgers, hot dogs and such, cooked by a mess sergeant, and drink profusely when off-duty. The main Officer's Club for the Depot was on the grounds of the 67th MedEvac Hospital, located right next to the 629th. It served a more elaborate, upgraded cafeteria-style mess for officers. Several nights a week there were lousy Filipino bands playing covers of American rock 'n roll songs rather badly. The song I heard most often was the Temptations' "My Girl". Even today, when I hear it, I am propelled back to remembering Vietnam.

Most days, during the hour-and-a-half lunch break in the middle of my shift, I would usually go to my BOQ room, which was conveniently across the street from 03 Bin Storage. There, I would consume a six-pack of San Miguel beer and maybe a bag of potato chips, while listening to music on the Armed Forces Vietnam Network. Most every night, I would go to the Officer's Club and eat the one meal a day I consistently ate, drinking a fifth of Drambuie, chased by many San Miguel Beers. Of course, I would sometimes write. Here's one of the several poems I wrote about what I observed at the 67th MedEvac Officers Club:

chief nurse

*bleached hair
strands wispy
limply fall about
flushed eyes*

running mascara
bluing the bright face
with the ready smile
which when curved wide
somewhat hides
the wrinkles
of a body
ounce-spreading
though still
supple-seeming

here in flare-flickering shadows
of frantic basecamp officers club
while pouring can after can of san miguel
down my unquenchable throat
i imagine her name is major marge
the fancy tonight of some colonel who buys drinks
and sneers while jerkily dancing
with a rather crooked beak
of one who leads desks and/or diagrams

the pity of it is
when young she probably loved children
maybe wanted one or ten
now she can only watch
them mutilated die
her surrogate sons
of my generation

by blistering day
she garbs herself
with scissors and gauze
stuck in pockets
of jungle fatigues
to guide those
younger than she
the nurses
who tend their would-be lovers
lost in this would-be war

Despite the general safety of my work in the Depot, there were, nevertheless, a number of occasions, when I was faced with some considerable potential danger. My death wish in Vietnam could very well have been realized. There were several potentially dangerous episodes:

Deranged Trooper

During the first couple of days on duty with the 629th, I had my first harrowing, potentially life-threatening experience. A soldier went berserk and assaulted his squad leader and platoon sergeant with a bunk adapter – a serious chunk of steel pipe. After he seriously injured them, he fled the company area. It was late afternoon. The Company Commander ordered all officers and NCOs to spread out throughout the depot complex to find him and bring him back to the company area. Not knowing much of anything about where I was, and certainly not what I was doing, I started looking in an adjacent storage yard where crates of truck transmissions, axles, and large CONEX containers were stacked high. I had no idea what I was doing, but was just following orders and looking for the miscreant. I certainly thought that he would have been long-gone and didn't have the foggiest semblance of a plan of what I would do were I to encounter him.

I turned a corner, and—bam! There he was, hulking in front of me. He was at least a foot taller and a hundred pounds heavier than I was. He crouched and froze with the bunk adapter raised menacingly over his head. I closed my gaping mouth and said, "How ya doing, solder?" He grunted, and lifted the bunk adapter more threateningly. He was huge!

"Getting kind of late, isn't it? Must be about chow time, I imagine. Aren't you getting hungry?"

He just stared at me, wide-eyed, sweat pouring off his face, panting heavily. It took me a moment to realize that he was just as terrified as I was. I relaxed a little and pulled out a cigarette, leaned against a stack of crates and offered him one.

"Smoke?"

He relaxed a bit also, lowering the bunk adapter, and took a cigarette. I lit it with my Zippo, saying, "Look, you're already in a bunch of trouble. You don't want to make it worse by hiding out and running away from me. Why don't you come back, get some chow, and we'll see how we can straighten this thing out."

To this day, I don't know where I got the sense or the courage to face him down, but I suppose he was kowtowed by my lieutenant's rank. He docilely came back to the orderly room with me, where he was seized by the MPs, handcuffed and taken away. He was court-martialed, and nine months later I visited him and a couple of other members of my company at down at LBJ—Long Bin Jail in Saigon. I still feel a tinge of guilt for telling him we could "straighten this thing out."

Ammo Dump

In the summer of 1967, I was assigned on the Battalion roster for a week's duty as the Officer-In-Charge of the guard detail at a large Ammo Dump complex in an isolated area that was several klicks—Army slang for kilometers—away from the main depot complex out in the boonies. It was built into the side of a small mountain that was covered with brush and jungle foliage. Fire lanes for M-60 machine guns had been cleared and claymore mines were interspersed around the perimeter. There were several guard towers on the perimeter connected by stacked bales of concertina wire. My duty was to sleep in the command bunker during the day and at night insure the readiness of the guards on duty by performing periodic radio checks. I would also walk around the perimeter doing random inspections of all the guard towers and defensive positions. I never caught anyone napping on duty for which I was most relieved. The week was mostly uneventful, despite my high level of anxiety and uncertainly about what to do in an actual combat situation. I played endless nightmare scenarios in my head about a probe or attack occurring on the ammo dump.

Nothing happened that week, except for one night in the wee hours of the morning when one of the claymores mysteriously blew. It put us all on full alert, scaring us half to death. We never found out what set it off and hypothesized that a small animal, likely one of the huge rats, which on occasion we saw scurrying about, had tripped it off. A number of months later the Ammo Dump was successfully blown up about 2100 hours one night. I happened to be riding down the main street of the Depot in my gun jeep on the way to the Officers Club when it happened. The force of the blast several klicks away not only shattered windows in the depot, but it also blew me out of the jeep.

I landed, hard, on my right shoulder and rolled into the ditch, partially filled with sewage water. Cursing profusely, I got up and brushed myself off as best I could and went back to the BOQ to change into a new set of jungle fatigues. I didn't think anything more about the incident until 1999, when I went to an orthopedic surgeon complaining about severe pain, numbness and tingling in my right hand and wrist that impeded my ability to write. I figured that I was suffering from carpel tunnel syndrome. Upon examination, however, the surgeon asked if I had ever suffered an injury to my right shoulder. I recalled being blown out of my jeep, landing on my right shoulder, and told him about it. He asserted that most likely I was suffering from Keinböck's Syndrome, a condition where the blood supply to small bones in my wrist had been interrupted as a result of landing hard on my right shoulder. Without blood, the small bones die, requiring them to be surgically removed. I was most disappointed when I was told I could not keep the bones to make a necklace!

Almost Dying Getting Laid

Any death in war is tragic. It's indescribably awful when a soldier, presumably fighting for a just and noble cause is KIA, killed in action, while defending his or her country, or so politicians, pundits and obituaries claim. But, it's especially appalling when a soldier is killed by mistake, by friendly fire or an accident or something horribly stupid, such as happened when a Chinook troop ship blew up, killing all aboard because it had been mistakenly hooked up to the wrong fuel. One of my closest encounters with death in Vietnam happened as a result of something that had it turned out differently, it could have been judged as being of the "horribly stupid" variety.

For three months, mid-May to mid-August, being junior officer in the company, I was assigned to the night duty shift from 7:00 p.m. until 7:00 a.m. The skeleton crew on duty during the night was responsible for processing priority orders for supplies and generally took an hour-and-a-half "dinner" break between 1:00 a.m. and 2:30 a.m. One night my NCOIC, noncommissioned-officer-in-charge, a Spec 5 good ole boy with a heavy drawl from Arkansas or the Texas panhandle, asked me if I wanted to go with him to visit a local Boom Boom Shack, where for a $5.00 MPC, one could relief themselves of their carnal desires.

"What the hell," I replied. "Sure, why not."

Off we went to a cluster of shacks in a fishing village about a 5-minute walk on the other side of Red Beach, the recreation area that during the day was the local R & R center for Army personnel in the Qui Nhon Support Command. In short order, we each had procured a more or less young lady of the late evening, with whom we lustily pursued carnal knowledge in the deep dark of adjacent cubicles. All of a sudden, the beaded curtains of the cubicles parted and the wrinkled, old Mamma-san, from whom we had procured our "dates", let loose a strident stream of Vietnamese. This seemed to create high consternation and anxiety in our not-so-young, not-so-lovely ladies. They quickly detached from our amorous embraces and hurried us out of the hut with words in Pidgin English to the effect of, "GI, Hurry. Hurry, GI. VC. VC Tax Man. Hurry. Get clothes. Hide. Hurry. Hide!"

Half dressed, dragging boots, rifles and jungle fatigues, we hurried as best we could to a back area of the village complex near the seashore. There, they frantically motioned for us to climb into a couple of large baskets filled with detritus from that day's sea catch. The large baskets were closed with wooden covers. Breathlessly, hearts pounding, we waited in the dank, smelly dark, sweating profusely and listening to the harsh yammering of several men and the Mamma-san back and forth in Vietnamese. After what seemed like an eternity or so, the covers of our baskets slid open to reveal a slice of bright, star-chipped sky and the grinning visage of the Momma-san. She grinned a betel-nut-black-toothed grin and told us, "Okay, GI. You go now. VC no find. No kill you, no kill me."

Trip to Phu Bai

In October of 1967, I was assigned an extra duty as company supply officer. On the property books were a couple of deuce-and-a-half trucks, a five-ton wrecker, water tanks, a jeep, field mess units, tents, etc., which had been temporarily assigned to a Task Force up in I Corps near Phu Bai. The company commander ordered me to go up to Phu Bai, inventory the equipment and formally transfer the items to the property book of the Task Force. Early the next morning, his driver took me to the Qui Nhon Army air field. The deal with Army Air Transport is that you report to the Sergeant in charge, handing him a copy of your orders. Then, you wait until your name is called for an available flight to wherever it is you are going. I was easily able to get manifested to Danang, but it was quite a different story getting a seat on a plane or helicopter for the short flight to Phu Bai, only about 40 klicks up the road. Because it was unsafe at anytime to drive though the area completely dominated by the communist insurgency, I had to wait for a plane or helicopter ride.

I spent several days in the Danang Army Transit Terminal, waiting to be manifested on one of the scarce flights up to Phu Bai. During the days, I was at the terminal waiting for a manifest. During the nights I would eat and drink at the Navy Officer's Club on the lovely Perfume River. Then, I would hitch a ride to the Transient BOQ on China Beach. There, one night, I survived my first and only rocket attack in Vietnam. About 0400 hours, I was awakened by a wailing siren and an orderly running through the BOQ, pounding on all the doors, as he yelled, "Alert!, Alert!, Alert!" I was very mocus, sleepy, and still drunk from my evening meal accompanied by much too much Drambuie and San Miguel. I didn't know what to do, so I got dressed, checked my weapon and crawled under the bed. The siren kept wailing, and I heard several explosions and yelling nearby. Then silence. I must have fallen asleep, most likely passed out again, because my alarm awoke me, dressed, curled up under the bed, with my weapon, an M-2 carbine, cradled in my arms.

Eventually, I got manifested on a Vietnamese Commercial DC 23 flight. The plane was very old, very rickety, very shaky, a real chewing-gum-and bailing-wire kind of a deal. It was quite hot in the plane with no air conditioning, and since the windows were open, it was also most dusty. The short flight started with a very bumpy take-off up to maybe 1500 feet or so for no longer than 15 minutes. This was followed by a sharp dive earthward, as tracers reached out for us from the jungle below. The pilot slammed into the tarmac of the landing strip, bounced for a terrifyingly short while and suddenly skidded around, revving the engines, whether braking or speeding up, I had no idea. I desperately gripped the seat in front of me, terrified.

An Air Vietnam Stewardess hastily motioned for me and a sergeant to get off the DC 23, jumping out an open door at the rear of the plane onto the hot tarmac. We barely hit the ground when we were nearly blown over by the prop wash, as the old bird quickly moved down the airstrip, up and away from Phu Bai. It only took me a couple of hours to complete my task of reassigning the property to the Task Force. The five-ton wrecker was not at the Task Force, but I paid that no mind at the time. Luckily, I was able to hitch a ride on the empty supply helicopter back to Danang in time to have a good meal accompanied by the usual bottle of Drambuie, chased by San Miguel beers at the O-Club.

Here are several other incidents from my year In-country. Though not necessarily dangerous, they remain deeply imprinted in my memories.

Dead MP

This next incident is a result of a dumb accident that sometimes happens in wartime. Though it posed no danger to me, it was a reminder of just how awful death can be. Did it temper in any way my firm intention to die in Vietnam? Maybe just a little.

Early one afternoon I was on my way out of the main gate of the depot compound one to go to MACV, the Military Assistance Command Vietnam, for a meeting. I saw there were a group of people milling around the guard shack, several MPs and a couple of officers. An Army ambulance was parked nearby. Off to the side, a young Vietnamese girl was crying hysterically, being comforted by several companions.

After we got through the bottleneck, I had my driver pull over. I walked back and saluted an MP Captain, who seemed to be in charge. I inquired what was going on, and he informed me that one of his men was horsing around with the Vietnamese girl, putting his .45 revolver to her head, after having taken the clip out. When she protested and started crying, he put the .45 up to his temple, not realizing that a round was chambered. He pulled the trigger, blowing his brains and the side of his head all over her and the guard shack. I looked in and saw his frozen look of shocked surprise, dark blue eyes wide, mouth gaped open, with blood beginning to dry matted through his short-cropped, blond hair. He was slumped against the guard shack wall in a deepening pool of brownish-dark red blood with Jackson-Pollackian swirls spread across the upper walls and ceiling. Seeing his death mask and the ghastly visage of his premature death gave me a shiver, causing me to momentarily question somewhat my ardent death wish. These many years later, that stark vision remains deeply imprinted within my memory. It makes me especially grateful that—despite my strong death wish to the contrary—I did not die in Vietnam.

Lost Thai Sticks

Many troops in Vietnam, and some officers such as myself, smoked Thai sticks, potent marijuana cigarettes that have been dipped in opium or hashish oil. My jeep driver was able to purchase 20 fat joints of potent Thai Sticks packaged in a number 10 business envelope from a Mamma-san he knew downtown for about $2.00.

Late one night, I was outside my second-floor BOQ room, two doors down from the latrine, grooving to the full moon playing hide and seek among scurrying clouds, while I puffed away on the first Thai stick from a new envelope. Suddenly, several doors away, a hard-ass Major lurched out of his room and stumbled towards me on the way to the latrine. I panicked and flipped the joint into the street. It seemed like it took forever for the lit end of the Thai stick to arc slowly several times over the street below, hit the street and bounce several times with a profusion of sparks. I was sure that the Major had detected either the pungent smell of marijuana or seen the mini-light show. I saluted him and hastily went into my room, where I stashed away the envelope, in which were the 19 other fat Thai sticks. I passed out and promptly forgot the incident had ever happened, as the next day melded into another endless round of slow-passing 24 hours. In Chapter 7, you'll find out exactly what happened with the envelope containing the 19 joints.

Busted

One night, I had my driver drive me to the Officers Club at the MACV compound on the beach in downtown Qui Nhon for a floor show, supposedly much better than the ones we got at the 67th MedEvac Hospital. As usual, I got drunk on Drambuie and lots of San Miguel beer. About midnight, when we were driving back to the depot, I decided I wanted to get us laid, so I directed him to take us to a brothel. We finished our business, but as we left the brothel, we were spotted by two MPs on patrol in a jeep downtown. We were promptly detained and booked at the headquarters of the Military Police in Qui Nhon.

As it turned out, the depot and Qui Nhon were under an alert, whether practice or for cause, I have no idea. So, I was charged with not only being off limits after curfew, but being off limits after curfew, during an alert—these were quite serious charges. Since my driver was just following my orders to drive him downtown, he was given an Article 15 and fined a half-months pay. I had to report to the Battalion Commander, a folksy Lieutenant Colonel from Arkansas, the next morning. However, he was quite stern as he restricted me to the BOQ, when not on duty, until it was determined whether or not I would be court-martialed. Thank goodness I was able to get my evening meal and booze at the tiny O-Club on the first floor of the of the BOQ.

It took a couple of long and agonizing weeks for a decision about court-martialing me to be determined. Had I been court-martialed, I would have perhaps had to serve my sentence down at Long Binh Jail near Saigon. This would have extended my tour in Vietnam for as long as I was jailed, and most likely meant I would get a dishonorable discharge as a felon. This was a very big deal! Finally, I was told to report again to the Battalion Commander's office at depot headquarters. Wearing my cleanest, most starched pair of jungle fatigues, I entered his office and sharply saluted him.

"Lieutenant Brinson, reporting as ordered, Sir."

Looking me up and down, he returned my salute, "At ease, Lieutenant."

"Yes Sir!," snapping sharply to parade rest.

After a few seconds, seeming like an eternity, he slowly drawled, "Well, Lieutenant, you sure fucked up."

"Yes Sir!"

"But, you've done a good job for us here at the Depot, so we've decided not to court-martial you."

"Thank You, Sir!"

"However, we have to give you some consequences for your fuck-up."

"Yes Sir!"

"You'll get another letter of reprimand in your file ..."

"Thank you, Sir!"

"And, we're cancelling our recommendation that you get a Bronze Star for your service here in Vietnam."

"My Bronze Star, Sir?" I could hardly keep from guffawing.

"Yes, Lieutenant. Now, you're not getting the Bronze Star we wanted to put you in for."

"Thank you, Sir. This is certainly a hard lesson for me to learn."

"Well, Lieutenant, we hope so. You're dismissed."

"Thank you, Sir!" I saluted him, did a sharp about face and left his office. It was one of my best acting jobs ever. That I didn't break out into a raucous belly laugh is most amazing. I'd like to think that he was just as amused about this charade of military justice as I was.

Another Alert

While much of my duty in Vietnam was relatively uneventful, there were periodic reminders that we were serving in a hostile combat zone. Whether for practice or for cause, we were regularly subjected to alerts, usually in the wee hours of an early morning. Believe me, there is nothing more disconcerting than a bunch of rear-echelon officers, disdainfully referred to as a bunch of REMFs,—Rear Echelon Mother Fuckers— stumbling out of their BOQ rooms in various stages of dress and inebriety, half-asleep, brandishing an array of unauthorized weaponry and rushing to get to their very important places of assignment.

Our unauthorized weaponry included AK-47s, Uzis, Thompson assault rifles and other special forces weapons from around the world. The weapon I carried was an M-2 carbine, illegally modified with a sawed off barrel and a pistol grip, accompanied by two banana 30-round clips, taped together with duct tape. An irony was that I never fired the weapon in a firefight, only several times at the rifle range and once during my last week in-country that I'll discuss in the next chapter.

My place of duty, after I became Supply Officer, was in the arms room to supervise the dispensing of M-16s and four clips of ammo to each of the troops. One night, during an alert I gave a weapon and ammo to a new man, who had just joined our unit that very afternoon. It was his second tour in the 'Nam, his first having been down in the Delta with the 9th Division. I could see he was adrenalin-pumped, as he took his weapon, expertly loading a clip and seating a round. He then rushed off to what he thought was the perimeter of our compound. It struck me too late that he wasn't aware our compound was smack-dab backed up upon the western boundary of the 67th Medical Evacuation Hospital compound.

"Oh shit," I panicked, quickly yelling after him, "Soldier, WAIT!" I leapt over the counter and sprinted after him, but not before he had emptied a clip into the dark shadows across the sewage creek between our concertina-topped cyclone fences into the hospital compound. I explained to him that our compound bordered the compound of the 67th MedEvac Hospital.

"What? Our guys are over there?," he incredulously queried.

"Yes, they are, soldier" I replied.

"Are their security people pointing their weapons at us, Sir?

"I suppose so."

"Well, Sir, with all due respect, that doesn't make any sense."

"You're right there, Soldier. It surely doesn't."

This is another glaring example of the reality that in the military, or for that matter any large, complex organization, such as AA, too often the right hand often does not know, nor thinks to coordinate with, what the fuck the left hand is doing …

Chapter 6—Gun Jeep

The last six months of my tour, my platoon was assigned a gun jeep with an M-60 machine gun mounted in the back seat. As the platoon leader, I sometimes escorted small convoys of specialized weapons and other sensitive supplies throughout the Central Highlands of Vietnam in this gun jeep. I flew a green flag with a prominent red rose from my radio antenna. I flew this Rose Flag instead of one with the usual gung-ho dictums, such as "Get Some," "Kill Cong," "Can Do" or "45 Killing Days Until Christmas!," perhaps the most obnoxious slogan I saw while in Vietnam. I would also wrap garlands of plastic roses around the gun mount and in between the sandbags on the windshield. Sometimes, I stuck a lotus blossom in the barrel of the M-60 machine gun barrel, emulating the famous picture from the October 21, 1967 "Levitate the Pentagon" protest of a young blond hippie boy, sticking a flower into the barrel of a soldier's M-14 rifle.

Occasionally superior officers, uptight, gung-ho majors or captains, once a lieutenant colonel, would bellow, "Lieutenant, what the fuck is going on with all this flower stuff?"

"Well Sir," I would respectfully reply, "I adhere to the love/hate philosophy of Edward Albee, evident in such works as *The Zoo Story* and *Who's Afraid of Virginia Woolf.* I believe in mixing my firepower with flower power, Sir!"

One of my several letters of reprimand while serving in Vietnam was for refusing to remove my Rose Flag. That from the lieutenant colonel, a visiting dignitary from the Pentagon. To this day the flag is framed and hanging in my office, one of my most prized possessions. Another letter of reprimand I got was for dancing on the stage of the Depot Enlisted Men's club with two Australian Strippers, which the Battalion Sergeant Major reported to the Battalion Commander. In it I was reprimanded for fraternizing with enlisted men—they had much better floorshows than the O-Club did—and for conduct unbecoming an officer and gentleman.

The Mang Yang pass was one of the most desolate places I've ever experienced. It was denuded of most vegetation by the defoliant Agent Orange. The landscape on both sides of the road was littered with wreckage of disabled vehicles damaged by ambushes. Damaged vehicles would be bulldozed off the road, their cargo scattered in rotting heaps, so that other vehicles in the convoy could speed through the hostile terrain. Here's a poem I wrote about a convoy from Qui Nhon to Pleiku that I escorted through the Mang Yang pass in the gun jeep on Valentines Day of 1968:

valentine's day, 1968

dust cakes into pores loosened by streams of sweat
the back and butt rebel at each rutted jolt
eyes tear with irritation and grime

fear like a tickling dream
scurries wetly about in gut

i gaze up the steep barren-stumped cliffs
and down in valleys below where scattered
about like carcasses of dried locusts are
debris of other war machines that didn't make it
as we wind a snail's pace way up
somewhere beyond the far ridge line

behind me
a grinding rev-straining
deuce-and-a-half
filled with crates of 105 ammo
presents of death for sir charles
on this valentine's day
lumbers through the dust
trailing after my gun jeep

i wait watching i wait
listening jerkily all
around for swish
of rockets plop
of mortars thud
of grenades whine of
bullets the terrible
swift suddenness of
one mine which
others missed

much of me wants one of these to occur—it's why I came here
BUT

flitting visions pass the mind in quick revolutions:
  –a girl baby tiny and cuddled cooing
  –one woman young lonely and fretting
  –parents stoically speaking to a uniformed stranger
  –sisters huddled around a flag-draped closed coffin
  –a muted plea for some god somewhere to maybe forgive
  –the disturbing perfectly sane query:

  WHAT THE HELL AM I DOING HERE???

for small comfort is one meager carbine grasped more tightly

Christmas Eve and the Bob Hope Show

On Christmas Eve of 1967, I was Battalion CQ, Charge of Quarters. This duty entailed me to stay in Battalion Headquarters all night, manning the radios and phones, where I would be the point person to respond to any untoward event or incident that happened within the Battalion's areas of responsibility overnight. Since I was on duty all night, I couldn't get shit-faced drunk as I usually did every night, a real bother. My BOQ roommate, Bernie, was the Battalion S-2, the staff officer in charge of garnering intelligence information for the Battalion Commander, the Executive Officer and the company commanders to plan for our convoy operations and our defense of the Battalion if attacked. Bernie and I sat for several hours that evening in his office, discussing the current tactical situation. According to maps with plastic overlays on which intelligence information was posted in varying colors, the situation looked extremely dire. Huge arrows showed the movement of VC, Viet Cong insurgent units, and the NVA, North Vietnamese regular army units that had infiltrated into South Vietnam from North Vietnam along the infamous Ho Chi Ming trail that ran through neighboring Laos and Cambodia. Several stark arrows were converging on the Depot and the city of Qui Nhon.

In April of 1967, General William Westmoreland, Commander of US Military Forces in Vietnam appeared before Congress to request additional troops for the war. He assured US law makers that unlike the situation in 1965, when Vietnamese Communist insurgents were winning, that in 1967 American and South Vietnamese forces were defeating the communist insurgents and their supporters from North Vietnam. In November of 1967, during another visit to Washington, DC, he addressed a news conference, in which he was widely quoted as saying, "We have reached an important point, when the end begins to come into view." He even repeated the words of others, referring to a "light at the end of the tunnel" to describe improved U.S. fortunes in Vietnam. Westmoreland was convinced that the VC and NVA were trying to recreate a decisive military victory at the Marine Corps base in Khe Sahn, near the Laotian border and the DMZ separating South Vietnam from North Vietnam. He asserted the enemy commanders were attempting to replicate what the Vietnamese had successfully done at Dien Bien Phu in 1954 to defeat France in the First Indochina War. Out of hand, he disregarded any suggestion that the communists were instead planning massive attacks against major population centers all along the coastal areas of South Vietnam. The troop movements, he asserted, were attempts to divert our attention from Khe Sahn. Oops, choose once again, good General, Sir! About ten weeks later, the notorious and devastating Tet Offensive began on January 30, 1968.

The next day, Christmas Day, I was exhausted and dead tired. Nevertheless instead of drinking per usual in my BOQ room until I passed out, I decided to go to the famed Bob Hope show at nearby Phu Cat Airbase. I dozed in my shotgun seat during the short drive out to the airbase, where I joined some 30,000 other US servicemen to experience the comic remarks of Bob Hope. As well, we greatly enjoyed a bevy of go-go girls, led by Ann Margaret, dressed in knee-high white leather boots and blue pastel miniskirts, dancing to the music of Les Brown and his Band of Renown. How do I remember these details, you query? I didn't, but last year I googled Qui Nhon and came up with a 2014 Brisbane, Australia travel article about Qui Nhon, in which the Bob Hope show I attended was prominently noted. The article included the details above, and a photograph of Hope, Welch and the go-go girls—it was a most bizarre walk down memory lane.

It happened that I sat near a classmate of mine from Xavier's ROTC unit, James, who was now a Captain. He related that he was a Battery Commander at a nearby fire base. He looked considerably older and extremely careworn. We hardly spoke, but we did comment about what sitting ducks we were jam-packed together in a valley surrounded by mountains. It was especially daunting for me, having seen the maps in Bernie's office with the ominous arrows of VC and NVA forces aimed precisely where we were. Several well-placed rockets would have killed or wounded hundreds of us.

In 1983, I wrote the following poem after seeing a news program during another special Bob Hope show, this time in Lebanon, following the October 23rd bombing of the Marine barracks in Beirut:

Bob Hope Show, 1983

Christmas Eve
Waning days before the year of Big Brother
The TV flickers cross-fading images of the Bob Hope Show
Another ritual of entertainment for American grunts
Being maimed and killed in another far-off land

His eyes silkenly sincere
Straight into the lens of the nation's soul
Our President yearns for peace
But steadfastly vows to keep the troops in place

Hot damn we're doing it again
Keeping the world safe
For some democracy
While our precious youth
Spurred forward by patriotic myths
From fantasies of armchair warriors
Are brutalized in a cross-fire
Of centuries-old blood-hatreds

The soundtrack croons John Lennon's "So this is Christmas"
And I'm flooded with memories and tears
Never able to forget my Bob Hope Show
Christmas Day of '67 at Phu Cat Airbase
On the once verdant coastal plain of Vietnam
Where too weary from witnessing too much death
I couldn't snicker much less laugh as he quipped
"Some police action, huh boys!"

I rock my sleeping son
holding him tighter
Pray for a time
When our beautiful land

*Can be as diligent in waging peace
As it still is obsessed with seeking war*

The An Nhon Orphanage and R & R

In November of 1967, about the time that Westmoreland was assuring Congress that victory was forthcoming, I volunteered to be the Civil Affairs Officer for my battalion, the 98th Supply and Service Battalion. Our primary project was the Ah Nhon orphanage, located about 25 klicks out in the boonies. The orphanage was operated by an order of French-Vietnamese nuns, mixed-race themselves, who cared for some 40–50 Vietnamese orphan children. Most of the children had been fathered by American GIs. These "half-breed" children, as well as the nuns who cared for them, were spurned by their Vietnamese families and Vietnamese society at large.

I organized a campaign similar to the Toys for Tots campaign, sponsored every year by the Marine Corps. We garnered about $200 worth of Christmas goodies from friends and families in the US, which we distributed to the children at a gala Christmas party in late December. It was such a delight to enjoy the laughing and giggling glee of the children as they opened their presents. To thank us, we were invited to a sumptuous feast of Vietnamese delicacies at the orphanage the third weekend of January, 1968. I was especially fond of the deep-fried peacock sausage served with núóc-mám, i.e. fish sauce, made from fermenting fish heads with copious amounts of sea salt, a staple of Vietnamese cuisine.

The next week, I was scheduled for six days of R&R (Rest and Relaxation) in Hong Kong. I spent the days shopping and luxuriating in a hotel on the tip of the Kowloon peninsula next to the Star Ferry pier with a gorgeous view of Hong Kong Island and the busy Victoria harbor. During the day, I would shop, getting drunk window-shopping. In every shop, whether a tailor shop or a camera store, an electronics outlet or what have you, I would be offered a quart bottle of San Miguel beer. By early afternoon most days, I was pie-eyed drunk. One morning, I took a tour bus up to the boarder between Hong Kong and Communist China. I sat for a couple of hours eating lunch at a café overlooking Communist China. It didn't look much different from the farmlands and tenements of Kowloon I had seen on the hour bus ride up to the border. I was most disappointed that I couldn't actually go into China or purchase any of the exquisite jade that China produces, since it was an "Enemy State".

At night I would cruise the bars and strip clubs, eventually procuring a lady of the evening to accompany me back to my hotel room. On my last night in Hong Kong, however, I met a delightful young women, Jackie Larn. I procured her for the evening from a withered madam with extremely long and curved fingernails. Jackie and I immediately established a very powerful, karmic connection. She was different from the other prostitutes I had experienced previously in Vietnam and in Hong Kong. She spoke fairly good English and had a delightfully witty sense of humor. We fell passionately and hopelessly in love, as the following poem describes:

a love lament for Jackie Larn from January, 1968

though shared, through only the short space
of a few swift-passing moments, love is,
perhaps, a magical potion and precious

she turned her tawny face
and leaning closer kissed my shoulder
with just the tip of a delicate finger

we rested in early evening's dusk light
limbs and spirits joined quietly anticipating
the next sensitive explosion to come

underneath satin sheets musing upon the slow undulations
of ceiling fan and tangy smell of long flowing dark hair
i traced a perfect circle upon the curvature of her thigh

later while walking the deserted Hong Kong streets
we paused to laugh through our broken words and gestures
at the delicious wonder of chipped starlight

ah hem – but tears swiftly
followed at daybreak
and neither of us
could quite understand
what compelled me to return
like others she had spent time with
to the urgencies of killing

now in my state of duty
surrounded by strewn earth
incessant confusion

*and the sweet sick stench of burnt flesh
while behind me
the never-ending booms
tear away at all living
scattering bits
of distant blue ridge line
in lazy haphazard arcs
all i can do
is regretfully bask
in fading memory
and tenuous worlds
of if only and maybe*

While still in Vietnam, and after I returned to the US, we exchanged correspondence across the vast space and distance between our very different worlds. However, during the late summer of 1968, after I wrote her another letter, I never received a letter in reply. I have no idea whatever became of her. She became one other major unrequited lover, about which sometimes I would cry in my beer. Just the other day, I came across her Kowloon address that is still in my little black army notebook.

Saigon French Meal

A week after I got back from R&R in Hong Kong, I was sent to Ho Chi Minh City, which will always be Saigon to me, on temporary duty for several days. This was the result of a policy change initiated by Captain Parker, the second CO of the 629th. Captain Parker was a Mustang, a Regular Army Master Sergeant, who also had a Reserve Officer Commission. He was as different as bright day is from darkest night, compared to the total asshole, Queeg-like Captain Lauck, the previous CO, who took all such plush assignments for himself.

At the end of each month, an officer from every company had to travel to Saigon to visit company members incarcerated in LBJ – Long Binh Jail. We had to have a "counseling session" with company prisoners, giving them pay vouchers and any cash left over that hadn't been deducted for fines and forfeiture of pay from their court-martial. Since I was at the time the senior lieutenant in the 629th, he sent me on this nice in-country R&R to Saigon. After New York City and Portland, Oregon, for sure, maybe Paris also, Saigon is my favorite city in the whole wide world. I've been fortunate to be able to make two return visits to Saigon, once in 2002 and also in 2004.

I flew into the busy Ton Son Nhut airbase mid-afternoon of Saturday, January 27th. I have a vague memory of seeing F-4 Phantom jets in their concrete revetments along the runway as we taxied to the main terminal building. When I returned on my first trip back to Vietnam in 2002, I saw the same revetments along the runway, which we had built during the American War in Vietnam. They were now protecting Russian MIG 21 fighter planes, which belonged to the Vietnam People's Air Force. I have a trace memory of the Army bus ride into downtown Saigon and seeing a large golden Buddha glittering in the distance a couple of hundred meters or so across the glistening rice paddies. However, during the intervening four decades Saigon had expanded to encompass Ton Son Nhut airfield. Upon my return visit in 2002, I could discern no Golden Buddha nor any rice paddies between Ton Son Nhut airbase and downtown Saigon during the bus ride—there was nothing but crowded urban sprawl.

I got a BOQ room in the Rex Hotel, then next to the USAID building on Nguyen Hue Street near the old French Opera House, which today houses the offices of the Saigon People's Politburo . A statute of Ho Chi Min is today in the flowered square across the street. In 1968, there was instead a large statue of a South Vietnamese ranger, charging an enemy position with fixed bayonet. Amazingly, on both return trips, I stayed again in the Rex Hotel.

On Saturday night, I ate a wonderful meal and drank my usual bottle of Drambuie accompanied by San Miguel beers with other young officers at the rooftop restaurant of the Rex Hotel. There, we literally watched the war being waged in the outer suburbs of Saigon. Firefights, flares, and gunships provided a constant, cycloramic light show. Especially gorgeous from a distance was Puff, the Magic Dragon, a heavily armed AC-130 Hercules gunship, which was reputed to be able to lay down a barrage of mini-gun fire so thick that every inch of a football field would be covered with lethal lead. It was like watching a fantastical 4th of July fireworks show, until with a sinking feeling in my gut, I realized that the deadly fire was raining down upon the densely populated civilian suburbs of Saigon.

A loud crash in the street below, followed by a stream of high-pitched Vietnamese invectives, interrupted our conversation. We rushed over to the ledge to look down at the drivers of two lorries that had crashed into each other on the crowded street. They viciously yelled at each other until some White Mice—our racist GI nickname for members of the brutal Saigon Police, diminutive in statue, who wore white shirts with black ties and white helmets—came to straighten out the accident scene with maximum application of their nightsticks upon both miscreants. We laughed at the impromptu Vietnamese Keystone Cops scene below us.

Since there were no visiting hours at LBJ on Sunday, I had the day to just chill in the fascinating French-Vietnamese City of Saigon, known as the Paris of the Far East. I spent an hour or so walking through the open stalls of the downtown Saigon Ben Thanh Market, where there was a cornucopia of goods from around the world, many no doubt stolen from US facilities by the thriving Vietnamese black market. I also walked all around downtown Saigon, finding the port area along the Saigon River. I was fascinated by the several classic French Peugeots and Citroëns I saw parked on residential streets. I also spent several hours at the Saigon Zoo, where I took Kodachrome slides of elephants, giraffes and monkeys. Somewhere in my belongings they are safely packed away. Maybe during the long winter months some year, I'll look for them.

Monday was spent traveling to LBJ in an Army Bus, getting the pay vouchers for the two incarcerated members of the 629th and visiting briefly with them. One of them was the large black troop I had encountered during my first night in Qui Nhon. At first, he was very surly and only grunted in response to me. I apologized to him for misleading him that we could work it out by going back to the company area. As I left, he saluted me and thanked me for apologizing.

Tired, dusty and bored, after spending much of the day traveling to and from LBJ, while playing the typical Army game of Hurry-Up-and-Wait, I decided to go out on the town instead of eating at the Rex Hotel Rooftop officers mess. After I showered and put on a freshly cleaned and starched pair of jungle fatigues, I walked out into the still crowded Saigon streets and found a small, French restaurant nearby. A French-Vietnamese hostess, dressed in a stunning black silk ao dai with an intricate golden-thread pattern, led me to an empty seat at the French-style long table down the middle of the restaurant. My intention after the meal was to check out the infamous Tu Do Street, to see about perhaps getting laid in Saigon.

Across from me was a distinguished-looking Vietnamese gentleman, smoking a cigarette in a long, black holder with whom I struck up a conversation. He spoke excellent English, relating that he had been a student in the US for seven years that included graduating from Harvard with an MBA. He was the General Manager of the American Tobacco Company subsidiary in Vietnam. We had a rambling conversation about politics, culture, business, the war, movies, Broadway plays, etc. He was extremely well read, including the latest bestselling novels in the US. He had just finished reading James Michener's *Hawaii*, a book I had also read and thoroughly enjoyed. One of his favorite movies was Elizabeth Taylor and Richard Burton's *Who's Afraid of Virginia Wolf?*, also a favorite of mine.

After I finished my meal, he asked me if I wanted to continue our talk at his nearby Villa. I was pleasingly high, invigorated by the best conversation I had had in months, so I agreed, forgetting about Tu Do Street. He insisted on paying my bill, and we left the restaurant. As soon as we walked out the door, a Mercedes sedan pulled up to the curb, and we got into the lavish leather backseat. Momentarily, I had second thoughts, but forgot about them when he lit up a Thai stick. After a short ride, during which I mostly quelled panicky visions of being kidnapped by the VC, we pulled into his gated French Villa somewhere on the Saigon River. It was absolutely sumptuous.

We settled in to heavily cushioned easy chairs on a screen porch overlooking the lights of Saigon quivering on the river. With a bottle of Courvoisier we continued our conversation for the next hour or two. By this time, not only was I considerably drunk, but I was quite exhausted, barely able to stifle my yawns, much less put together a coherent sentence. He suggested I stay the night in his guest suite rather than disturb his chauffeur to take me back to the Rex. I gladly agreed. He summoned a manservant, who escorted me to a guest cottage with a large sunken bath, in which was drawn a hot bath, complete with a laid-out silk bathrobe. After my bath, I crawled into a huge King-size four-poster bed inside a custom-made mosquito net, still a bit drunk, but considerably refreshed.

On the bedside table were several books and current issues of American magazines. I was paging through the most recent issue of *Life*, beginning to drift off, when there was a demure knock on the door. I queried who it was, and the door slightly opened to reveal a most attractive Eurasian woman with a long, shiny black, ponytail wearing a lovely negligee. She inquired if I would like her to spend time with me. How could I refuse? We, indeed, spent a most lovely hour or so together. When I awoke the next morning to the sounds of birds and Saigon traffic, she was gone. I sometimes wonder if it actually happened. Maybe I just had a very vivid wet dream!

I got dressed, checking that nothing had been stolen, and enjoyed a breakfast of strong French-Vietnamese coffee, strong espresso coffee sweetened with condensed milk. It was accompanied with freshly baked croissants and fresh fruit, including one of my favorites, dragon fruit. When done, the manservant summoned the Mercedes driver to take me back to the Rex Hotel. My duty in Saigon finished, I got my gear and checked out of the Rex Hotel. I hitched a ride with a Captain from the Americal Division back to Ton Son Nhut air base. I was glad I had a paperback novel with me, Eli Kazan's *The Arrangement,* as I recall, because I waited the rest of the day and much of the night in the hot, sticky, primitive air terminal at the Ton Son Nhut airfield. I was finally manifested on the last scheduled flight that day to Qui Nhon, which left Saigon about 10:00 pm.

Though exhausted, I drank a San Miguel beer or two, talking with my roommate Bernie, catching up on the latest VC and NVA troop movements, which were still converging upon Qui Nhon. Exhausted, I soon fell fast asleep. Not for long, however. A couple of hours later, we were rudely awakened by the wailing siren of yet one other alert. We didn't know it, but the brutal Tet Offensive of 1968 had begun in earnest. Due to miscommunications from North Vietnam, it began a day earlier in the Central Highlands than in the rest of South Vietnam.

The Tet Offensive

The devastating Tet Offensive of 1968 had indeed been launched. I was most glad I had eaten the wonderful meals in Saigon, because for the next week or so I had nothing to eat but C-rations, not so affectionately called C-rats by GIs, and warm water from our canteens. No booze at all—it's lucky I didn't go into DTs. After I had distributed weapons and ammo to the men of the 629th, I went to a primitive CP, command post, behind the first platoon AO, area of operations on the depot perimeter. For the next several days, we were continuously on guard with only catnaps for sleep. We also went unwashed in the same jungle fatigues and flak jackets. Portions of the Depot Complex and the city of Qui Nhon were under sustained enemy assault for the first and only time during my tour of duty. Primary targets in Qui Nhon were the airfield, radio stations, MACV headquarters downtown, the petroleum tank farms and the ammo dump north of the main depot.

Since we were in the middle of the large Qui Nhon Depot complex, we did not experience any direct small-arms fire, and we were most fortunate not to sustain any rocket or mortar rounds, which haphazardly fell all around us in the depot. Artillery, naval bombardments and air strikes occurred continuously throughout the day and night all along the mountains to the west and north of the depot area. Early in the second week of the offensive, my driver drove me in the gun jeep through downtown Qui Nhon to attend a meeting to coordinate Civil Affairs efforts for the thousands of refugees that had been forced out of their fishing hamlets and villages by the pillaging VC and NVA during the first days of the offensive. The refugees had been gathering in open fields of the An Nhon district near the orphanage. Scattered throughout the city streets were many dead bodies—bloated, oozing, stinking, grotesque in rigor mortis—bodies of VC, NVA and South Vietnamese Army soldiers, as well as many civilian bodies, including men, women and, most distressing, children.

Several days later, I accompanied a three truck convoy of 5-ton tractor-trailers full of lumber and supplies to build housing for the displaced persons in the refugee camps. Since the orphanage was nearby, I had my driver take me over to it, while the trucks were being unloaded. I was shocked when I drove through the familiar gates of the orphanage. Part of the compound had been devastated, a couple of buildings mostly destroyed and burned. From the intact buildings came mewing, whimpering sounds. Heart pounding, I walked up on the same veranda where several weeks earlier we had enjoyed such a festive feast. One of the nuns, limping badly on a homemade crutch came out to greet me. She sobbingly embraced me, and we spoke in her Pidgin French-Vietnamese-English. Apparently on the second or third day after the Tet offensive began, the Orphanage had been caught in a brutal cross-fire between a North Vietnamese unit and a Republic of Korea unit. A number of the children and staff had been killed. Many others had been critically wounded. She took me around the orphanage, and I saw several children being held and rocked by other children, all crudely bandaged, deeply in shock. They were in incredible pain and suffering terribly. To this day, I still vividly recall the blank looks of utter dismay and horror within their young, innocent, questioning eyes !~!~!

When the trucks had been unloaded, I drove back to the main depot compound in somewhat of a fugue state. Later, that evening, I went to the Catholic Chaplin's office to speak with him about how devastated I was about what I had witnessed. In passing, I mentioned that at least the orphans were in a better place, at peace in heaven. The Chaplin waved a stern finger at me, saying something to the effect, "Well, lieutenant, you know that if those children had not been properly baptized, they won't be in heaven. Perhaps in limbo, but certainly not in heaven!"

Initially, I was shocked. Almost immediately thereafter, I became apoplectic. Since he was a Captain, I remember stifling an impulse to tell him to go fuck himself. I vaguely recall standing up, mumbling something, saluting him and walking out the door to the Officer's Club, where once again I got royally drunk. This was another quasi-final straw that broke the back of me seeking any kind of solace from religion, especially from the Christian brand of religion. This incident deeply instilled in me an abhorrence of organized religion, any organized religion.

One of my last convoy runs in early March of 1968 was to a forward operating base of Task Force Barker, the command element of Lt. Calley's platoon, which was responsible for the My Lai massacre. It's still hard for me to fathom that this infamous day took place on March 16, 1968, some 49 years ago, while I was still in Vietnam. I did not shoot any civilians in a ditch, nor did I torch the hootch of any Vietnamese family, but when I visited My Lai on my first return trip to Vietnam, I realized with some chagrin that I had supplied the troops who did perform those heinous deeds—I sometimes refer to myself as a combat-support war criminal!

During the last week of my tour, I accompanied Bernie on a tour of several fire bases within Binh Dinh Province surrounding the depot, which had sustained brutal ground assaults overnight. One fire base very nearly was overrun by numerous squads of VC sappers. It was most disturbing to see the stacks of Vietnamese youth, horribly disfigured and blown apart from claymore mines and the withering fire from M-16s, M-60 machine guns, M-79 grenade launchers, artillery strikes, and napalm sorties from F-4 Phantoms. With a macabre fascination, of course, I was compelled to take several pictures of this Guernica-like gruesomeness. Their grisly death masks haunt me still today.

Later that night, getting drunk per usual in the Officers Club, for some reason, maybe a cover of a song from my high school days by a Filipino band, I remembered the summer, six years previously, when I fell in love with Barbara. This memory inspired me to write the following poem, utilizing considerable poetic license:

stark memory

*you looked up at me
with the precise peculiarity
of your smile
touching me
with a distinct embrace*

*my hand trembled
upon the round smallness
of your soft breast
the flesh quickening
with slight quivers*

*i knew then
i would remember you
in some place far-off
alien and strange*

*now
in this early morning light
drowsily munching stale c-rats
i am comforted
by your stark memory
gazing at silhouettes
of shredded viet cong
dangling mute
in concertina wire*

Coming Home

During the last week of my tour I was very ambivalent, mightily disappointed even, that my time in Vietnam was coming to an end, and I had not been killed. Despite the limits of my noncombat assignment as an Ordnance Supply Officer, I had volunteered for every extra-hazardous duty assignment that I could.

Early in my tour, during my scant time off, I trained to qualify to ride shotgun on MedEvac Helicopters from the 67th MedEvac Hospital contiguous with the 629th Company. On the weekend, when I was scheduled for my first assignment, a memorandum came down from MACV headquarters in Saigon that no longer would junior officers or senior noncommissioned officers, be allowed to ride shotgun. The reason? Because too many were getting killed or seriously wounded.

Compared to other Ordnance Supply Officers in my company and Battalion, nevertheless, I had been exposed to much more danger than most. One lieutenant, Charles, the fellow with whom I roomed at Ft. Lee, Virginia, never left his compound throughout his entire year tour except for the week he went on R & R. I at least was able to travel throughout much of Vietnam, visiting Danang, Phu Bai, Cam Ranh Bay and Saigon. I also escorted some twenty convoys throughout II Corps in my gun jeep. I was never involved in an ambush or firefight. Other regularly scheduled convoys of supplies were often hit. Rather ironic that. One afternoon after I returned from R & R, I watched a firefight that included F-4s dropping canisters of napalm on a village about 4 or 5 klicks—some 2 to 3 miles away—across rice paddies from the road on which I was traveling. I stopped and took a roll of pictures with the new Nikkormat Ftn camera I had bought in Hong Kong. Unfortunately, I mis-loaded the film canister and none of them were exposed. That's the closest I came to actual combat.

Late one night during my last week in Qui Nhon, very, very drunk, I roused my driver and my machine gunner, ordering them to get the gun jeep. Then, at my command, we went on a midnight drive out into the boonies far away from the depot. Sporadically, we would fire the M-60 machine gun and my modified M-2 carbine into the dark jungle. No one, friend or foe, ever fired back! The next day, I believe, was March 31, 1968, when horribly hung-over, I listened to LBJ announce he would not run for re-election. I and Jesse (Sgt. Rock) cheered. Did we high five? I don't remember.

My last night in Qui Nhon, my platoon threw a raucous farewell party for me. I got very drunk and high from smoking fat Thai sticks. Jesse procured for me a lovely, full-bosomed lady to celebrate my last evening in the 629th. I have no memory about how I got to Cam Ranh Bay from where I flew back to the US of A early in the morning of April 5, 1968. When I left Cam Ranh Bay, Vietnam I was still very drunk and blitzed. I don't remember anything about getting up that morning, getting dressed, getting to the Cam Ranh Bay airfield, and getting onto the chartered Tiger Airlines 707.

I do, however, vaguely remember taxiing along a long runway in a pink-tinged dawn, seeing palm trees and parked F-4 Phantom jets silhouetted against the distant triple-canopy jungle and the jagged ridge lines of the coastal mountain range as we gathered speed for takeoff. Quickly, with stomachs sinking, we whooshed away in a steep climb. I could see, far down below, the fading demarcation of land and sea. There was a skein of white sand beaches that merged into the blue-green sparkle of the South China Sea. And just like that, Vietnam was over for me. Despite my best intentions I had escaped Vietnam with nary a scratch, but with a horrendous itch, since I brought home a virulent case of crab lice, from the full-bosomed lady with whom I had spent my last night in Vietnam, up in Qui Nhon.

I remember nothing of the transpacific journey. It's gone, forever, a lost memory. It was dark, when I landed at McChord Air Force Base, Washington just before dawn on April 4, 1968, having crossed the International Date Line to gain back the day I lost the year before, living it again. Typically, it was lightly raining, and I was chilly in my rumpled khaki summer uniform. While eating my "Welcome Home" tough-and-greasy-steak-with-eggs breakfast, a Captain suggested I change into civvies before going to the Sea-Tac International Airport to book a flight to Washington, D.C., so I wouldn't be hassled by my college-aged peers. Incredulously, I followed his advice, changing into casual civilian clothes in the latrine of the mess hall before I got a taxi to Sea-Tac.

Luckily, I got a seat on a mid-morning flight direct into National Airport —it'll never be Reagan for me. I was really psyched about this, since I had never flown into D.C. before. A couple of years earlier, in a drunken stupor, one evening at twilight, during a visit with my best high school buddy, John Albert, we had gazed in awe at planes noisily making their final approach into National Airport. I remember nothing of the flight across country. I probably slept a lot, maybe read some, no idea what, and drank. Of course I drank, as much as I could.

Mostly I recall being in a dissociated fog, very disconnected and removed from what was happening. It was difficult for me to truly believe I had survived Vietnam, including the Tet Offensive, when much of my reason for having volunteered to go to Vietnam in the first place was to get killed. It was also hard for me to fathom how radically my life had changed during the past year. I was now "Coming Home" to a fledging family of my wife, Kathy, and our 5-month-old daughter, Rebecca Cher.

About 7:00 p.m. Washington time, the Captain announced that we were making our final approach into National. He related that we would see just what I had hoped we would see. With a rumbling thrill in my gut, I peered out the window and was able to detect the darker shadow of the Potomac River among the lengthening shadows of evening. Soon, the lights of suburban Virginia and Maryland, on either side, began to pack more tightly together, as steadily descending I could see the buildings and crisscrossed thoroughfares of Georgetown and D.C. merge into view.

We made the sharp right turn, with the lights disappearing to become a silken, dark-blue sky with specks of starlight and a half-full moon rising from the far horizon. Then, right on cue, a sharp left bank brought us right over the top of the Lincoln Memorial. As we leveled out, all of downtown Washington was spread out before me. There were the Reflecting Pools, the Washington Monument the Smithsonian Buildings, the Mall, the Capitol—wait a minute, what the fuck? I rubbed my eyes, peered out the window again, thought I was hallucinating, or dreaming, was much drunker than I thought I was.

I became very frightened and couldn't believe what I was seeing. Fuck It! I had just left this kind of a scene a day or so before and 12,000 miles ago! Why was Washington burning? Huge, dark, black, spumes of billowing smoke from it looked like all of Washington behind the Capitol, burning, burning, burning brightly, in angry orange-red, yawing sheets of licking flame. I was stunned. Speechless. Dead inside. Numb. Don't mean nothing. Don't mean nothing. Don't mean nothing. Same as it ever was.

We landed with a screeching of tires on tarmac. I finished my drink, impatiently waiting for the plane to taxi to the gate, so I could get the hell out, light a Pall Mall cigarette, get another Drambuie on the rocks, and find out what the fuck was going on. About 15 minutes later, I was sitting, alone, in an airport bar with my duffel-bag, a lit cigarette and four-fingers of Drambuie, watching the news, staring numbly at the scenes of the aftermath of Martin Luther King's assassination in Memphis several hours before I landed in D.C. Much of Washington, and other ghetto areas in cities across our red, white & blue land, were burning from the keening rage of blacks taking white-hate out in self-hate upon themselves.

"Welcome Home, Son."

Yeah, right! Some homecoming! Welcome Home your freakin' self...

King had been murdered by James Earl Ray, who grew up in one of the tough river towns of the "Little Dixie" region, on both sides of the Mississippi River in Illinois and Missouri, a breeding ground for white Christian Supremacists of the Ku Klux Klan!

Chapter 7—Becoming A Civilian Again

So, despite myself, I survived Vietnam to come safely back to the World, the grand PX in the sky, as we referred to it in Vietnam, the United States of America. I had not died after all. Didn't happen. Now, I had returned to a ready made family of wife, Kathy, and five-month-old Rebecca Cher, our daughter, who had been born on November 16, 1967. A couple of weeks after I got her birth picture, very drunk late one night in my hootch, while Bernie snored, I stared in mystified awe at her picture. I could not fathom that this picture of a scrunched baby face with closed eyes and splotches on her cheeks, looking exhausted after the ordeal of a difficult birth that required an emergency caesarean section, was my daughter. I was utterly baffled, distraught, overwrought. It made no sense to me that I was now a father, that the tiny face in the picture was my flesh and blood, my DNA, my daughter. This reality seemed too bizarre, too alien, too improbable. I felt myself slipping over the brink into a dark abyss of full-fledged insanity.

In a panic, I took my lit cigarette and put it out on my left forearm. The pain snapped me back into some semblance of being connected to myself in a here and now reality. Some 49 years later, I look at this scar today with immense gratitude. Why gratitude? I am most grateful that I did not fulfill my ardent death wish to die in Vietnam, that I survived my year in Vietnam, very much despite myself, so as to have been able to live the most full and enriched life I have experienced all throughout recovery in AA.

Kathy and Rebecca were staying with her parents in Milford, CT. Before I joined them, I took a couple of days by myself to decompress from what I had experienced in Vietnam and to adjust to the reality that I had, indeed, returned home instead of being killed in Vietnam. I took a cab from National Airport to a hotel in downtown Washington, DC with the surreal glow of the ghetto fires burnishing the nighttime sky. I starkly remember being terrified in the cab, "speeding" at 40-45 miles per hour over the mostly empty 14th street bridge into downtown DC with little traffic. It terrified me. I was petrified, sitting drunk in the backseat. I gripped the back of the drivers seat, remembering how I had gripped the M-2 Carbine on Valentine's Day in the Mang Yang Pass. In Vietnam, the maximum speed limit was between 15 and 25 miles per hour at the most. I hadn't travelled that fast in a vehicle for a year.

One of the things that haunted me most on the long flight back across the Pacific on the Tiger Airlines 707 "Freedom Bird," and also during the American Airlines flight across country into Washington, DC, was that no way could I continue drinking the copious amounts of booze that I had consumed daily in Vietnam. My lieutenant's pay was not enough for a daily 5th, often a quart, of Drambuie plus two or more six-packs of San Miguel. For those first couple of days, I began weaning myself off of booze all together. I impulsively decided to go cold turkey.

I slept in late the next morning and took the train from Washington's Union Station to Penn Station in New York. I booked a room at the same hotel that I had stayed in three years earlier with my family after I broke off the engagement with Roseanne. I spent the late afternoon and evening walking up to Central Park and around Times Square.

Vietnam was still very much in the forefront of my mind, but I could see that it meant nothing to any of the passersby I encountered. It was hard for me to fathom that there was so much death and dying happening in Vietnam and that "We the People" back here, back home, were mostly oblivious to it. That night, I began my intention to go cold turkey and had only two Colt .45 beers, since I couldn't get San Miguel's with my pastrami sandwich at the Carnegie Delicatessen. I loved Colt .45! The next day, I took a Metro North train to Milford and reunited with my young family and her parents.

Since Vietnam had been my first active duty assignment, I still had six months remaining to fulfill my two-year active duty obligation to the Army. For that half-year, I was assigned as an instructor at the Army Ordnance Center and School. I would finish my active duty requirement where I had begun it a year-and-a-half previously, at Aberdeen Proving Ground.

I remember very little of the 30 day leave before I had to report for duty at APG. Most of it was spent with Kathy's family in Connecticut, except for a week when Kathy, Rebecca and I flew down to Mississippi to visit my family. After leave, we returned to Aberdeen Proving Ground to live in Army housing on post, while I finished my active duty obligation.

During the several months we lived at APG, life settled down into a somewhat humdrum existence, compared to what I had experienced while in Vietnam. I would go and teach young Ordnance officers, such as I had been in 1966, an introduction to supply management course. I taught during the weekdays, and spent evenings and weekends with Kathy and Rebecca in our Army apartment. During nice weather on weekends we went on picnics or took day trips to Washington, DC or nearby Baltimore.

One afternoon, I came home as usual to our apartment and was met at the door by Kathy, who had a most stern and concerned look on her face. She held out the envelope with the 19 fat Thai Sticks in it, demanding to know what they were. After I told her what they were, I queried, "Where did you find them?".

"In the briefcase with all your letters from Vietnam," she replied. Being co-dependent, I didn't think to be upset that she had been snooping around in my stuff.

"So that's what happened to them," I exclaimed. "I knew that I had put them somewhere, but the next day I couldn't find them, so I just got some more."

I told her about the incident with the Major going to the latrine, when I was so paranoid that he had detected me smoking a joint. I remembered the next day thinking that I had put them somewhere in my room, but by noon I had forgotten all about the incident. The whole event had been wiped from my memory, until Kathy confronted me with the envelope of 19 fat opium-laced joints several months later. I turned Kathy on to them, and we consumed them over the several months or so. Later, I'll relate a couple of stories about us getting "high", after we left active duty and were living in the Maryland suburbs of Washington, DC. It strikes me now how fortunate it was that they were not discovered in the hold baggage that I shipped home from Vietnam. I surmise that since I was an officer that my hold baggage was not perused by drug-sniffing detection dogs.

With the obvious exception of the four year period from 1861 to 1865 during the American Civil War, 1968 was perhaps the most tumultuous year in our nations history: the Navy Destroyer, *Pueblo,* hi-jacked; the Tet Offensive; MLK and RFK assassinated; Columbia University shut down; police riots at the Chicago Democratic Convention; Czechoslovakia invaded by the Warsaw Pact to end the Prague Spring; Black Power protests at the Mexico Olympics, etc. etc. etc. I remember drinking and screaming at the TV during the nightly news programs. It was a perfectly awful year!

Somehow I found out about a production of *Brecht on Brecht* down at John Hopkins University in Baltimore. I attended auditions and was cast in a major supporting role. After being cold stone sober for all of several weeks at the most, I began drinking again, maybe after RFK was assassinated. After rehearsals, driving back to APG from Baltimore in my Javelin SST, I would stop at one of the many taverns along US Route 40. I loved that Javelin SST pony car. I had ordered the Javelin at the Qui Nhon PX my last week in Vietnam, when I accepted that I wasn't going to die, and I picked it up at a dealer near Kathy's house in Milford, CT, while on leave.

While drinking, I began writing poetry again in my journals. Here's a poem from that time, which indicates how haunted by Vietnam I continued to be:

I move in high circles

Run rings with the best of them
Often am I equally at ease
In conversation important
And discussion peacock-puffed strategic
With colonels majors career-toughened NCOs
And the young eager student officers
Dedicated accomplices to murder all are we
The pay may be small
But large and looming are the posters

With a feeling of patriotic pride
I sometimes strut falsely
In my rut of accomplishment

One day
This morning as a matter of fact it was
After having just lectured
Lucidly and gallantly
Impressionable newly-minted officers
Feeling dutifully important
'bout being a VN veteran
I happened to see lying on the ground

Its severed head God knows where
A dead, quite brittle chipmunk
Half-buried by brightly-turned leaves

It jolted me
Deflated me
Like a pin-pricked full balloon exploding

For a long, long moment
Choking back deep, deep tears
I was off track
Wishing I could go back
Maybe start differently
All over again

Upon my return from Vietnam I became more rabidly against the war than I had been before I went. When Eugene McCarthy entered the Democratic Primary race as a peace candidate running against President Johnson, for a couple of weeks I had a McCarthy bumper sticker on my car until I was told by MPs at the APG entrance gate that this was a violation of the Military Code of Justice. I also attended a candlelight peace protest at the White House, wearing my field jacket, where I advocated for the US to cease hostilities in Vietnam.

It turned out Rebecca had esotropia, a crossed-eye condition. Her left eye needed surgery so that she wouldn't be cross-eyed. Therefore, I extended my active duty requirement for several months so that the surgery could be done with the government paying for it at Kirk Army Hospital. In July of 1969, I was discharged from active duty with the US Army and our little family moved into a new apartment complex in College Park, MD. I had gotten an administrative assistant job with the Association of Military Surgeons of the US (AMSUS) in nearby Bethesda, MD. I remember very little about this job. However, I do remember that I desperately wanted to attend the Woodstock Music and Art Festival up in New York, with a couple of office mates. Big bummer, it was impossible for me to do so, since we had just gotten out of the Army and all of our money had gone towards moving expenses.

I remember getting very drunk once in our College Park apartment, during which I threw an empty—thank goodness—bottle of Boone's Farm Apple wine at the living room wall, smashing it into a thousand pieces. Luckily, I didn't throw it against the large picture window overlooking the balcony, which likely would have shattered it, costing a bunch to replace. Another time, drunk, I nearly drowned in the Chesapeake Bay during an outing with office mates, when I fell off the boat owned by the Executive Director, a retired Army general. I remember how disoriented I was, gasping for air, and how difficult it was for drunken me to climb back on board the boat. It took three of the men on the boat to help haul me back into the boat.

My dark state of mind during this period is depicted in this poem written, drunk by myself, in a local bar on July 20, 1969. I remember nothing about watching the landing on the moon, but I wrote this poem about it while getting drunk, as Neil Armstrong and Buzz Aldrin successfully achieved the first manned landing on the moon:

moontalk 1969

i say
if the
violated moon
were to look
down upon me
and say,
"yon young man
rapidly growing older
gaze upon me still
with wonder
with awe
as ever before
for lo' though
i've been tainted and befouled
by your corporate technology
verily may i yet evoke in you
fathoms of rapture
hectares of love!"

well
if the moon
were to say
something
like that
to me
i'd probably
glance for

*a moment
somewhat
skeptically
into the now too familiar
pock mocked face
and murmur,
"what kind of
doddering
outmoded
old fool
is this?"*

I hated working for AMSUS, an organization that was connected to the military, so I applied for graduate school at Catholic University's graduate school of theatre. At the time with Yale, it was one of the two most acclaimed graduate schools for theatre studies in the US. Otto and Diane had graduated from Catholic University, so they were quite helpful in getting me a fellowship to pursue an MFA in theatre arts. I started classes in January of 1970, and I worked in the theatre shop, building sets for productions.

Before I started classes, we found a cheaper apartment closer to Catholic University in West Hempstead, MD. It was a sub-basement apartment with windows at ground level, looking out upon the parking lot in front of the building. It was much smaller and older than the College Park apartment, but also more reasonably priced for a graduate student couple with a small child. Kathy got a job with the local telephone company.

Earlier I related that Kathy had found the envelope with the 19 opium-laced Thai sticks. One night we were smoking one of the Thai sticks in the sub-basement apartment, when a ruckus happened out in the parking lot in front of our building. Yelling and screaming were followed by a police car siren screeching and bubble lights flashing. A police car skidded to a halt in front of the entrance to our building. We both panicked, becoming instantly paranoid, a state sometimes induced by marijuana.

I instructed Kathy to stand over the toilet with the remaining Thai sticks, ready to flush them down the toilet at my command. I peered out the sub-basement window from our darkened living room, but I couldn't see a thing. Not thinking, being buzzed to the max and adrenalin-pumped, I reached back and turned on the light, so that I could see what was happing. Instead, I was illuminated, standing butt-naked, peering out the window. Luckily, the police had left, and we didn't have to flush the remaining Thai sticks down the toilet!

On another occasion, we each smoked a Thai stick while visiting a friend of Kathy's from Goucher College and her fiancée. Besides heavily drinking and smoking more pot, we gorged ourselves on hors d'oeuvre and snacks. Very hungry, I had gulped down pigs in a blanket, tiny hot dogs wrapped in buttery pastry with bacon. When we left the party, I had horrible indigestion. Since we were both blitzed on the booze and dope, we couldn't find the exit from the apartment complex to get onto the street. We must have driven around the complex five or six times before we finally found the exit to the street. Each time I drove over a speed bump, I experienced a yawing surge of indigestion that felt like it would engulf me in a tidal wave of burning nausea. It was one of the most awful experiences I ever had under the influence of alcohol and drugs.

I tried out for a production of *The Bacchae* by Euripides during my first couple of weeks in class and was cast as the Messenger, who relates to the Maenads the terrible demise of Dionysius at the hands of the Titans. It was quite an honor to be awarded this role, since I beat out some forty other actors auditioning for the role, a number of them second year acting students in the MFA program. Being cast in a major production meant I was automatically accepted into the highly competitive MFA acting program, but I turned it down to focus instead on an MFA in directing. Since I was married with a small child, I thought it more prudent to pursue a career in theatre, teaching and directing in the theatre program of some small, liberal arts college somewhere, such as mentors Otto and Diane had done, rather than trying to make it as a working actor between New York and Los Angeles.

To this day, I still have some regrets about this decision. I was a gifted actor. I sometimes parrot Marlon Brando's iconic line from *On the Waterfront,* "I coulda been a contender!"

During the summer of 1970, I was hired as Box Office Manager at Olney Theatre, a professional summer theater in suburban Maryland, then owned and operated by Catholic University. Here I met the talented actresses, Patricia, who would be most influential to me getting sober a couple of years later.

I began drinking daily again, on average a case of Colt .45 a day. I switched to Colt .45 because it was much less expensive than imported San Miguel, and besides, I loved it. Unhappy in the marriage with Kathy, I began having affairs. One night, during a cast party that Kathy attended, I was out in the bushes having relations with one of the student interns. The company stage manager, Molly, found us, telling me that Kathy was worried and concerned about where I was. Sheepishly, I returned to the party and mollified Kathy. Our solution to repair our tottering marriage was to have another child. With the prospect of having two children, driving the sporty Javelin, which I mightily loved, was most impractical. One of the saddest days I ever experienced was trading in the sporty gold Javelin SST for a brown Opel Station wagon, the epitome of a suburban house-dad vehicle.

As box office manager, after each performance I had to close out the box office receipts for the day and deposit the cash and checks in a bank branch about 25 minutes away. I was able to drink 16 oz. cans of Colt .45 all throughout the day and evening, so I would be fairly well lit-up by the end of the long day. Occasionally, on the way to the bank, I would go on long drives through upper Maryland into the foothills of the Appalachian Mountains in Pennsylvania. Sometimes, I would play a game of chicken, more appropriately Russian roulette, with myself, driving through the mountain back roads. I not only drove while drunk. I continued to drink while I drove, throwing the empty cans into the backseat of the Opel. I would usually have a six pack of Colt. 45 in my lap, and a six pack riding shotgun in the seat next to me. I'd get lost and try to find my way back to the bank. Sometimes, I'd turn off the headlights and drive recklessly as fast as I could on the wrong side of the road until I chickened myself out. I never had an accident nor got arrested for driving while intoxicated. It's almost enough to make me believe that somewhere there is a god who watches over me—NOT !~!~!

Late one night, after one of these passive suicide missions, I was halfway home before I realized I had not made the night deposit. I was too drunk and tired to drive back to the bank, so I just drove on home. When I got home about 15 minutes later, I forgot that I had forgotten to deposit the money and checks, totaling some $1000. I left the bank deposit bag sitting in the front seat of the Opel Station wagon. Of course, the next mid-morning when I left to go to the Olney Theatre, the bag was gone. Driving to the theatre, I realized what had happened. Though panicked, I made a decision to just stonewall it. After a couple of hours working in the Box Office, during which I practiced the stonewalling in my head, I was called into the administrative office, where I was questioned about the bank deposit.

Poker-faced, I queried, "What about it?"

"The bank just called wondering where our deposit is," the administrator told me.

"Well, I deposited it, last night in the night deposit of the bank after I closed out the box office, like I always do."

"Let me call the bank back." She did and was told again they did not have the deposit.

I just kept denying it, insisting that I had made the deposit. It was a stonewalled case of my word against the bank's word. It was perhaps the best acting job I had ever done. With the passage of time, the impasse eventually was forgotten about, although I continued to feel guilty and be fearful that I might be accused of stealing the money and expelled.

Debbie, My Second Wife To Be

Kathy's and my relationship, despite her being pregnant with our second child, continued to unravel. We were both miserable and often argued vehemently. My having affairs and being drunk most of the time was a major theme of our disputes. One night, when she was about seven months pregnant, and I was, as usual, drunk, we had an awful argument that was more violent than usual. I lunged at her in a screaming rage, and she fell over, hard, on the floor. This scared us both, and we decided that perhaps it would be best if she and Rebecca went to stay with her parents in Connecticut until she was scheduled for the cesarean birth of our second child several weeks later in March.

One night in late February of 1971, I was in the Catholic University student bar, the Rathskeller, drinking with a friend, Jack, from the Theatre Department. He had a date with him, Debbie, a senior studying social work, who was from New Rochelle, NY. Debbie and I flirted—it was lust at first sight. Since Kathy was away in Connecticut, I ended up taking Debbie home that night and deflowering her in Kathy's and my bed. Hey, the booze made us do it, you know?

Debbie and I began a torrid affair. A couple of weeks later, Kathy returned to Washington to have the cesarean section. One of the most terrifying couple of hours I've ever experienced was sitting and fretting in the waiting room of the maternity ward, much too sober, in the mid-afternoon of March 9th, 1971, awaiting for the birth of our second child. I recalled in gory detail the ghastly scene a couple of months earlier when Kathy and I had violently argued. Most fortunately, however, our second daughter, Jennifer, was born perfectly healthy.

Debbie and I moved into a basement apartment a friend, Mike, got for us in his building in the Kalorama Triangle area of Washington, DC. I also convinced her to be named co-respondent in the divorce suit from Kathy that I had initiated on the grounds of my infidelity. I provided Kathy's lawyer with copies of our love letters, and Mike agreed to testify that Debbie and I were living together "in sin." Using the grounds of infidelity was the quickest and easiest way to end the marriage with Kathy in Maryland. Hung over, one mid-morning, I sat in the darkened shadows at the rear of the Family Court of Prince Georges County, MD, watching the proceedings of my uncontested divorce. Yes, my life was most unmanageable.

Debbie was a BIC—Bronx Irish Catholic. A nickname I had for her was my "Tough New York City Chick". She was also an ex-nun, whose family had moved to New Rochelle, NY, where she had gone to high school, and where her father was the town drunk. She joined the nunnery to escape the ravages of alcoholism in her home. At the end of her first year in the nunnery, there was a ceremony where she would take her first vows. Her father very much wanted to attend. However, the nuns sternly told him, being the notorious town drunk, that he would have to be stone-cold sober in order to attend. So, he decided to go cold-stone turkey, and in the middle of the celebratory mass traumatically died of delirium tremens. Debbie left the nunnery and went to Catholic University to pursue a social work degree instead of becoming a nun.

Protests Against Vietnam

During the Spring of 1970, Nixon's invasion of Cambodia along with the student killings at Kent State and Jackson State mobilized extreme opposition by college and university students to the war in Vietnam. All across the nation, college and university campuses began going on strike. As a Vietnam Veteran against the war, I became a member of the ad hoc student committee to plan for and initiate a similar student strike at Catholic University. I vaguely recall speaking to a large crowd from the steps of the Mullen Memorial Library. Students, undergraduate and graduate, had massed together on Pryzbyla Plaza, spilling all the way into the distant parking lot for the National Shrine of the Immaculate

Conception. Also on hand were men in hats and trench coats, obviously FBI, observing the crowd and taking pictures.

During the turbulent period of the sixties, while living in the Washington, DC area, I marched in most of the large protests against the Vietnam War. I had been against the war before I went to Vietnam, and what I experienced in Vietnam did nothing but make me more rabidly in opposition to the war when I returned home. The only major protest against the Vietnam War that I missed between 1967 and 1971 was the initial gathering of some 100,000 people near the Lincoln Memorial in West Potomac Park on October 21, 1967, while I was in Vietnam. A March to the Pentagon was followed by an effort, initiated by Jerry Rubin and Abbie Hoffman, to "Exorcise and Levitate" the Pentagon.

On October 15, 1969, I participated in the Candlelight Moratorium Against the War, being among some 100,000 people who marched in a silent, candlelight march around the White House. A month later on November 15, 1969, I joined the huge Moratorium Day Peace Parade with a crowd of some 500,000 persons massed to protest the war in Vietnam in Washington, DC. We were delighted to hear Pete Seeger sing the newly released song by John Lennon, "Give Peace A Chance." During the march down Pennsylvania Avenue, I wore my Army Green uniform jacket, no doubt a serious violation of the Uniform Code of Military Justice. In one of those serendipitous encounters that sometimes occur, I ran across the brother of the light-skinned African American dancer and actress whom I dated briefly while at Xavier. He was carrying, more accurately dragging, a huge wooden cross down Pennsylvania Avenue. He asked me if I wanted to relieve him for a spell, and I agreed. However, after maybe 50 yards at the most I had to relinquish it back to him. That cross must have weighed a couple of hundred pounds at least.

In 1971, the Vietnam War was still raging with no indication from either the Nixon Administration nor Congress that there was any viable initiative to end it. Debbie and I started attending meetings of the Mayday Tribe. Coordinated by Rennie Davis and other radical, much more militant anti-war organizers, the Mayday Tribe was planning for massive protests on the anniversary of Nixon's invasion of Cambodia. During the May Day weekend of 1971, we planned to conduct a massive series of large-scale civil disobedience actions throughout Washington DC with the rhetorical intention to "Stop the Government."

Early on, Debbie and I concluded that the primary objective of the Mayday Tribe organizers was to get a bunch of students' heads busted, perhaps for the negative PR effect on the Nixon Administration. Their tactics were based on getting large numbers of students to rampage through the commercial areas of Washington, smashing windows and blockading some 21 key bridges and traffic intersections in waves of affinity groups. Thus, we would prevent government workers from getting to their jobs in government offices, thereby "Stopping the Government."

Debbie and I unsuccessfully advocated for a different tactical plan. Instead of rampaging through commercial areas and blocking traffic in our hippie attire, why not dress up as young government workers going to work and stop our vehicles in the middle of bridges and intersections? This would mean we ditch our hippie attire, cut off our beards and long hair and wear establishment, business clothes. We were soundly denounced as counter-revolutionaries and purged from the Mayday tribe.

We also met a couple of times with DC representatives of the Berrigan brothers, who were brainstorming plans to use homemade napalm for burning government records, like they had done in 1968 with draft records, or pouring blood on them, like they would later do with the Plowshares movement.

Nixon thwarted our plans to disrupt Washington, DC by mobilizing units of the 82nd Airborne Division and the Marines to augment the DC police and National Guard in patrolling the streets and guarding the monuments of Washington. Nixon announced that all measures would be taken to maintain and preserve law and order. I have pictures of the 82nd Airborne being dispersed throughout Georgetown and guarding the Washington monument. Early on the Sunday morning of May 2nd, an actor friend from Catholic University, John Heard, and I went down to West Potomac Park where some 35,000 protestors were camped out in preparation for the protests on Monday. We were waiting for an all day concert and rally that had been planned for the next day, Sunday, in the park. About 2:00 a.m., Nixon cancelled the park permit, ordering that the park be cleared by the police, supported by federal troops. In chaos, we were rousted out of the park with hordes of other protesters.

I walked back to our apartment, where I shaved off my beard and cut my hair. I have a picture that shows me in my full-blown hippy attire, then with long, flowing, beautiful hair and wearing large yellow-tinted aviator glasses. I relished saying that I preferred to look at the world through piss-colored glasses! Just as we had proposed for the Mayday Tribe, Debbie and I dressed up, she in a business dress and me in a suit and tie with shorn hair, no beard and an old pair of Army glasses, as young government workers going to work. We "stalled" my Opel Station wagon on the 14th Street Bridge, blocking traffic for several minutes. We panicked when we saw mounted police moving toward us on horseback, and were able to drive away, so as to escape being arrested.

Later in the day, however, we were tear-gassed and arrested in an illegal sweep by cops and armed National Guard troops of all young people in the vicinity of the US Department of Justice on Pennsylvania Avenue. I have a picture of one of the entrance signs, which had been spray-painted to read US Department of INJustice. As we were being herded onto a school bus with other protesters, I looked around as students, some bleeding, seriously injured, fled armed police and soldiers. Tear gas filled the air and helicopters flew overhead. With a chill, I had an intrusive recollection of what I had experienced in Vietnam. It was hard to comprehend that these were the freedoms that I supposedly had fought for in Vietnam to protect. We joined several thousand other protestors who were illegally detained behind a hastily constructed wire barricade for several hours in a practice field of the Washington Redskins next to RFK Stadium.

Being involved with the Mayday Tribe, attending classes, and being in the new love relationship with Debbie, I was totally unaware of another major protest, Dewey Canyon III, conducted by the Vietnam Veterans Against the War. Held between April 19 through April 23, a number of protest actions occurred, including Vietnam Veterans returning their medals by throwing them upon the steps of the US Capitol. I would gladly have participated with my Vietnam Vet Brothers and sisters had I known about it. Along with not continuing in the Acting MFA program at Catholic University, I regret that I did not know about VVAW, so I could have participated with other veterans in this historical event of the successful GI protest movement against an unjust and unnecessary war. In a subsequent chapter, I'll discuss my continued peace activism as a result of the invasion of Iraq as a member of Vietnam Veterans Against the War and Veterans for Peace with young veteran activists of the recent and continuing wars in the Middle East.

Institute of Modern Languages

In the spring of 1971, both Debbie and I began working part-time for IML, the Institute of Modern Languages, which was shortly thereafter acquired by the American Express Company. IML, soon to be American

Express Language Centers, was a prominent language teaching organization with government contracts to teach English as a Second Language all over the world. Debbie had graduated with her social work bachelor's degree from Catholic University in June and moved to New York to live with her aging mother in New Rochelle. She got a full-time job with an American Express Language Centers pilot program, teaching English to Puerto Ricans, in Spanish Harlem.

At the American Express Language Centers in Washington, I was promoted to a full-time job as editor for English as a Second Language publications, while also taking the last of the required courses for my MFA in directing at Catholic University. This editorial job was a dream job for a functioning alcohol addict in the gathering throes of his addiction. I didn't have to punch a clock, but could make my own hours, which often didn't start until early afternoon. My boss was a heroin addict, and we sold marijuana he got from friends in Mexico out of his office. I was able to keep six packs of Colt .45 in a small refrigerator in my office, consuming them throughout my work day, which often went late into the evening. As long as I kept on schedule editing the English as a Second Language textbooks, all was copacetic.

Every weekend, either Debbie would come to Washington and stay in our apartment, or I would go up to New York where we would stay in a two star hotel down in Greenwich Village on 11th Street that we could afford. With my rampant alcoholism this was the perfect living arrangement—during the week, I could drink by myself and get as shit-faced as I wanted, while on weekends we would have our young-lover weekends in either New York City or Washington, DC, two of the most glamorous cities on the planet, getting drunk with her, but not too sloppily or darkly so. It was probably the best time of our relationship. Though I did not deny I was a drunk, having identified with bar drunks at Xavier, I was in total denial that I would ever have to deal with my drinking. Our relationship flourished, and we made plans to get married in New York in July of 1972.

After completing my course work and stage-managing a major production of Hamlet, which was going to be the basis of my thesis project for the MFA in directing, I was too drunk to be coherent on the written comprehensive examinations. I royally failed them. Being too proud and embarrassed to take them again, I dropped out of the masters program in a huff. Thus, I flunked out of a second graduate school program due to my excessive drinking. It really didn't matter that much to me, because I had a new life with Debbie and a full-time job with American Express

Language Centers, who had just been awarded a contract to expand the Spanish Harlem program throughout other Spanish-speaking areas of the New York City metropolitan region. I applied for and was promised a job as the director for one of these expansion programs in Perth Amboy, NJ. A childhood dream was about to be manifested ...

Chapter 8: Marrying Debbie and Finally Becoming a New Yorker

Since childhood, New York City had always been the Mecca of my mind. When Jackson got its first TV station in 1954, I was enthralled by shows situated in "The Big Apple," which included *I Love Lucy* and *The Honeymooners*. Even Jackie Gleason's variety show with the overhead camera shots of the June Taylor Dancers, looking like an ever-changing kaleidoscope, fascinated me—just because it was conceived of and produced live in New York City. With envious daydreams about the sophisticated high life of the Big City, I watched *The Thin Man*, starring Peter Lawford, along with his sassy wife, Nora, played by Phyllis Kirk. They captivated my imagination during high school. Everyday while delivering papers on a morning paper route, I would dream dreams of glory and accomplishment as a grown-up in Manhattan. However, the show which most stoked my youthful imagination about New York City was *The Naked City*. I especially appreciated the ending of the show, when the narrator intoned the iconic line: "There are eight million stories in the naked city. This has been one of them," as the camera panned Manhattan's nighttime skyline while the credits rolled. I desperately yearned to make my story one of those eight million stories in Manhattan.

During the first weekend of May, 1972, just after after my 29th birthday, I finally achieved my youthful dream—I became a New Yorker. I made three round trips between Debbie's and my former apartment in Washington, DC and our new studio apartment in a Brownstone building on W. 82nd Street. Across the street was the 20th Precinct of the New York Police Department, and the Museum of Natural History and Planetarium were nearby.

I joined Debbie teaching English as a Second Language in the American Express Language Centers pilot program in Spanish Harlem, while waiting for the expansion program to open that I had been hired to direct. Every weekday morning, we would ride the 79th Street crosstown bus to the Eastside, where we'd transfer to the Lexington Avenue Subway at the 77th Street station. We'd ride the subway up to the 103rd Street station and have a three block walk to where we taught in a community center on E. 106th Street. On the way we'd get a bagel and a *café con leche* from a street vendor before class. It was a very New York kind of a thing to do, and I relished becoming a New Yorker.

The building wasn't air-conditioned, and I recall how sweltering hot the classes would become. Since we usually went out drinking after work with friends who also taught there, Sophie and Ross, I also recall being horribly hung over some mornings. We also did a lot of heavy partying with other associates from American Express Language Centers. At some of these parties, we used poppers, vials of amyl nitrate that give you a rush, and smoked dope we bought from my boss, since the Thai sticks were long gone.

Often at these parties, I ended up in a dark corner somewhere, drinking by myself and muttering about dead babies in Vietnam. I was no more of a party animal in New York City than I had been anywhere else. Debbie was beginning to experience what the real me was like when I drank. She hadn't been aware of this side of me and wanted me to just be a good-time-Tommy-party-boy, something I had never been.

Ross was a wanna-be actor, one of thousands in New York City, who had a friend, Ed Moore, who was an actual working actor, who played supporting roles on Broadway and Off Broadway, as well as on television and in films. Ed had written a play, *The Sea Horse*, about a handsome merchant marine sailor, who has a long-standing and tumultuous affair with an overweight woman, who owned a bar named the Sea Horse in a port city. The first theatre work I did in New York was to design a set for a workshop production of *The Sea Horse*. It eventually played in a critically acclaimed Off-Broadway production by the noteworthy Circle Repertory Theatre. This play won for Ed a Drama Desk Award as being the Outstanding New Playwright of 1974. Due to the unmanageable final weeks of drinking, and later being involved in early recovery, I was unable to participate in the evolution of *The Sea Horse* from workshop production to a successful Off-Broadway production. This is one of a number of "close-but-no-cigar" opportunities I've missed out upon throughout my long life—no five seconds of fame and fortune for me to experience momentarily the fast-passing of celebrity.

Marriage and Honeymoon

Debbie and I got married in July of 1972 in her childhood parish in New Rochelle, NY. I don't remember us taking any pre-Cana classes for this marriage, as Roseanne and I had to endure in Cincinnati. Though agnostic, I didn't mind getting married in a Catholic Mass and marital ceremony for the sake of her mother and sister, Dorothy, who was the maid of honor, and for my mother, who came up for the wedding with Dad from Mississippi. We both drank heavily afterwards at the wedding reception. The best man, a dear friend from college, Bill, drove us to the City, where we checked into the honeymoon suite of the Plaza Hotel. At dusk, we took a horse-drawn carriage ride through Central Park. For a young man who grew up in Jackson, MS, this was an ultimate fantasy come true: being most grown up and super cool, practically like Nick and Nora Charles, in New York Freakin' City.

Following the carriage ride, we went up to our suite and quickly downed the complimentary bottle of champagne. After making sloppy love, we both passed out—for the entire night !~!~! We missed out on all of the perks given us as a honeymoon couple at the Plaza: free drinks at Trader Vic's, 15% off dinner in the Oak Room, complimentary desserts in the Palm Court. We also overslept the next morning, nearly missing the flight to New Orleans for our honeymoon. Somewhat hungover, we nevertheless got to the New Orleans airport, where we rented a BBG—for Big Bad Green—1972 Javelin in honor of the Javelin SST I had when I returned from Vietnam. We honeymooned for two nights in the Cornstalk Hotel, named for its wrought iron fence with prominent cornstalks, on Royal Street in New Orleans' famed French Quarter. Or course, we got drunk, drinking Hurricanes at Pat O'Brien's and carousing at other nightspots in the French Quarter. I also took her for a meal accompanied by two or three bottles of wine at Tu Jacques, and in the mornings, or early afternoons, we had *café au lait* and beignets at Café Du Monde.

We drove along the Gulf Coast with me showing her the hotel where the Catholic Youth Organization made such a ruckus in 1961, and the nightclub where Flo's father took us. I had wanted to take her to the famed Angelo's Seafood restaurant in Gulfport that had a live oak tree growing out of the middle of the main dining room, but it had been destroyed during Hurricane Camille in 1969. Instead, we had a wonderful catfish lunch at Aunt Jenny's in Ocean Springs.

On the way to Jackson, we drove to Monticello, MS, where I spent summers as a pre-adolescent. Grandmother had died in 1969 and her house was empty, but we were able to look in the windows and cuddle on the front porch swing where I had sometimes read. After spending several days with the family, visiting a few friends in Jackson, and showing her all the old haunts from high school, we flew back to New York to resume our normal lives in the humid heat and dog days of August in New York City.

In mid-August we got a shock. President Nixon impounded the Department of Labor funds for programs such as those for teaching in Spanish Harlem and the proposed program in Perth Amboy. American Express decided to get out of the language teaching business and began closing down offices, laying off employees. Debbie was one of the first to be laid off and immediately got another job with the Federal Reserve Bank. I continued teaching until late-September, when I was let go.

I remember a couple of bad drunks after I was laid off. One was with Ross drinking in a shit-kicking bar on 8th Avenue all afternoon and into the evening. Another was when Debbie and I went to the Hell's Kitchen apartment of Sophie and Ross for dinner. Both Ross and I got very drunk that night and passed out. I don't remember how Debbie and I got home. It was one of the few total blackouts I recall having.

While Debbie was at work, I was supposed to be looking for work, but I was petrified about not being able to find another job. I would look at the New York Times classified ads and circle potential administrative assistant jobs, or the like, but was terrified to make any actual calls. Instead, like a good alcoholic, I would just drink until I forgot about it.

On Tuesday, October 10th, I cooked a nice chicken dinner for Debbie to celebrate her getting a promotion at the Federal Reserve Bank after only a few weeks working there. By the time we sat down to eat, however, I was hammered. I took the steaming hot chicken out of the stove and sloppily began carving it. It kept burning my fingers, so I flew in to a drunken rage and flung it into the faux fireplace next to our small dining table. Debbie screamed, believing I had thrown it at her. I had not. I was just frustrated and drunk and in a rage because my fingers were being burned. Nevertheless, she fled our apartment in terror and wouldn't come back.

I drank, as usual, around the clock for the next several days, while desperately seeking Debbie. When I couldn't find her, I made several pitiful, drunken attempts to kill myself.

One night, shit-faced drunk as usual and most remorseful, desperately missing Debbie, I took a handful of her tranquilizers and pain pills. Instead of sliding into oblivion, I woke up late the next morning, groggier than usual.

A friend of ours lived up by the George Washington Bridge, and late one night, after literally crying in my beer with him and his wife for a couple of hours, I walked out to the middle of the bridge, but I couldn't figure out how to get up and over the tall cyclone fence to jump into the dark and murky waters of Hudson River far below. On the way back to my parked car in Washington Heights, I leaned over one of the highway approaches to the bridge and contemplated propelling myself headfirst onto the speeding lanes of traffic, but I got vertigo and chickened out.

Once, on a crowded subway station, I had an impulsive urge to jump in front of a subway train, but a flash of the mess I would make caused me to gag, so I forgot about it.

My last aborted suicide attempt was an hour or so before my last drink while driving to my mother-in-law's apartment in New Rochelle, NY, looking for Debbie. Driving along the Cross County parkway, I saw a wide expanse of curving concrete wall before me. I revved up the car, the Opel Station wagon I hated so much, and aimed straight for the gray-white concrete wall rushing towards me. I could feel the bumps and rattles of the car as I drove onto the shoulder, chugalugging a can of Colt .45, and yelling, "Bonsai, Mother Fucker !~!~!

BLACKOUT!

I came to several minutes later, aimlessly driving around the upscale neighborhood of Scarsdale. This was my moment of "pitiful and incomprehensible demoralization." I was a complete and utter failure – I couldn't even properly kill myself. I drove to my mother-in-law's on Stonelea Place in New Rochelle, hoping to find Debbie. She wasn't there. Yelling obscenities at my mother-in-law, I had my last drink there, a Rheingold beer—yuckkkkk! I slammed out of the apartment. There were two unopened 16 oz. cans of Colt .45 on the front seat of the Opel. My intention was to drink them, buy another case of 16 oz. cans, and continue to drink until somehow I found a way to kill myself.

Just as I have no explanation as to why I ended up not smashing into the concrete wall, I also have no explanation as to what happened next. Walking out of my mother-in-laws apartment my firm intention was to continue drinking. Walking down the three flights of stairs, my firm intention was to continue drinking. Walking across the lawn and onto the street where the Opel Stationwagon was parked, my firm intention was to open and continue drinking the two cans of Colt .45, stopping on the way back to Manhattan to get another case. But, when I got into the car, I did *not* open one of the cans of Colt .45. In a fugue-like state, instead, I drove through a blinding rainstorm back to our apartment on W. 82nd Street in Manhattan.

There, I spent the first night in a number of years without drinking my self into a stupor. I tossed and turned, shaking horribly with night terrors, but I did not drink again that night. I desperately wanted somehow to get my wife back. It was a beautiful, cloudless, bright October Sunday morning that I woke up to the next day. The thought occurred to me that maybe, if I stopped drinking, maybe even going to AA, I could convince her to come back. So, I didn't drink the rest of that day. Instead, I cleaned out over a hundred empty cans of Colt. 45 from the back of the Opel Stationwagon. In retrospect, I can see that my last day drinking, which was a coolish, rainy mid-October day with blinding rainstorms, and my first day day sober, which was a gorgeous, clear fall day with clear skies and bright sunshine, is an apt metaphor for my life in recovery.

Nor did I drink on Monday, when I called Intergroup to inquire about an AA meeting. They gave me the address of nearby meetings on Thursday evening. Since I wanted to get Debbie back desperately, I clung to the idea that maybe, if I stopped drinking and went to AA, I could convince her to come back, to rejoin me in our apartment.

Somehow, I continued not to pick up a first drink on Tuesday, or Wednesday, or Thursday, the day I attended my first AA meetings. I have no recollection of what I did during those several days, but I know I did not drink. I don't recall having any acute cravings or desperate urges to drink, but I do remember feeling awful, terribly missing Debbie, having the shakes, and feeling horribly hung-over.

I certainly didn't know it at the time, but I had had my last drink and was about to embark on a totally new life, one in recovery through Alcoholics Anonymous.

Part Two

What Happened, Getting Sober in New York City

Chapter 9: First AA Meetings

Several years ago, my wife Jill and I were visiting my daughters and grandkids in Frederick, Maryland. We found an open discussion meeting listed on the Internet at a nearby Methodist church. Held in a classroom, neither the window shades for the 12 Steps nor the 12 Traditions were in sight. No slogans either. A small book of Christian meditations, *The Upper Room*, was at each seat. Before the meeting started, I asked the chairperson if this was an AA Meeting.

Rather arrogantly he replied, "Absolutely, this is AA the way it was supposed to be."

"Excuse me?" I queried.

"Yes, we follow the original format used by the Akron Oxford Group as formulated by Dr. Bob and his wife, Anne."

"What do you mean?" I further inquired.

"We all surrender on our knees in prayer to Jesus Christ, Our Savior. Then we read from our meditation book and seek guidance in quiet time for 15 minutes. We then share with each other the guidance we have received from our Lord and Savior, Jesus Christ."

Jill and I were appalled. We rapidly left the meeting, sharing perhaps just a bit too vociferously that this definitely was in no way any kind of AA that we wanted.

This incident made me most grateful for my first AA meetings in New York City.

On Thursday, October 19th, 1972, I attended my first AA meetings at the Renewal West group in the large basement of the Church of St. Paul and St. Andrew at West End Avenue and W. 86th Street. I had gotten the time and address of these meetings from a call to Intergroup the previous Monday. I had a hazy concept of AA being something to do with broken-down old men. Watching late night movies, probably drunk, I had seen old films about AA on TV. The impression I had was that AA consisted of a bunch of old men, who had been on skid row, and who talked about God a lot. I was 29 years old. My second wife had left me. I was an utter and total failure. I couldn't even fucking kill myself!

The product of a Jesuit education, I was proud to be a skeptical agnostic. Sure enough, the speaker at the beginners meeting and the three speakers at the following open speaker meeting were all old men, who had been on the Bowery, the skid row of New York City, who talked about God a lot. No way did I identify with anything any of them related. I did not feel any rush of relief. I did not feel like I was at home with like-minded people. I did not feel warmly welcomed. I felt like a fish out of water. I felt just as lost and miserable as I had been when I walked in to the meeting. I missed Debbie—bunches !~!~! I did not speak to anyone at these meetings, and no one came to speak to me. I was most grateful for this. Had someone tried to speak to me, I may have screamed and run for the hills. After the meetings, I walked home alone. BUT, I did not drink.

I continued not to pick up the first drink for each day of the following week. The next Thursday evening, I went back to those same two meetings. I went late and left early. I hunkered down by myself in the back rows of the meetings. My dark demeanor kept anyone from approaching me, and I certainly didn't reach out to anyone. In fact, I was terrified to speak to anyone, but also terrified someone would try to talk to me. I was so uptight about this that while walking to the meeting I stopped in a coffee shop on the way to take a piss. This meant I wouldn't have to relieve myself at the meetings. I didn't want to risk anyone trying to engage me in conversation while standing side by side at the urinals. Uptight? A social retard? Painfully self-conscious? In spades.

I had known and accepted for several years that I was an alcoholic. I described in Chapter 3 how much I identified with the old men in the shit-kicking bars around Xavier. I knew they were what I would someday become. Alcoholic was too decent, too nice a word for what I really felt I was. A hopeless ne'er-do-well drunk was what I was, a reprobate, a degenerate, a debauchee, a rogue, a good-for-nothing louse! Instead of denying I was alcoholic, I denied there was any hope that I could, in fact, get, much less want, to stay sober. Certainly not for any length of time. My previous effort to get sober upon returning from Vietnam lasted all of two or three weeks. Nevertheless, I desperately wanted Debbie back. This was my only motivation for going to AA meetings. I certainly had no intention to stay stopped drinking. I remember little about the two weeks I went to meetings, but incredibly, I didn't drink. I did the two absolutely essential behaviors necessary to stay sober—I didn't pick up the first drink a day at a time, and I went to those two AA meetings.

I am ever so grateful my fate had me experience the gift of recovery in New York City. Had I experienced a fundamentally Christian milieu, such as Jill and I later experienced in Frederick, MD, I doubt that I would ever have continued going to AA meetings. If I had been lucky, I would have died early of an alcohol-related cause, an accident, say, or by succeeding to kill myself. If I had been unlucky, I would have ended up on the Bowery or some other skid row, like the gentlemen I heard at my first AA meetings. I can't know for sure, but I doubt I would ever have gotten sober. It pains me to realize that in vast sections of North America newcomers are being turned away by meetings that focus upon the necessity of a Christian god as described explicitly and implicitly in the Big Book. The so-called Back to Basics movement has narrowed AA's "broad highway" of spirituality to a decidedly Christian religious cant—perhaps rant would be a more appropriate description.

First Identification and Meeting List

On November 2th, I went to my third set of AA meetings at the Church of St. Paul and St. Andrew. It was here that I first heard someone with whom I could relate. He was the very first person with whom I could identify. His name was Stanley S. Stancage, who led the beginners meeting my third week sober. Stanley was a large Russian Jew with hands the size of catcher's mitts. He was a chronic relapser, like Ebby Thatcher had been and continued to be throughout most of his life. Bill Wilson, nevertheless, always referred to him, even when he was most obnoxiously drunk at early New York City AA meetings, as his sponsor, because Ebby had brought the message of recovery to him.

Whenever Stanley drank, which was periodically, he got extremely violent. He would often end up in hospital emergency rooms after battling with cops. Upon release from the hospital, he would sometimes have to serve lengthy prison sentences for assaulting officers and resisting arrest. Stanley was ninety days sober again after another horrid relapse. His qualification was rife with F-bombs, as he gesticulated his huge hands all about himself. He quoted Nietzsche, Baudelaire, Shakespeare, even Marx. Not once did he mention god or a belief in any god or refer to the Big Book. He talked about how painful it was for him to continue drinking. He talked about how hard it was for him not to drink, but that he accepted there was no way for him to live any kind of a successful or decent life if he continued to drink. He was the first person whom I heard say that a day at a time he chose not to drink whether his ass turned to gold or whether it fell off. I was mesmerized. I thought to myself, "Fuck, if this asshole can get sober, maybe I can too." Finally, here was someone with whom I could relate and identify. To a great extent, I owe my subsequent years of longtime recovery to Stanley. It saddens me, even to this day, that a couple of years later he forgot what I had learned from him about not drinking no matter what. He ended up dying from alcohol poisoning, when he chug-a-lugged a quart of 100-proof vodka. Nevertheless, I will forever be grateful for him. Often, I remember him, and I thank his memory, whenever I do.

During the break between the Beginner's Meeting and the three-speaker open meeting, someone came up from behind me, ambushing me. Glen asked if I had a Meeting List.

"Huh? What's that?" I queried.

"A listing of all the meetings in New York City," he replied.

"You mean this isn't the only one?"

"Nope, there are hundreds," he informed me. He reached into his back pocket and gave me his copy of the thick New Your City Intergroup Meeting List, organized by boroughs, including meetings in New Jersey, Westchester County and out on Long Island. I was amazed there were so many meetings. I was really quite oblivious, and rather mocus, when I first got sober!

When I Decided To Stay Sober

Getting this Meeting List was vitally important for early recovery. It was essential in helping to keep me sober the next day, November 3, 1972, when I had a meeting with Debbie at her shrink's office down in Greenwich Village. It was the first time we had met since she had moved out of our apartment several weeks earlier. We did not have a good meeting. In fact, it was blooming awful! Here's what happened after the meeting.

I ran screaming out onto W. 11th Street at the corner of Waverley Place in Greenwich Village from the basement office of Dr. Wolf, Debbie's, therapist. I was wild-eyed. Most distraught. Raging. Heartbroken. In a panic. When hoarse, I stopped screaming. I vaguely remember looking around quite frazzled, thinking to stifle it because I didn't want to get arrested. I started walking rapidly, practically running, towards 7th Avenue. My mind was a blur, racing up, down, sideways, all around. I was in full-blown frenzy mode. Operating on gut instinct, I needed to get the fuck as far away as possibly I could from that horrible place—Dr. Wolf's therapy office.

What a most pretentious space it was! Low lighting, walls lined with bookcases stuffed with books and stacks of papers, stylishly decorated with obscure Beasley prints, knick-knacks, and tchotchkes, plush sofas with matching pillows scattered about. Forever more, it would be a most verboten place. This is where Debbie had just told me that despite my not having had a drink for almost a month, she had nonetheless moved out of our West 82nd Street Apartment. She had accomplished this feat that very afternoon, as a matter of fact, while I was applying for admission to an outpatient alcoholism treatment program downtown. Further, she adamantly refused to tell me where she had moved, what her new address was! The simpering, stern-faced Dr. Wolf nodded his pointy chin in approval.

So, there I was, striding up 7th Avenue, most discombobulated and rather in quite a dither. Really, why shouldn't I just go and get hammered, pissant, royally fucking drunk again? I mean, why the fuck not? After all, the whole reason I had stopped drinking and started going to AA meetings in the first place was to get Debbie back. She had left anyway—apparently for good. A modicum of sanity, however, reasoned that getting pissant drunk surely would not do anything to get Debbie back. Besides, through the fog of the three weeks of Thursday night Renewal West AA meetings, I had a glimmer of an idea that maybe, just maybe, if I stayed sober a day at a time, maybe my life could change for the better. Besides, Stanley's qualification actually gave me a tiny sliver of hope in the darkness of my dry-alcoholic despair about missing Debbie.

Also, I had the meeting list. I could check out other meetings. The list provided me with the means to continue not to drink and to become fully engaged within the AA Fellowship. I saw that I could attend AA meetings practically around the clock, all seven days of the week. With a wee bit of hope and the meeting list in my back pocket, I continued walking uptown. Along the way, I made a firm decision—I decided I did not want to drink that night despite being devastated about Debbie leaving. Further, I decided I would start attending other AA meetings.

On the walk uptown, on practically every block there was a bar, a nightclub, a liquor store, or a bodega, selling beer and wine, including a favorite, Boone Farm's Apple Wine. A wine connoisseur definitely I was not! Whenever I passed one of these booze-dispensing establishments, I would look at it and firmly say, "Fuck you!" This was all well and good, until uptown, somewhere north of Lincoln Center, as I recall, I delivered a "Fuck You" at a liquor store, not noticing a little old lady standing nearby.

"I beg your pardon, young man?" she indignantly accosted me.

"No, oh no, ma'am, I wasn't speaking to you, I—ah, well, oh, never mind." I mean, how do you explain to someone that you're telling a liquor establishment to go fuck itself?

When I got back to our empty apartment, I thought about maybe checking out another meeting in my neighborhood. For a while I looked through the meeting list and found several nearby. I saw there were even midnight meetings downtown on East 23rd Street. I also found an interesting sounding meeting down in the Village, the Perry Street Workshop group. Tired, however, and emotionally drained from the harrowing scene in Dr. Wolf's office, I instead decided just to stay home. Nevertheless, I didn't drink that night again, just like I had done a day at a time since October 14th, when I had my last drink, the Rheingold beer. I had successfully stayed sober one more day. This was rather momentous, because for the first time this is what I wanted to do *for myself*. Whether Debbie came back or not, I decided I wanted to get and stay sober by going to other AA meetings anyway.

My First Good Day Sober

The next day was a lovely Indian Summer day. I took the subway down to Greenwich Village, where I had an omelet at an inexpensive French café on Greenwich Avenue and walked around the Village, reveling in the hippy-influenced street scene of my baby-booming generation in the vicinity of New York University and Washington Square Park. I experienced the natural high of being a young man, sober, in New York City, the cultural and entertainment capital of the world. At 2:00 p.m., I walked over to the nearby Perry Street Workshop for the 2:30 meeting.

I sat along the wall near the entrance. There was a speaker's desk and chair up on a small dais in the middle of the long narrow room. Several rows of chairs were on either side with a dingy bathroom and coffee bar in the rear. Soon all the chairs filled up, and there was a blue haze of cigarette smoke, through which sliced beams of sunlight, shining in through the curtained front windows. The meeting started, and a well-dressed man a few years older than me qualified. He told a harrowing story of living on the streets drunk and shooting heroin. Clean and sober now, he worked professionally in the burgeoning new field of addiction treatment. I was riveted by his story. Within me was implanted the idea that maybe I too might like to work in the field of addiction treatment.

There was a woman on the far side of the podium, who looked somewhat familiar, but I couldn't place how I knew her. As soon as she spoke, however, I instantly recognized her as Patricia, an actress I had known at Olney Theatre in the summer of 1971. After the meeting, we hugged and spoke for a while. I asked her what she was doing there. She smiled and said the same thing that I was doing, trying to stay sober a day at a time. We laughed, talked for a while, then said goodbye. I didn't think to get her phone number. I didn't even know this was something that we do. It was a fortuitous, good omen, seeing Patricia at the very first meeting I went to, after having made the decision the night before to start a new life sober a day at a time in recovery. I've stayed sober ever since, and that was almost 45 years ago.

Several months ago, I read with sadness, but deep, deep gratitude, the New York Times obituary of Patricia Elliot who died at age 77 of a rare cancer. She had an amazing career as an actress, winning the Tony Award in 1973 for featured actress in a musical for her role as Countess Charlotte Malcolm in the Stephen Sondheim musical, *A Little Night Music.* For over 20 years she was a star on the soap opera, *One Life to Live.* I presume, since she had such a long and successful career working as an actress, she must have died sober. This pleases me immensely!

Chapter 10: First Year Sober—Getting Involved in the AA Fellowship

With the meeting list as a guide, I started going to meetings all over Manhattan. I became a meeting junkie. Since I was unemployed, I could attend lots of meetings. In the early days, whenever I spoke, which was hardly ever, I mentioned how yes, though my drinking was bad, I was also very concerned that I was crazy because of the crazy things I did drunk. A merchant marine by the name of Dan straightened me out, putting his finger sternly in my chest and gruffly saying, "Stay stopped drinking and much of the crazy will go away!" To a large extent, this has proven to be the case. However, I've been known to quote at meetings the iconic lyric from Paul Simon; though stone-cold sober, I can be "Still Crazy After All These Years."

My first home group was the Midnight Meeting which met Sunday through Friday at 156 W. 23rd Street on the second floor. To gain entrance upstairs, one had to ring the bell and someone would buzz you into the upstairs stairwell. It's been almost 45 years since I walked up that stairwell, but I can still recall the musty, dusty smell of it.

For many years, the Midnight Meeting met in the basement of the First Moravian Church at Lexington Avenue and E. 30th Street, where I regularly attended.

Funny thing, for the last couple of decades, the Midnight meeting has again been meeting upstairs, at 220 West Houston near 7th Avenue. Whenever I visit Manhattan I try to attend one of their meetings. On one of my recent visits I bought what has become one of my favorite T-shirts, black with white lettering saying, "Midnight Upstairs." It reminds me to forever be grateful for my first home group

The Midnight Meeting was notorious for being extraordinarily raucous at times. Bunches of active drunks would often attend, since it was about a mile from the infamous skid row Bowery. This would especially happen in winter, when folks would seek to get some relief from the bitter cold and to get a free cup of lousy coffee. It wasn't unusual for fights to break out. Once, a chair was thrown through the large picture window overlooking 23rd Street. NYPD officers would occasionally be called to restore order and to arrest miscreants.

After the Midnight meetings, a group of us would go around the corner to Bronco's, a western-themed diner at W. 22nd Street and 3rd Avenue in Gramercy Park. Regulars included Paulie, John, Jack, Bruce, Tom-Tom, Huey, Marianne, Dick and a few others, whose faces I recall but whose names I can't. By the time I celebrated my 10th Anniversary, a number of this first Group Of Drunks, with whom I hung out had not only relapsed and drank again, they had also died as a direct result of their drinking, like Stanley S. Stangage had done.

I was a member of the Midnight Meeting for several years and Chairman of the Thursday night Midnight Meeting during most of that time. I came to love and respect many of the night-owl members of the group, with many of whom I identified. One night when I was six or seven months sober, shortly after the Midnight Meeting had moved to the Moravian Church, I heard a gentleman speak whose lasting impact upon me has continued throughout my whole recovery these 45 or so years. He lead the Midnight meeting that night, dressed sharply in a suit with an ascot and brought his gorgeous wife with him. In his qualification he shared that earlier that evening he had celebrated eight years clean and sober.

I don't remember his name, but I remember to this day his powerful message, which resonated deeply with me, both then and now. A contemporary, he related that he had spent his teenage and early twenties drinking and using psychedelics around the clock, while flunking out of two undergraduate college programs. An arrest for driving drunk motivated him to get sober in 1965, the same year I graduated from college. He also shared that in a couple of months he would be completing his PhD in psychology from the City University of New York and starting a career in the field of addiction out on the west coast. He was the second person in AA I had heard speak, who was working in the growing field of addiction treatment. My interest and ambition was further enhanced to somehow become involved as a professional in this burgeoning new field.

In his qualification, he related two anecdotes which to this day I remember and sometimes share at meetings. First, he said he always wanted to consider himself a newcomer in AA, because as long as he didn't drink and drug a day at a time by staying actively involved in AA, he was always coming to new awareness, new insight, new understanding of his disease and how he could continue recovering from it by helping others. Secondly, he made sure not to let any of the many gifts he had received as a result of being clean and sober—his relationship, his schooling, his work life, etc.—get in the way of seeking continued progress in understanding how AA could continue to help him lead a better life. He remembered to be exceedingly grateful to AA for the good life he experienced.

I got my first Big Book from a young kid, Danny, who occasionally came to the Midnight Meetings. Danny was 17 years-old when I knew him, and had gotten sober in 1968 at the age of 13 down in Philadelphia. Early on, I tried reading the first 164 pages, but all of the emphasis on God bothered me, along with the archaic language and syntax. I've since come to appreciate much of what Bill conveyed in the Big book. To be truthful, considering the time when it was written, several years after the repeal of prohibition, it's amazing how much of what Bill wrote about alcoholism in the Big Book was spot on, how much of it was right.

It's The Stories, Sweetheart

I did, however, greatly appreciate the wisdom and inspiration I experienced from reading some of the stories in the Big Book. Today, I recommend to people whom I sponsor to read the stories, including Bill's story in Chapter 1. I don't focus too much on the rest of the first 164 pages, although I especially appreciate what he wrote on page 164, "Our book is meant to be suggestive only. We realize we know only a little." In my experience, the reason AA works is not so much imbued within the 12 steps and the "precise directions" delineated in the first 164 pages about how to work them. Rather, AA works because by relating our stories, we identify with each other, like I identified with Stanley.

When AA speakers lead a meeting, they generally follow the time-worn formula of qualifications. Speakers relate 1) How It Was (being addicted), 2) What Happened (to get sober), and 3) How It is Now (usually much better than when drinking). Not only do speakers relate their individual stories, but folks sharing during discussion also tell their stories. We relate stories to each other, anecdotes from our lived experience, about how we stay sober despite whatever challenges or obstacles we confront in living our lives, so that we can successfully stay sober in recovery a day at a time. John D. Niles, a Humanities professor at the University of Wisconsin-Madison, suggests that instead of being referred to as *homo sapiens*, a more appropriate description of we humans might be that we are *homo narrans*. We human beings shape our worlds through the stories that we tell each other. Certainly, this is what happens when we alcoholics relate our stories to each other of our addiction and the process and challenges of recovery in the meeting rooms of AA. Here are two stories that were crucially important for me to experience early on in recovery:

It's Never Too Late

This lady had gone to Hollywood in 1936 to become a movie star. She married a director and got involved in a heavy drinking lifestyle. She didn't become a starlet, much less a star. After her first divorce, she was introduced to AA in 1945, but she didn't stay sober. She had two other failed marriages and lived abroad in Europe and Mexico for many years. In the mid-60s after her third failed marriage, she again started going to AA, but this time she stayed sober. When I heard her qualify at a Midnight Meeting, she was seven years sober and a well known actress, playing numerous supporting roles in movies and on primetime television shows. She had achieved in recovery what she could not previously do in her youth or former life while drinking—she had become a well-known actress.

You Can't Take Sobriety for Granted

This next story really impacted me. This man in his 60s had ended up on the skid row of Philadelphia as a young man in his mid-twenties. He got sober in AA and within a few years became the successful owner of a major advertising company. He had a house and a family on the Main Line. He also became very active in AA, starting a number of meetings, being chair of Intergroup, serving as GSR, DCM, Area Chair and Delegate, etc., etc., etc. In retrospect, he was able to discern that at about 25 years sober, he had slowly begun to reduce his participation in AA. He was still going to meetings, but he stopped doing service work. After another couple of years, he was only going to one or two meetings a month. There followed a period when he hadn't been to a meeting for several months. Meanwhile, his life was continuing to be satisfying and successful, kids in college, lots of business deals, good home life, etc. On a cruise with his wife in the Caribbean, the maître d' asked he would have a glass of champaign to celebrate his birthday. Without hesitation he said, "Yes, one glass can't hurt."

Within six months he had lost everything again, the company, his house on the Main Line, his wife and family. In addition, he found himself again on Philadelphia's skid row. If this was the end of his story it would be tragic enough, but it got worse, at least as I related to it. He knew that for him to have any kind of a decent life again, he would have to get sober.

To get sober again, he would have to start attending AA meetings. But, because he had been so active and high profile in AA, his ego wouldn't let him go into an AA room again under the influence of alcohol. To him, this meant before he could go to an AA meeting, he would have to be three days sober. He spent the next five years, not drinking for two days, and drinking on the third day, all the while living in the degradation of skid row.

He finally got three days sober and went to his first AA meeting about a year-and-a-half before I heard him qualify at a Midnight meeting. He was most humbly grateful to be sober again, so he could enjoy a much simpler life than he had previously lived. This included regular visits with his several grandchildren. His story demonstrated to me that there are perhaps worse outcomes than dying as a result of a relapse. It made the 24-hour plan, of not picking up the first drink a day at a time, very feasible and critically important. It impressed upon me the reality that there are no cures or guarantees in sobriety.

For several months while separated from Debbie, I lived with Joe and John, two mainstays of the Midnight meeting. We also participated in treatment together at the Outpatient Clinic across from Cooper Square, where I participated in bi-weekly groups and individual counseling. The dayroom was a safe, sober place in which to hang out, watching TV or playing cards and conversing with other clients. The three of us shared a walkup tenement apartment on E. 11th Street between Avenue B and C in Alphabet City. It was on the sixth floor, up a dingy and narrow staircase with windows opening out upon an air shaft. We shared a toilet in the hall with other tenants on our floor and had a bathtub in the middle of our kitchen. We were the only white folks on the block, populated mostly by Puerto Ricans, Cubans and Haitians. We were eyed suspiciously by many of our neighbors, both in the building and on the block. They probably thought we were undercover cops, since several months before we lived there two New York City cops had been assassinated by members of a drug-dealing Black Liberation gang. Joe and John were among a number of close Midnight Meeting friends who died as a direct result of relapsing by the time I was ten years sober.

Another close friend who died was Huey, not necessarily because he drank again. I don't know for sure if he drank again or not. Huey was most handsome, the epitome of a man's man. He was a regularly working actor with minor roles in theatre, movies and on TV shows. Here's a poem I wrote about watching him with one of the chronic street drunks who regularly attended the Midnight Meeting:

compassion

*nick hobbled in
shuffling his cane
serenely drunk again
lobotomized by gallo*

*he gazed about him
quick-moving darts
of blurry eyes
as if uncomprehending
fully what he saw*

*stumbling
he found a seat
gratefully empty
sat heavily
marrow-achingly tired*

*shivering
huddled small
within his over-sized coat
both hands clutching
the top of his cane
which unsteadily
propped up
his scruffy chin
he stared
stared with guilt
stared with isolation
stared with self-alienation
trying to focus
some semblance of meaning
out of his wet-brained fog
of gut-twisting
bowel-shaking
throat burning
belched wine
as forgotten spittle*

*dribbled down
the stubble of his scrubby beard
onto the dirt-splotched coat*

*i watched him
with mild derision
soul briefly stirred with gratitude
but for the grace of ... and all that
stayed rooted however in complacency
turning my attention
to fragile fantasies
of maybe some tomorrow's
erotic embraces
by the lovely object
sitting demurely
across the room
sternly ignoring
my random glances*

*looking back at nick
i saw with him huey
a strong-jawed
blond-mustached
big-boned man's man
who was as virile
as beautifully male
as any model
on any cover
of any GQ or
Soldier of Fortune
magazine*

*huey was gently
holding nick
stroking him
assuring him
relating with him
letting him just be him
and loving him
loving him so heart simply*

*a burning tear
slid down my face*

as i watched with awe
nick's streaming tears
steadily flow
through the gray stubble
missing the coat
to puddle on the floor

During the Vietnam War, Huey had been a young Marine, stationed on Okinawa. A couple of nights before his unit was scheduled to ship out for Vietnam, he got drunk and cold-cocked his squad leader. Instead of going to Vietnam with his unit, he was in the brig and shortly thereafter was dishonorably discharged. One night in Bronco's after the meeting, we spoke about my experience in Vietnam. He related to me how disappointed and ashamed he was that he had not served with his Marine Unit. In 1977, he volunteered to serve as a mercenary trooper in the Rhodesian Light Infantry, a well-trained and disciplined, extraordinarily proficient anti-guerrilla commando unit in Africa during the Rhodesian Bush War. He was killed during one of their operations. I attribute his death to his alcoholism, whether he drank or not, and to survivor guilt he had from not going to Vietnam.

During the first several months of early recovery, I would often go to one of the daily mid-day meetings at the Mustard Seed, followed by lunch at Sarge's Diner on 3rd Avenue. Sometimes, a buddy of mine at the time, Shelly, and I would walk over to the Intergroup office then on W. 22nd Street. There, we would do volunteer work, such as stuffing envelopes, collating newsletters, or other such clerical tasks. We were a bi-polar Mutt and Jeff—Shelly, from a prominent New York City Jewish family, was a manic, fast-talking con-man, who was a part-time antiquities dealer. I, on the other hand, was a shy, insecure and at times suicidally-depressed, mostly mute, Vietnam Veteran from Jackson, MS, who rarely spoke, since I was so painfully self-conscious. We were a perfect match to balance out each other's bi-polar extremes.

When I was about two months sober, I qualified for the first time. Bill K., a long-timer, who occasionally attended the Midnight Meeting, asked me to lead a meeting he was chairing at the Tuberculous Ward of Bellevue Hospital. I vaguely remember the dark, dank room in the basement filled with elderly men and a few women, who were mostly in wheelchairs. As I recall, I spoke for over an hour, oblivious to the reality that most of the audience had slumped into their wheelchairs fast asleep. They may not have heard much of what I had to say, but I recall to this day the wonder and gratitude I felt from speaking and hearing aloud for the first time my whole story. It sealed for me the truth that I belonged in AA.

My first service commitment was making coffee for the Young People's Meeting, which met on Friday nights at the Friends Meeting House across from Stuyvesant Square. This commitment kept me sober, when after about six months of recovery, I had decided to, was determined to, get drunk again. I had plenty of reasons. I hadn't gotten Debbie, my wife, back as yet. I still didn't have a job. *And*, I had just turned 30 years-old, which was way over the hill, according to the youthful arrogance of my hippie generation. However, I had this coffee commitment at the Young People's meeting, which I felt obligated to fulfill. I mean, what would they think of me if I didn't show up? So, I went to the meeting and made the coffee. I also had to stay for the meeting, since part of the commitment was to clean up afterwards. I couldn't not finish doing my service job, right? Whatever would they think of me?

My firm intention was to get royally hammered later that night and during the wee-hours of the following morning. This was my favorite time to get drunk by myself, listening to oldies but goodies and literally crying in my beer in remorse over lost loves from my past. Most especially, I would be crying in my beer over the loss of my current love, my wife Debbie, who wouldn't reconcile with me. The speaker that night was "Elevator Tom," a vibrant, successful young man, who was a foreman, supervising installation of elevators in high-rise buildings. His lead was scintillating, full of the humor and hope and joy and gratitude, all of which are the natural products of not drinking, going to meetings, and helping others. Despite my dark state of mind, I identified with him and experienced again H.O.P.E.—Hearing Other People's Experience.

I am convinced that this "human power" of hearing the stories that other addicts share in meetings is the primary healing dynamic of AA. I experienced again what I often do at meetings, even to this day in longterm recovery, an Attitude Adjustment! The result was I stayed sober for another day and did not follow through with my intention to get shit-faced wasted after the meeting.

Identification Is The Key

Stanley and Elevator Tom are just two many instances of identification I experienced during the first year of recovery. All throughout the ensuing years of longterm recovery, they are typical of what I always experience in AA, because I don't drink, I go to meetings, and I help others whenever I can. The way I experience how this works is that whenever I share with a newcomer, I not only hear and identify with their story—I also hear again and identify with *my* story. I have a sensory recall of how horrible my drinking was and how much better my life is today, sober in recovery. I thereby re-experience the gift of my story—both the horror of the former dark life drinking, and renewed hope to stay sober one more day, even if, at times, it is through gritted teeth. Through mutual identification with each other, we both are enabled to experience the gift of a "daily reprieve". Our spiritual experience is hearing and identifying with each other. I am utterly convinced that AA works because of this identification. We alcoholics identify with each other, both in our shared malady and through our continued recovery together. Essentially, the healing we experience in AA is due to our ability to deeply identify with the shared stories of our recovery together. This is the *Human Power* of AA !~!~!

Ernie Kurtz, the foremost historian of AA's rapid growth and evolution during the 20th Century, agrees. On page 61 of his seminal academic history of AA, *Not God,* he writes:

> *The antidote for the deep symptom of denial was identification marked by open and undemanding narration infused with profound honesty about personal weakness. The process of identification was offered without any demand for reciprocity or for anything else.*

In a 2002 article, Kurtz further notes:

> *The secret of Alcoholics Anonymous, the thing that makes AA work, is identification. As Marty Mann is reputed to have said to her fellow sanitarium inmate on returning to Blythwood from her visit to the Wilson home in Brooklyn Heights for her first AA meeting: "Grennie, we aren't alone any more".*

I am ever so grateful that I am always able to "not be alone any more," simply by going to an AA meeting, where I can readily identify with the experience, strength and hope of other alcoholics. In New York City AA meetings, I got a thorough grounding in what to me are the three basic essentials of staying sober: Don't Drink. Go to Meetings. Help Others. These are the effective supplements to the dictum I first learned from

Stanley at my third beginners meeting, "No matter what, don't drink, even if your ass turns to gold or if it falls off."

About a month after hearing Elevator Tom speak at the Young People's Meeting, I experienced a situation where my "ass turned to gold"—Debbie and I reconciled. She finally let me know where she lived and asked me to move into her apartment a block from Stuyvesant Square. Her apartment was short walks, as it turned out, from the meeting locations of both the Midnight Meeting and the Young People's Meeting. It was the happiest day I had so far experienced in recovery, when I walked my scant belongings in a couple of suitcases from Joe and John's dingy apartment up the several blocks to Debbie's apartment. Her apartment was much nicer, cleaner and had a full bath with a door that closed for total privacy.

One weekend we drove my beat-up Opel Station wagon out to Merrick, Long Island to visit a work associate of Debbie's. Driving back to the City on Montauk Highway, the car broke down, and I couldn't get it started again. We decided the best thing to do would be to abandon it. We took the expired Maryland license tags off the car, taking them and the car registration with us. Since I had had lived at several different addresses in Maryland, Washington, DC, and New York City, I figured the authorities would never be able to trace the car to us. I was wrong. Several weeks later there was a knock on the front door and two burly Nassau County police officers handed me a summons for the car. They told me where I could retrieve the car at a lot for impounded cars in Long Beach, NY. They also told me to bring the title and registration for the car with me.

This was not the only summons I had gotten with the Opel Station wagon. In my last months both driving drunk and during early recovery, I parked the car illegally with impunity. I parked in no parking zones, in front of fire hydrants, in loading zones, on crosswalks, in handicapped only parking spaces. I did with the many parking tickets I got what I had previously done with empty cans of Colt .45—I blithely tossed them in the back seat of the car. During this period, since New York City was in dire financial straits, there were severe scofflaw penalties for unpaid parking tickets; fines escalated drastically each month they went unpaid. I must have had some 50 or 60 unpaid parking tickets in the backseat of the Opel. No doubt, I would owe a couple of thousand dollars, maybe more, perhaps a lot more, to resolve these summonses.

To say I was terrified, as I took the Long Island Rail Road train from Penn Station out to Long Beach, would be a massive understatement. I guess I prayed frantically, not so much to any god, but to the Kosmos, to Karma, to my higher self, to something I had no idea about for help. I prayed not so much believing that anything would help me, but mostly to calm myself down. With trepidation, I walked from the Long Island Rail Road Station to the address of the junk yard where the car had been impounded. I handed the summons to the large man sitting behind the counter.

"How much is this going to cost?" I gingerly asked.

He found the appropriate paperwork in a thickly bound book, and muttered, "$25 dollars. Do you have your title and registration?"

"Ah, yes, I do," I replied. "Why do you need them?"

"Well, he said, "You pay the $25 dollars for this summons, give us your registration and sign your car title over to us. Then you can go your way."

"That's it," I incredulously inquired.

"Yup, that's it. We then own your car and sell the parts to reimburse us for towing it and the storage fees."

It was a nice scam the towing company and junkyard had going with the Nassau County cops. I, however, was greatly relieved. Apparently, no one had looked in the back seat of the car to see the numerous parking tickets I had thrown there during the past year. I suppose somewhere in the deep bowels of New York City police department, there are still copies of these unpaid tickets. It was a much different train ride back into the city, during which I pondered the deeply imprinted lesson that convinced me that no matter what, as long as I don't pick up, any seemingly dire situation has the possibility of turning out prodigiously better than just okay. It's an article of faith that I have experienced many times throughout my longterm continuing recovery in AA. I've experienced it in regards to lost relationships, lost jobs, sickness, travel difficulties, and relocating, some seventeen times, both overseas and in the US since 2001. As long as I don't use, things have a way of turning out for the best, much better than I could ever plan or imagine.

———

Debbie and I settled in to a tenuous reconciliation of our marriage. From the start, she made it clear that she would not join me in not drinking. She queried whether her drinking would bother me. I assured her that I had the drinking problem, not her. Further, I had no right to impose any of my restrictions onto her. In retrospect, I can discern that I was also extremely codependent on Debbie, and bent over backwards to accommodate her, so grateful I was that we had reconciled. Sober, I was eventually able to observe that Debbie might very well have had not only a drinking problem, but a problem with prescription pills as well. We were one of those households where if you opened the medicine cabinet a cascade of doctor's samples would fall out—percocets, davocets, tuinals, seconals, quaaludes, poppers (alkyl nitrate) etc.

I never queried her about where she got her drugs. She was always complaining of various aches and pains, having regular visits with several doctors for various ailments. Plus, her sister was a nurse at a hospital up in Westchester County, and some of our friends were heavily into party drugs. Perhaps they may also have been supplying her. Seven years younger than me, she was at the height of the age-appropriate heavy-using cohort of her peer group. Plus, she experienced no apparent negative consequences as a result of her using. She was a heavy and hardy party woman in her early twenties, very much the opposite of me in my years of drinking and drugging.

Shortly, after I moved into Debbie's apartment, I answered a New York Times Help Wanted ad for an Administrative Assistant at a small company, Assured Salesmakers, Inc., owned by Irv Zuckerman. Irv lived in super upscale, Scarsdale, NY, and owned the company offices that were located in three floors of a Brownstone on E 38th Street, just off Madison Avenue. The company created sales training materials for the sales forces of major multinational corporations. These included SONY, Volvo, VW, Singer and HILTI. Irv was a genius, who would sit for hours in his office, dictating off the top of his head the scripts for complicated slide shows presentations. Irv's dictations included instructions for what the graphics would look like and instructions to produce the handouts, workbooks and other training materials, which would accompany these presentations.

I edited the materials and coordinated with Jan, Irv's Creative Director, two graphic artists, a typist, and various vendors, to produce all of these materials for the elaborate sales training presentations that Irv would present at national sales force meetings. A decided advantage of this job was that it was a short walk from the many meetings at the Mustard Seed each day of the week. I could catch a meeting early in the morning before work, another around noon, or one of several meetings after 5:00 p.m. I also continued to attend Midnight Meetings, always the Thursday night meeting I chaired, and at least one other as well. Other meetings during the week including the Manhattan Group, a couple of blocks away from our apartment. I also made several half-assed attempts to develop a relationship with a sponsor, but nothing really ever worked out during my first year. Essentially, like I had been when drinking, I was a loner.

With us both working full time, we settled into a normal routine as a young professional couple in New York City. During the week we worked during the day, and met friends for drinks and meals one or two nights a week. At least once a week we would meet with former associates from American Express Language Centers, now reverted to its original name IML, the Institute of Modern Languages. On other nights, we prepared meals together in her apartment and watched television. Sometimes, we went to a movie or a concert.

One of the patterns we developed early on is that we would meet early after work with friends, and then I would leave her with friends while I went to AA meetings. On weekends, we would travel up to New Rochelle in Westchester county to have dinner with her mother and sister. Occasionally, we would drive her car to one of the beaches on Long Island. I remember us going to Coney Island and Jones Beach. Once we visited her cousin out in Mastic Beach, NY for a holiday weekend. During that weekend, we made a first trip to Montauk, which we both loved and visited several times that summer.

In the fall, to celebrate Debbie's one-year anniversary of working at the Federal Reserve Bank, we hosted a party with several of her close work associates and a number of our friends, including several from the Institute of Modern Languages. I got a bit of of a resentment, when she asked me to walk across town to a bakery on 7th Avenue in the Village to get a heavily rum-soaked specialty cake she had ordered to serve to her guests, but which I knew I couldn't dare taste. I bought myself two sticky-sweet pecan rolls to indulge in instead on the walk back to the apartment.

Neg-Fans

Soon after I was reunited with Debbie, I began to obsessively fantasize that she was having an affair. I would develop elaborate scenarios of her being unfaithful to me. I would imagine her with a girlfriend, with one of our former associates at IML, with a stranger who picked her up on the street, with the entire visiting team of the Pittsburg Penguins, when they played in Madison Square Garden—the more perverse my fantasies, the better. It was like there was a video-player in my head, playing an endless loop of X-rated porno films of various scenes of her infidelity with no off button.

I later came to describe these as neg-fans, negative fantasies. I was haunted by these dark imaginings of her being unfaithful. I was also consumed with trying to find corroborating evidence of this. I even sunk so low as to examine and sniff her panties, trying to detect evidence of her love juice or a lover's cum.

Every Wednesday night, she had a therapy group at her therapist's office in Greenwich Village, the same office I described in the previous chapter. The group, she told me, went from 7:00 - 11:00 p.m. Afterwards, she and several other members of the group would go to a nearby coffee shop on 7th Avenue, where they would converse for another couple of hours or so. I became convinced this was a cover story, so she could have a weekly tryst with a lover. One chilly, rainy night at 10:00 p.m., I walked across town to Dr. Wolf's office, crouching behind some garbage cans across the street. I waited for her and her lover to leave. They didn't. Instead, as Debbie had related to me, several members of the group left the office together and went to a nearby coffee shop. Heart-pounding, I followed them a half a block away, and stood in the doorway of a hospital clinic across the street until they all came out together a couple of hours later. I followed Debbie walking by herself, and when she stopped at the crosstown bus stop, I had to hurriedly hail a cab to get to our apartment before she did.

How did I feel? I was disappointed.

First Anniversary

On Tuesday, October 30, 1973, I celebrated my first anniversary at the Manhattan Group. I just saw in the meeting list of the Intergroup Association of New York AA that the group still celebrates its members' anniversaries on the last Tuesday of each month. The history of the Manhattan group goes all the way back to the original New York AA meeting, which started in the basement of Lois and Bill's Clinton Street Brownstone in Brooklyn when Bill returned from Akron. When they were evicted in 1939, the meeting migrated to New Jersey, where they lived in an early member's summer camp for several months. Other early meeting places of what became the Manhattan group were the tailor shop on 5th

Avenue, owned by Bert, another early AA member, and the original 24-Hour Clubhouse in the carriage house at 334½ W. 24th Street. The group eventually settled in at the Christ Lutheran Church on E. 19th Street near 1st Avenue, where it met for many years. This is where I celebrated my first anniversary.

A couple of years ago I googled the Church and found out that it is no more. In 2006, due to a diminishing congregation, the church was sold to a developer, who promised to build a condominium on top of the church facade. However, the project ran out of money. After the church had been gutted, the facade, exposed to the elements, collapsed into a pile of debris in 2007. For several years the lot stood empty, until another developer cleared the lot and built another condominium. In late October of 2015, some 42 years after I celebrated by first anniversary there, I walked by and took a picture of the nearly completed condominium. I was extremely moved by a mixture of grief that this iconic place from my early recovery was now gone, like a whisper on the wind. Simultaneously, however, I was filled with incredible gratitude that I was still sober after so many years.

Debbie accompanied me to the Tuesday evening meeting where I celebrated my first year anniversary. Each of us celebrants had 5 or 10 minutes at the podium, and there was a large cake that we shared at the meeting. I have no recollection of what I said, but I distinctly remember the pinched, scowling look on Debbie's face while I was at the podium. She never really accepted that I was an alcoholic. Nor was she impressed by my attending AA meetings. After all, her father had died the notorious town drunk after being in and out of AA for many years. She really didn't want me to stop drinking. She just wanted me to drink like a hail-fellow-well-met kind of a good-time-party guy. Instead, I used to get sloppy drunk and became all morosely maudlin, crying in my beer about dead babies in Vietnam and shit like that.

―――

The weekend after I celebrated my first anniversary, Debbie was away for the weekend with a girlfriend from work, or so she said. It was also the weekend of the Bill Wilson Annual Dinner Dance, celebrated every year at the New York Hilton Hotel. A gala affair, I had scrounged a ticket and went with a group of people from the Midnight Meeting. This included Fran, a lovely lady, visiting from Montreal, who had attended a number of Midnight meetings several days before the dance. We experienced lust at first sight, and I was sorely tempted to work the 13th Step with her. However, I was committed to remain faithful to Debbie. I did, however, thoroughly enjoy the evening with her, conversing and dancing. It was my first time to boogie without being smashed. I was most comfortable sober, interacting with other friends in recovery. It opened up a whole new dimension of life in recovery for me. I realized that I had considerably more fun partying sober than ever I did when shit-faced drunk.

At one of the Midnight Meetings, Fran shared an anecdote about how Michelangelo sculpted the famous stature of David. He took a defective piece of marble, one that other artists in Florence had rejected because it had a crook in it, and he chipped away everything that was not David! The defect, the crook, Michelangelo was able to envision as being the basis for the distinctive bend of David's posture. She related that her experience had been that AA was slowly doing the same process with her, chipping away all that was not her authentic self. Some 44 years later I still relate this anecdote at meetings, which so impressed me then, as it still does today.

The Power of Negative Thinking

A couple of weeks later, sick with a horrid head cold, I came home an hour-and-a-half early from my service commitment as chairperson of the Thursday night meeting of the Midnight group. I walked into our apartment and found Debbie in bed naked with a lover and our dog, Dylan. I'm unsure, even to this day, about what upset me more, that she was in our bed with a lover, or that they were both in bed with our dog. With a flash of insight, I realized that the obsessive Neg-Fans I had indulged in the previous several months had come true. Her lover, Tom, a fellow worker at the Federal Reserve Bank, hastily got dressed and left our apartment. We spent the next several hours arguing and discussing our situation, going round and round with no resolution, only mounting counter-accusations of raging resentment and disagreement. Turns out they had been together for the first time the couple of weekends previously when Debbie had been away with "a girlfriend."

In essence, Debbie's and my conundrum boiled down to an intractable impasse—she couldn't live with my not drinking, and I didn't want to drink again.

In disgust, feeling horrid, mentally, emotionally, and physically from the head-cold, I packed a couple of suitcases with some clothes and my most prized possessions, the poetry and several short stories I'd written, the collected poetry of e.e. cummings and a book of Rod McKuen's poetry. I found myself sitting, sobbing and sniveling, in nearby Stuyvesant Park, where we had daily walked Dylan. Dully, I watched a cold, wan sunrise. I was devastated, heartbroken, most distraught. I had no idea what I was going to do, where I could go. *But,* I knew one thing for certain—I did not want to drink on this awful new day either !~!~!

I now understood why I had been so obsessed with Debbie having an affair, why I had been disappointed when I followed her to the group, when she didn't leave with a lover. I had been on a raging dry drunk. The alcoholic part of me counted on my discovery of her having an affair as being an excellent reason to get drunk again, especially since the only reason I had initially stopped drinking in the first place was to get Debbie back. As terrible as I felt, my tears of utter desolate grief were soon transformed into tears of gratitude for my involvement with AA during the previous year. Because I had stayed sober a day at a time and was actively involved in the AA Fellowship, including service work to help others, I did not want to drink that awful day either—What an incredible gift !~!~!

Chapter 11: Unity and First Meditation Experience

At 8:00 a.m. Friday morning, I took a cab up to the ASI offices with my two suitcases of belongings. I was determined to distract myself with work. Thank the Kosmos, I was extremely busy that day, putting the final touches on a major presentation Irv was presenting to the Singer Corporation over the weekend at a conference center up in the Catskill Mountains. I had no choice but to buckle down and focus on "First Things First"—don't drink and do my fucking job!

Since the ASI brownstone building had a mini-studio apartment where Irv on occasion stayed, I decided to crash there for the weekend. I have no recollection of what I did that weekend, but I imagine that I went to lots of meetings to insure that I would stay sober. When Monday came, I decided to continue to crash in Irv's mini-studio for awhile. This was all well and good for the next several days until Jan, Irv's partner, walked in at 7:00 a.m. one morning, and found me sleeping on the couch. She told me in no uncertain terms that I had to move out that day. For the next several days I stayed in a number of single-room-occupancy hotels in Midtown. A couple of them were rat and roach infested. Finally, I found an affordable room to share with three Bosnians, who spoke little English, in an apartment way uptown at W. 146th Street and Riverside Drive.

―――――

Throughout the 70s and 80s many people in 12-step recovery would attend the Unity Center of Practical Christianity, where Eric Butterworth had a New Thought ministry. Every Sunday morning, he would nearly fill Avery Fisher Hall at Lincoln Center. Upwards of a half of the audience were in one recovery program or the other. Eric taught that Jesus was just one of many enlightened beings, such as Buddha, Krishna, Muhammad, Krishnamurti, etc. These avatars, or "way showers," were not considered to be divine or gods, but by following their teachings and example, one was enabled to discover how to manifest the spark of divinity that lies within each human being. Essentially, New Thought is neither monolithic nor doctrinaire. Eric further taught that life essentially was for loving by extending unconditional compassion and forgiveness to others. Meditation was the tool used to look within oneself to discover and evolve the divinity within, so one could spread loving compassion and forgiveness.

A number of my friends from the Midnight Meeting were regular attendees of Unity, not only to hear Eric on Sundays, but also to experience guided meditations from his assistant, Justin Morely, every Wednesday at noon and 6:00 p.m.. One Wednesday, I decided to attend Justin's noon meditation session. It was my first time to meditate. What follows is an account I wrote about this "white-light" experience. Though vastly different, it rivals in intensity the one reported by AA co-founder Bill Wilson:

> *It's a sunny, late Wednesday morning. I'm walking to Unity Center in the old Abbey Victoria Hotel in Midtown from my office just off Madison Avenue. I'm on my way to attend a first meditation experience. I'm most ambivalent as I walk on this crisp, bright, late fall day in mid-November of 1973. I'm in a most discordant state of mind, rather of a dither really. Several days ago, I discovered my second wife having an affair. The closer I get to Unity Center, the more ambivalent I become:*
>
> *"This is stupid. This is dumb. What good will meditation do? I want my wife back. I want to kill, or at least seriously beat up, her lover, Tom."*
>
> *I'm forlorn, I'm heartbroken, I'm raging. As I approach the entrance to Unity on W. 51st Street, I'm seized with rebellion, "Screw this. I'm outta here."*
>
> *Just then Nancy,, the wife of a friend of mine in recovery, greets me enthusiastically. She's most grateful to be sharing the Unity experience with someone else in recovery. Docilely, I follow her up the steps and into the large auditorium. Nancy joins some friends, and I sit by myself in the middle of an empty row of seats. The houselights dim, and a magenta spotlight illuminates the face and upper torso of Justin Morely, who will lead the guided meditation. After several bars of soft, lilting music, Justin begins to speak in a rich baritone voice. Gently, he suggests that we quiet our minds and focus upon our breaths. We are instructed to breathe deeply in and to deeply breathe out. It's difficult sitting still.*

It feels like bugs are crawling all over me. I have to stifle a tickle in my throat, so it doesn't explode into a cough. My legs begin to ache. Carefully, I shift them, most self-conscious about disturbing others nearby.

My mind races with obsessive thoughts, multitudinous variations on the theme, "This is so stupid!"

It takes every ounce of will-power to resist the frantic urge to run out of the auditorium screaming at the top of my lungs, "I gotta get outta this place!"

Despite my scattered consciousness, I slowly begin to calm down. Imperceptibly at first, but surely gathering fullness deep within me, I become aware that in the darkness behind my closed eyelids a cascade of streaming galaxies flow in all directions. I'm mesmerized by this infinity of light, a seemingly endless Niagara Falls of streaming light, cascading within me. Suddenly a huge, dark door superimposes itself over the streaming galaxies. I can still see them flowing in all directions behind the door. I don't hear a voice, nor read any words, but solemnly, deep within me, this thought is imprinted:

To join this infinity of light, all you have to do is open the door.

Slowly, with tears of gratitude flowing down my face, I watch my hand steadily reach up and open the door.

It's forty-five years later. I'm still sober. I live a contented and successful life with fourth wife, Jill. Though in the late autumn of my life, I am most grateful still to be able to recall with clarity this first meditation experience.

One of the most valuable lessons I learned from Eric and Justin at Unity was the concept that everything, absolutely everything, comes to pass, not to stay. This includes relationships, jobs, happiness, depression, troubles, the good, the bad, the beautiful, the ugly and everything in between.

The apartment I shared on the far Upper Westside had a gorgeous bay window that overlooked the Hudson River, the lights of New Jersey. and the George Washington Bridge. Many a night I would sit at the window, reading, writing poetry, listening to classical music or Alison Steele, the late night DJ, who called herself "Nightbird." Here's a poem I wrote there:

nightlight

i sit at my window
against which whistles and whirls
in pane-rattling, scurry-pounding bursts
early spring's blustering wind
commingled with late winter's bitter chill

i look out the window
across the dark void of night
under which unseen the hudson silently flows
distant pinpricks of misty light splay out
in awkward angles upon jersey's shore
unstrung pearls a glimmer in scattered disarray

i reflect upon
how much this scene starkly symbolizes
my oft times state of soul which allows
self-induced inner darkness to falsely cloud
the divine infinities myriad of light
safely glowing within always me

i am still ...
focusing on the disjointed bits of light
until they merge are telescoped
like rushing chips of a kaleidoscope
into the reality right this instant
here before now me

                        one
                                ness
                                      is

Rock Roots

During this period, I began experiencing a "Rock Roots" meme. It began manifesting itself in journal entries and in my dreams. I'd be walking along the streets of Manhattan, and the phrase would just pop into my mind, "Rock Root," "Rock Root," "Rock Root." It just bubbled up from the vastness of my subconscious. In retrospect, I believe that I was deeply experiencing the stirrings of what some refer to in 12-step recovery as a "spiritual awakening." One of the affirmations I wrote out or said to myself dozens, maybe hundreds of times, each day was "I trust the rock-root certainty of my Higher Self."

Though I applied at the very last moment, I was accepted for a weekend Unity Retreat at a conference center up in Greenwich, CT. I even had to borrow money to attend the retreat, something I hated to do. On the cold Saturday lunch break, I took a walk on the retreat grounds. It was a cloudy, overcast day, and soft, large flakes of snow gently fell and swirled about me. I wandered around a lovely lake partially bounded by a steep escarpment. I was truly in a wondrous winter wonderland. Everything glowed with an inner luminescence. Looking up, I happened to see, a foot or so above my head, growing straight out of a sheer surface of rock, several hardy "Rock Roots." I was utterly delighted! I interpreted this as a talisman that no matter how painful the separation from Debbie had been, seeing them was an indication of better things to come. I was right – during that weekend, I met a most lovely lady, Nancy, with whom I had a brief, but poignant affair. I also met Peter during the weekend, the man who was to become my sponsor for the next 33 years until he died in late August of 2006.

There's another instance of my experience of this "Rock-Root" meme. In the summer of 1995, I spent several days down in my hometown of Jackson, MS. On a whim, I happened to go to an art auction at a gallery nearby my childhood home in North Jackson. It was run by Larry McCool, someone I had been slightly acquainted with during high school. One of the pieces being auctioned was a mixed media painting, "Cliff Falls," by Rex W. Robinson. It prominently portrayed several "Rock Roots" growing out of a cliff, around which cascaded a waterfall. I had to have it and was successful in bidding for it. Today, it is one of my most treasured possessions.

———

The first lady in recovery with whom I had an affair was Nancy. I met her at the Unity weekend retreat. She was the privileged and beautiful daughter of a prominent Hollywood director. A yoga teacher, mostly out-of-work actress, and wannabe artist, she lived off her considerable trust fund. She had survived the tragedy of finding her husband, the father of her two teen-age children, hanging drunk but dead in their Upper Westside co-op apartment. For several months, we had a delicious, whirlwind affair, meditating, doing yoga, attending many AA meetings, and making love several times a week. Here's a poem she gave me, describing a cold walk we took through Riverside Park on Christmas Day, 1973:

Growing Light

Tiny black and grey figures moving
Across a bleak blackbrown winter
Christmascape of park deserted
By all but wrens and indigents
Moving, gesticulating, laughing, hugging
Under a greyed cotton-batting skycover
Heavy with winter's silence and promise
Under nests and bridges, listening;
Watching hardy avian domesticity;
Shivering at watersedge, gulls swooping
Over the greasy green riverswells
The figures merged, and after lightly,
Bounding up the seven-league steps
Towards warmth/music/coffee-tea cups
Each seemed to have absorbed a
Little of the other person's radiance
         NNC
         12/25/73

On New Year's Eve, we attended a delightfully raucous, but sober, AA party in the Lincoln Towers penthouse apartment of Sam Baker. The apartment had a glorious view of the Hudson River and the opposite Jersey shore. I still recall the excitement of sweatily dancing in the New Year to the rhythmic beats of Barry White's, "Love Theme."

Sam was one of two people I knew who died sober, when I was in early recovery. An avid skier, he died of a massive heart attack up at a Vermont Ski Resort, where he had a vacation condo. People who witnessed it said he was smiling broadly as he flew down a ski slope. Suddenly, he dropped his ski poles, grabbed his chest and tumbled several times, dead in a heap. Another man, Bob, whose last name escapes me, died similarly, surfing for his first time out at Kismet, Fire Island.

Nancy taught me a lesson about how cunning, baffling, and insidious our disease can be. In mid-February, her face dark and downcast, but steadfastly firm, Nancy broke up with me. She related she had a one glass of wine slip. She had to break up with me, she explained, because she was a newcomer again and had to focus solely on staying sober a day at a time. Over the next several years, I was aware of several other one-glass-of-wine slips she had. However, she never stayed sober long enough to be able to do the requisite healing of her trauma within and to experience self-forgiveness. In other words, she never experienced "a personality change sufficient to bring about recovery from alcoholism," as it is discussed in Appendix II of the Big Book.

I last saw her in the mid-1990s in a bookstore on 57th Street near Carnegie Hall. She had aged badly, was overweight, bloated, her face red-splotched. She reeked of alcohol, that pungent oder of vodka-spiked sweat. She had lost her co-op apartment, so I walked her across town to where she was living with a sister on East 57th between 1st and Sutton Place.

Chapter 12: First and Only Sponsor, Peter …

I made several "half measure" attempts at being sponsored during my first year of recovery. One of these was the founder of Adult Children of Alcoholics, Tony A., who wrote the renowned "Laundry List." However, I didn't deeply connect with a sponsor until early in my second year of recovery, after I discovered Debbie having the affair. I mentioned in the previous chapter that I met Peter at a Unity Weekend Retreat up in Greenwich, CT. I chose him to be my sponsor because he was solidly back in AA again after a horrid drunk, when he discovered his second wife having an affair—I did not want to likewise get drunk !~!~! Peter was instrumental in helping me to go through the process of my divorce from Debbie.

We started discussing the steps. I had no problem with the first step. I knew alcohol made my life not only unmanageable, but also unbearable much of the time. I had some considerable difficulty with the second step, because no way could I accept any "power greater than myself" being some kind of distant sky god up above somewhere unknown and unseen. I did not, however, have a problem at all about needing to be restored to sanity – I accepted I was sometimes crazy as a loon.

"So," Peter queried me, "Can you stay sober by yourself?"

"Uh, probably not," I hesitantly replied. "I know I need meetings."

"So, there you have it," Peter said.

"Huh," I puzzled, " Have what?"

"Your higher power is the group of drunks, g-o-d."

This made sense to me! Thus, Peter helped me to solidify my Higher Power as being AA. He helped me realize and accept that I could not stay sober without the Fellowship of other sober members in AA. Peter also made the third step easy for me accept. He pointed out that I don't turn my life and will over to some nebulous big daddy in the sky far, far away. He taught me instead that I turn my life and my will over to the *care* of a higher power, in my case the human power within groups of drunks in AA meetings with whom I related. I could readily accept that I was cared for, certainly by Peter, as well as by other men and women in the rooms of AA.

Eventually after several months of procrastination, I finished my first 4th Step. Here's what happened. On Thursday night, October 26, 1973, several days before I celebrated my first anniversary, I was Chairperson of the Midnight Meeting. I discovered I had left my keys at home after I had cleaned up and was ready to lock up the First Moravian Church. No way could I leave the church unlocked, so I had to stay there all through the night until the next day. Luckily I had plenty of coffee and cigarettes, even a radio to listen to Alison Steele's all night radio show.

After reading the chapter on the 4th Step in the *Twelve and Twelve*, what I did was to make a listing of some 45 adjectives and phrases that described qualities and characteristics that I didn't like about myself. It didn't occur to me to consult the Big Book, because when I glanced at the layout of the three columns, I didn't see how any benefit could come to me by doing a 4th Step following those "precise directions". In New York AA meetings during in the 1970s, the Big Book was not revered as sacred text nearly as much as it is currently throughout much of North America. My intention was to use this list of 45 descriptors as the basis for completing my first 4th Step during the following week. Largely due to separating from Debbie, being involved with the affair with Nancy, and living way up on the Upper Westside, I didn't actually sit down and finish the 4th Step until some seven-and-a-half months later, on May 11, 1974.

I just re-read this first 4th Step—yes, I've kept it, along with other 4th step inventories I've handwritten, or composed on my computers, these many years later, packing and moving them with other meaningful and valuable items. This first 4th Step is written in longhand on eleven legal-size pages. The first nine pages describe in exquisite detail the negative mental and emotional states I have experienced from earliest recollections and how I experienced my drinking. In the last two pages, I combined the initial listing of 45 characteristics into a list of 29 descriptors with further explanation and notations.

Two thoughts strike me upon re-reading it. First, as a result of not drinking and going to meetings, hearing the experience, strength and hope of other alcoholics seeking progress, not perfection within AA, I was enabled to effectively utilize the human power of our Fellowship to gain valuable insight and forgiveness of myself for those qualities of my character that through my alcoholism have harmed others, most certainly including myself. Secondly, I'm amazed at how accurate this description of myself is and how relevant it still is today some 44 years later. Recover*ed*, I definitely am not !~!~!

Nevertheless, I have made steady and continuing progress throughout the years of my longterm recovery. Despite the sometimes painful consequences of my behavior, both for myself and for others, especially those with whom I am most intimate, I am considerably more enabled to accept and forgive myself. I am not consumed to nearly the same degree as I was then with the following description of myself in the first paragraph of the Inventory:

> *So much of my life has been dominated by self-induced fear, insecurity, anxiety, self-doubt, self-loathing and depression.*

The following week, Peter and I met at a meeting out in Brooklyn Heights, where he was speaking. We went for a dinner after the meeting, and I shared the 4th Step with him, reading it in the candlelight of our table. He listened intently, and afterwards told me it was an authentic and most honest effort, that he was most impressed with the insight and willingness I had to be honest, not so much with him, but most importantly with myself. These long years after, I'm still deeply moved recalling this feedback, perhaps more so now than I was when he said it. On the long subway ride home back to my apartment way up at 146th and Riverside, I had the thought that the long list of 29 negative descriptors of my character maybe would never be fully removed. Nevertheless, they would not have to completely dominate me nearly as much as I perceived they always had. I felt great hope and relief about this new perception of reality in recovery.

More A Friend Than A Sponsor

For the most part after this meeting, we stopped doing the steps together formally as sponsor and *pigeon* or *baby*, the somewhat derisive terms used then to describe the people with whom a sponsor works in New York City AA.

Once in February of 1975, I shared an 8th Step list with him. Frenetically, one cold night when I was unable to sleep, I made a list of everyone I could remember from childhood on. I rationalized that if I had known them, I had to have caused them harm in some way. The list went on for sixteen legal-size pages. After fifteen or so minutes of my reading him the list, he abruptly interrupted me and suggested that perhaps I was being just a wee bit anal. He suggested that there was really no need for me to look up and make an amends to my kindergarten teacher. Over zealously scrupulous? Just a tad !~!~!

After this, we rarely discussed the steps specifically, but we often related to each other about the generic, humanistic, moral and ethical principles that undergird the 12 steps. Such principles can be found in every spiritual tradition our species has formulated throughout the millennia. We morphed into being peers, equals, close friends, who shared recovery together. We related with each other as man to man, as recovering person to recovering person. We talked about our experiences, we shared what we were reading and thinking about, what moved us to tears, what depressed and enraged us. Instead of being a sponsor with a sponsee, we deepened our mutual friendship. This included sharing a sober house with other New Yorkers on Fire Island for several summers.

We spent hours discussing our various spiritual pursuits. We meditated and did yoga together. We read voluminously from the world's spiritual traditions, astrology, yoga, New Thought, many New Age gurus and authors. Among these were Ram Dass, Alan Watts, Bubba Free John, Werner Erhard, Marianne Williamson, Gary Zukov, Matthew Fox, Stanislav Grof and Shakti Gawain. During the 1980s, we also both became very involved with *A Course In Miracles*. Yup, we were prime examples of our "woo-woo" baby-boomer generation, deeply intrigued with the multitudinous forms of "New Age" spirituality.

In sum, we shared our "experience, strength and hope" with each other sober, as peers, as equals, as co-sponsors. I experienced with Peter a level of trust and unconditional acceptance that is the essence of intimacy: *into-me-see*, and equally he let me see fully into him. We also shared our rage, anger, resentments, despair and dismay about what we judged to be mostly a fucked up world and society, filled with injustice, suffering, poverty, and never-ending war. In spite of this, we often laughed, deep, raucous belly laughs, one of the most spiritual and healing of behaviors, I believe, we humans can experience together. Our deep and frequent bouts of laughter were perhaps the most precious gifts we shared with.

His Last Ten Years

For the last ten years of his life Peter drank, more or less successfully, with the aide of a rampantly co-dependent and enabling fourth wife. We continued to stay in regular contact with each other via email, even after he and his wife relocated to South Africa, while I lived for two years in Sri Lanka from 2003 to 2005.

Peter died in South Africa on August 6, 2006, from an aortic aneurysm. He remained until the day he died full of humor, hope, wonder and curiosity. Though he could be very dark, archly cynical and sarcastic at times, he was also full of awe, wonder and most of all great gratitude. I never stopped learning from his wisdom and sardonic acceptance of life as it is, despite how awfully fucked up it often may appear to be. He always was considerably more grateful than he was despondent.

Like Bill did with Ebby, I have never stopped referring to Peter as my sponsor. The son of a street hooker in upper Manhattan during the mid 1930s, he lived a rich and full life, both in recovery and after he drank again. He was my sponsor for 33 years for whom I shall always be grateful. His humor, knowledge, wisdom and light-hearted approach to life and living always inspire me.

It still does. I periodically communicate with him. On my MacBook Air is a document entitled "Missive to Peter." In the mystery of the Kosmos, which the science of the recent blockbuster movie, *Interstellar*, hypothesizes, I magically believe he somehow hears me, and I also believe in some unknown, mysterious way he continues to commune with me. Hey, as an aging hippy-dippy baby-boomer I may have morphed into an agnostic nontheist, but I'll always be somewhat "woo-woo"!

Whenever I help others I remember with gratitude the memory and certainty of Peter's human power which sustains my recovery today in my 45th year of sobriety in AA as much as it ever did. I am also sustained in continuing recovery today by everyone who shares in the several AA meetings I attend each week, whether they are new to recovery, coming back from a relapse, or have been fortunate like myself to have years in the ever-changing process of recovery. I am newly inspired by the infinite variety of the human powers related in the stories of continuing recovery we share with each other in the rooms of AA.

Several weeks ago, An old computer crashed. On it were several years of email correspondence between Peter and myself. They are now whispers in the wind of my memories. It's another opportunity to apply the lesson I learned from Unity's Eric Butterworth and Justin Morely during my second year of recovery, "It all comes to pass, not to stay … "

So, as the new year of 1974 dawned, I was firmly ensconced within the AA recovery process. I was not drinking. I was attending several meetings a week. I was deeply connected with other members in the AA Fellowship. I was regularly communicating with a sponsor and working the spiritual principles of the 12 steps. This is "What Happened" to launch the continuing day-at-a-time lifelong restoration process to heal the damage I had done to myself and to others during the active addictive process that I described in Part One, "How It Was."

Part Three, which follows, shall describe "How It's Been" for the past 44 years since, as a direct result of experiencing the "daily reprieve" gift of the AA recovery process.

Part Three

What It's Been Like Since

Chapter 13: The "R" Word – Relationships

"Regarding having a relationship with someone in the fellowship, the odds are good, but the goods are odd."

December 15, *Beyond Belief: Agnostic Musings for 12 Step Life*

Joe C.

Throughout my recovery during the past 44 or so years, one consistent threat to continued sobriety has been the "R" word, Relationships, as in romantic relationships, to be specific. Along with two other "R" words, Resentment and Rage, my recovery has been most threatened by difficulties and challenges I've experienced with romantic relationships. These at times triggered massive Resentment and Rage. The unpleasant experiences I encountered with difficult, dysfunctional, depressing romantic relationships were often a threat, certainly to my serenity and peace of mind, but they also could have resulted in my return to active addiction had I not been well-tutored in the formula for achieving longterm recovery in New York City AA—Don't Use, no matter if your ass falls off or if it turns to gold. Go to meetings. Help others.

13th Stepping

It's been my personal experience, as well as what I know from AA history, that 13th-Stepping has always been prevalent within the rooms of AA. 13th-stepping is becoming romantically involved with a fellow member of AA, who is of the opposite sex—or the same sex, if one is gay or lesbian. Bill writes about this most common human phenomenon within AA meetings in *Twelve Steps and Twelve Traditions*, "It is only where 'boy meets girl on A.A. campus,' and love follows at first sight, that difficulties may develop." According to three of his biographers, Nan Robertson, Susan Cheever and Frances Hartigan, Bill may very well have been as responsible for the 13th step as he was for the preceding twelve. Nan Robertson relates in her book, *Getting Better: Inside Alcoholics Anonymous* that

> … Bill Wilson was a compulsive womanizer. His flirtations and his adulterous behavior filled him with guilt, according to old timers close to him, but he continued to stray off the reservation.

In addition, Cheever and Hartigan discuss that Bill was involved in a long-term relationship with a woman, Helen Wynn, whom he met when she was a newcomer. A former actress, 18 years younger than him, Bill got her a job with the *Grapevine*. She later became editor and was included in his will, in which she was granted 10% of the royalties his estate got from the sales of AA literature he wrote. When I got sober during the 1970s, this was common knowledge among New York City AA members.

In 1982, I had the occasion to meet Lois Wilson, while doing research about Ebby Thatcher at the AA Archives. Nell Wing, the first AA Archivist, Lois and I went to lunch with Margaret McPike at whose drunk farm near Ballston Spa, NY, Ebby died in 1966. Margaret and I at the time were collaborating to write a book about Ebby. However, after she died, I let the project go dormant. In the mid-1990s, I gave the materials Margaret and I had developed over to Mel B., who wrote the book, *Ebby: The Man Who Sponsored Bill W*. Published in 1998 by Hazelden, Margaret and I were prominently thanked in the acknowledgements.

During the lunch with Lois, most inappropriately, I asked her about Bill's affairs. A sheet, like ice-cold, burnished steel, quickly snapped shut over her countenance. She curtly replied, "Bill was never unfaithful to me in his life." With a shock of understanding, it made sense to me that she had to convince herself of this falsehood—otherwise she may have been compelled to divorce Bill. This would have disastrously impacted not only AA, but Al-Anon as well, since she was a co-founder. Fellow *AA Agnostica* author, Bob K. in his excellent book, *Key Players in AA History,* perhaps describes the situation best:

> *It is worth remembering that this was a different era, an age in which many wives of the men of power or prestige, wealth or genius, turned a blind eye to a certain amount of sexual philandering, if they were able to "keep up appearances."*

Even in more modern times, this phenomenon is true. Witness Jacquelin Kennedy's tolerance of JFK's dalliances, and Hillary Clinton's acceptance of Bill's peccadillos with Monica Lewinsky, Gennifer Flowers and others.

Within the first several weeks of my sobriety, I was 13-stepped by an attractive, older women who invited me to her Greenwich Village apartment one evening for coffee after a Perry Street Workshop meeting. One thing led to another, and we indulged in considerably more than coffee. I remember almost nothing about the evening, not even her name.

I do, however, remember being horribly ashamed, because I had been unfaithful to Debbie. I still have the Hazelden *Twenty-four Hours A Day* book that she gave me.

A rather misogynistic quip I heard around the rooms from hardened oldtimers early in my recovery was this: "Behind every skirt is a slip!" This chapter will relate some of the more significant romantic relationship challenges I dealt with—and survived—throughout early recovery. Certainly what I experienced with Debbie and Nancy, related in Part Two, were dire threats to my sobriety. As disturbing as these two instances were, however, they were just two of a number of similar threats to my sobriety, resulting from romantic relationships gone bad throughout the ensuing first decade of recovery.

New York City AA during the 1970s was like AA in any urban metropolis in the USA. From what I've been able to discern from talking to folks in recovery from other large cities, the name of the relationship game could best be described as "Relationships Du Jour." This differed somewhat from recovery in the first three decades of AA's history prior to the sexual revolution of the 1960s. When AA was founded, it was mostly composed of middle-aged white men from the middle and upper classes. Initially, there was strong resistance against women being involved in AA meetings. The fear was that they would distract the men from getting sober. When Dr. Bob was approached about helping Sylvia K., a rich heiress from Chicago, it's described in *Dr. Bob and the Good Oldtimers* that he threw up his hands and said, "We have never had a woman and will not work on a woman." Lois had to browbeat Bill to allow Marty Mann, the first woman to achieve lasting recovery in New York City, to attend early meetings in the basement of their Clinton Street Brooklyn Brownstone.

Starting in the 1960s, however, young people of all sexual genders discovered the wonders of recovery. New York City AA meetings, especially in Manhattan, were awash with young adult singles including high school and college students, as well as the rich and famous "beautiful people." AA became quite a happening scene, one even non-alcoholics frequented, cruising on weekends for one-night-stands, or pick-up dates, known in today's parlance as "hook-up" connections. I succumbed to such a "hook up" one night after a regular meeting near Lincoln Center by a woman who I never saw again at a meeting. I experienced some considerable shame about this, fearful I would be labeled with the derisive term, "pigeon fucker."

After my divorce from Debbie in 1974, I had several relatively short relationships with women, most of whom I met in the rooms of AA, which averaged generally three to six months. I was, therefore, a devoted serial monogamist, the sociological term for someone who has a number of serially monogamous, relatively short-term relationships.

I was still desperately seeking *the* one and one only woman companion with whom I could share a forever lifetime. However, the majority of women with whom I hooked up were most incapable—much less willing—to provide me with a longterm committed love relationship. Most of the women with whom I related were highly liberated and commitment phobic to boot. It got to the point where I was somewhat infamous throughout New England Young Peoples Conferences for quipping that I could tell how sick the woman was by how strongly I was attracted to her. Mind you, this was not taking her inventory. Instead, like a lemming off the proverbial cliff, I was attracted primarily to women who were most incapable of providing me with the longterm committed relationship I insisted I wanted. My rendition of the popular Carley Simon song was, "I always had time for the pain."

Leslie, however, was one exception. She was quite a lovely lady with gobs of money, who lived at 1010 Fifth Avenue across from the Metropolitan Museum of Art. She moved into my large studio apartment with her two Persian cats shortly after we met at the Black Duck, a house we shared out on Fire Island during the summer of 1978. Goo-goo-eyed one night, Leslie looked deeply into my eyes and informed me breathlessly that all she wanted to do was to marry me and have my babies. I felt like I had been doused with a bucket of ice-cold water. It panicked me that she actually wanted to marry me and have my babies! She bored me to distraction; even our sex was pedestrian. I quickly beat a hasty retreat. While I was away at another Young Peoples AA Conference in Montreal, I enlisted two friends to help move her and the two cats out of my apartment.

I did get one lasting benefit out of the relationship with Leslie. When I returned from Montreal, I realized I missed her two Persian cats much more than I missed her. So, one fall morning I went down to the Manhattan Bideawee on E. 38th Street to adopt a cat. After I had filled out the application and been vetted by their staff, I began examining the many cages of all kinds of different cats. I came upon one all-black cat with piercing yellow eyes. I opened the cage to pet her, and she leapt onto me, digging her claws into my coat. She adopted me, much more than I adopted her. I couldn't bear to put her back in the cage, so I completed the adoption process and took her to my apartment. Named Shashu, she lived with me for the next 19 years, moving with me to Albany and back down to Long Island. She was a most adept huntress and was the alpha cat whenever I had other felines, which was most often the case.

I began to reevaluate my thinking about who was commitment phobic. You see, during an intensive 4th step inventory where I examined all my romantic relationships, it was evident that I had the uncanny knack of picking women who where most unsuitable and incapable of providing me with the longterm relationship I insisted I was looking for. This led me to ponder—perhaps it was I who was commitment-phobic. Maybe I was the one incapable of a committed one and one only romantic relationship. After all, I kept picking women, who on some level I had to have known couldn't, or wouldn't, give me what I protested so firmly I wanted. Here are a few of the more significant, relatively short-term relationships I had during the 1970s:

Gloria

Several months after Nancy dumped me, I befriended a newcomer named Gloria. Several years older than me and a beautiful second generation Ukrainian woman, she had once been one of the many party-girls of the famed Rat Pack of Bogart, Sinatra, Martin, Davis, Jr. etc. For a couple of years before coming to AA, she had been the girlfriend of a professional boxer, who would occasionally use her as a punching bag. I helped her move out of their Hell's Kitchen apartment and into an apartment way up on the far upper eastside. A couple of years later, I helped her move again into a small apartment in a brownstone on E. 58th Street just off First Avenue underneath an approach to the 59th Street Bridge.

Our first date was a round-trip ride on the Staten Island ferry, where I bought her a hot-dog. It was not the kind of treatment she was used to, and she never let me forget how cheap she thought I was then. It didn't matter to her that my sole source of income at the time was New York State unemployment benefits. She was used to being—and expected to be —treated like a lady as she had been by the Rat Pack bunch. We had a strong connection, which was much more familial, like siblings, than romantic. Nevertheless, I would on occasion try to seduce her into a romantic relationship. Here's a poem, I once wrote after we had sex:

gloria

fingers of the gray-mottled mist-covered dawn
creep upon empty rain-streaked streets
and in through the window
to caress me with shivering coolness

in this early morning light
stark still silent-centered
a gathering warmness
spreads through all of me
at the memory firmly etched
within my awakened consciousness
of earlier your wet-widened womaness
yielding upwards to enfold
my strong-for-you maness
thrusting deep within you
as i came bursting a profusion
of white hyacinths and perfumed gardenias
as you in tiny spasms cried out
"duzhe dobre, duzhe dobre, duzhe dobre"

we drifted spent
into close slumber
as from my shoulder nestled
you turned gently away
murmuring satisfied smiles
reaching far behind you
to take my wandering fingers
that tapped a tantric melody
upon your silken back
and clasp them tightly
around your firm nipple-quick breast
smoothed by the lingering moistness
of my hungering kisses

warm oneness
is ... was
then ... now
contentedly complete

My seductions ultimately didn't work out. After several months, I accepted that she was unavailable as a romantic partner. Nevertheless, we remained close, dear platonic friends throughout the 70s and 80s, during which we both remained sober. Once, I bought her dinner at a French Restaurant near 3rd Avenue and 55th Street. I remember this because we foolishly ordered creme brûlée for our desserts. Unbeknownst to us, it had been spiked with a strong liquor. It was very strange to feel the brain stem go numb, since I hadn't had any alcohol for several years. I suppose both of us were lucky that it didn't trip off compulsive cravings for more alcohol.

She had a rather tragic ending. For the Easter weekend of 1979, she planned to visit her family in Cleveland and was waiting for a standby flight. I was one of the last of her friends to speak with her late on Easter Thursday evening. One of the things we discussed was her concern about how strong her ego was, how she couldn't accept growing old and losing her considerable beauty. She opined that something drastic would have to happen to help her deal with her ego.

None of her close circle of friends heard from her on Friday. We presumed she had gotten her flight to Cleveland. But a couple of days after the Easter weekend was over, when no one had still not heard from her, we began to get concerned. On Wednesday afternoon, another friend and I broke into her apartment. We found her lying on one side on her living room floor. She had suffered a stroke and had lain there for several days. In the ICU where she was taken, the nursing staff told us that it was most unlikely she would awaken from the deep coma she was in, that she had suffered a massive stroke, that if she survived, she might very well be in a vegetative state.

That evening several of her friends, including her sponsor and a sponsee, gathered around her bed. We each spoke to her, telling her how much we loved her, and said the Serenity Prayer over her. The next morning she woke up and asked for cold cream to put on her face that had been badly disfigured by the pooling of blood, when she had lain immobile on the floor for several days. She was paralyzed on her left side, but her speech functions were unaffected. We maintained periodic contact for the next several years. When my son was born in 1980, she became his godmother. She became increasingly disabled with the passage of time, both from the stroke, and from the many drugs she was prescribed, which included strong opiate painkillers. On occasion, I would call her or visit her, sometimes taking her godson, Tommy, with me.

I hadn't heard from her for a number of months, when I got a panicked call from her during the late fall of 1987, the night before I was leaving on a business trip. Sobbing, she related she was being forcibly evicted from her apartment and moved into a state hospital somewhere upstate for the disabled. There was nothing I could do. When I returned from the business trip, I tried calling her, but only got a message that her phone had been disconnected. I never heard from her again.

Barbara

Barbara was a tall, absolutely stunning model and actress from a wealthy family in Florida. We met in AA, and were part of an Off-off Broadway Actor's Equity Showcase Theatre company comprised mostly of sober people in AA. She was also the "arm candy" of one of Broadway's most successful theatrical producers. She had her own apartment just off Central Park West on W. 71st Street, but spent a good part of her time either traveling with the producer or staying at his brownstone townhouse on the Upper Westside. For several weeks early in our relationship, I did odd jobs, painting unfinished furniture, installing bookshelves and such, in his townhouse.

Barbara told me early on in our relationship that she was very attracted to me, that I was one of the best-looking men she had ever encountered. I was flabbergasted. My low self-esteem kept me suffering under the delusion that I was still that gawky, geeky pimply-faced kid I thought I had been in high school. As beautiful as she was, her wanting to be with me certainly cured my misbelief that I was unattractive. Here's a poem I wrote for her:

afterglow

you sleep carefully enshrouded
in Titania's translucent web

i am moved
to such poignancy
by the slight curve of your smile,
the curled tendril of just washed hair,
your long lean form nestled snug neath its comfort

but most brilliantly
am i mesmerized
by the memory sharp

*of earlier your face in ecstasy
my sweat streaming
upon your upthrust breasts
as I fill you with my most
bursting me*

Barbara told me I was the only one with whom she had experienced an orgasm. Several times after sex, we would cuddle in bed and fantasize about someday perhaps getting married and having a family. The rub was she remained most devoted to the producer and his family. She also wanted to date and have sexual relations with other men to see if she could be orgasmic with others beside me. When she missed the opening night of a production I directed at the Off-off Broadway theatre due to a commitment she had with the producer's family, I was extremely hurt and upset. This was the final straw that broke the illusion of the one-and-one-only fantasy that I kept projecting onto her. We drifted apart, and I shortly found another hostage.

I last saw her was in late-July of 2005, after I returned from living in Sri Lanka for two years. We met for an hour in her office, and she told me how she had been present when her producer friend died of a massive heart attack in 1989. As tears softly trailed down her cheeks, I fully understood for the first time, and accepted, how devoted she had always been to him. In one of those quirks of fate, she had married an emergency room nurse, who looks like the producer looked in the 1970s. And, guess who else with bad head and rotund midriff looks like the producer? Yup, yours truly !~!~!

Aneen

Aneen was another woman several years older than me, from Darien, CT. Before I knew her, she had lived the sedate life of a 1950s suburban housewife married to the CFO of the J. C. Penny Corporation. An MSW graduate student at Columbia University, she had a teenage daughter and a 20 year-old son. We met at the first job I had in the field of addiction treatment, where she was doing a field placement internship. Since we both lived on the upper westside, we shared long subway rides uptown from the lower eastside facility. One night, she asked if I would like to have dinner with her at her apartment near Columbia University. We consummated our strong attraction to each other that night. Here's a poem I wrote about that evening:

connection

gentle rubbings
quiet glances
subtle movements
        of gentle hand on arm
        or that look which cuts across
        the borders of language
make of me
something
to hold onto
forever

to bear life
with love maybe
to drift for eons longer
in dreams diaphanous

As most romantic relationships go, at first we shared deep conversation, laughter and lots of love, i.e. sex. She introduced me to her circle of friends that included a prominent professor of social work at Columbia University. I started taking social work courses at Columbia with the goal of eventually also getting an MSW. At the end of the school year when she graduated and got a job in the field of addiction treatment, her son and I helped her move into an apartment in Park Slope. This included picking up furniture she had stored in Connecticut. We rented a U-Haul truck and spent a day-and-half moving her furniture from Connecticut to her apartment. While up in Connecticut, I picked up an antique golden oak, drop-down desk and secretary that Kathy had given me that had been stored at her Milford, CT, childhood home. It had a beautiful rounded glass door with an engraving of a medieval lion on the desk top. Late on Sunday night, exhausted, after we had unloaded her furniture, I left the secretary unsecured in the back of the U-Haul truck and drove it back to my apartment on the Westside. When I opened the back door to unload it, I was confronted with a million little pieces of splintered wood and glass. I should have taken the time to secure it!

Aneen owned a house built through a mountain in the south of France in the tiny village of Ménerbes. You entered the house from the street and walked through the house to come out upon a sunlit patio, overlooking a gorgeous valley in Provence. In September, I took the first overseas trip since I had traveled to Vietnam to visit her in France. We drove a Citroën deux chevaux, a small two cylinder car, all through Provence, along the

Mediterranean, visiting Nice, Roman antiquities and the museums of Vincent van Gogh and Paul Cèzanne. We had a marvelous, idyllic time. But as most relationship stories go, when we returned to the States, she soon grew weary of our monogamous relationship and wanted to be sexual with other men friends. Of course, I couldn't tolerate this, and so our relationship, even as friends, skidded to an abrupt end over a cliff of vastly different desires.

Another Nancy

During what turned out to be my last couple of months living in New York City, a lovely advertising copywriter, also named Nancy, propositioned me one night during the secretary break of an Eastside AA meeting. She told me she had a steak marinating and would love it if I would share a meal with her followed by an evening in front of her fireplace. How could I refuse? Of course, I wrote a poem for her:

sensations

your body
i love
the firm form
which nestles
quick
and the soft
crease of odor

when with you
i tingle
at the tiniest
flick of a smile
in which your face
is a blossom
that flowers
even in the fall
of snow

> &
>
> *like lightning*
> *i become large*
> *stretching the seams*
> *just barely when*
> *the soft point of*
> *your tongue*
> *brushes*
> *mine*

We dated for the next couple of months, which included a five-day trip to St. Thomas in the Virgin Islands. A decided impediment to the relationship was that she was the fantasized love-object of a schizoaffective former professional boxer. Tommy had developed a highly complex delusion that he and Nancy would be the founders of a supremacist white race. I posed a considerable threat to his being able to achieve this fantasy. Nancy had been dealing with his "affections" for months. He would mail reams of correspondence to her, complete with pictorial renditions of the master race they would spawn. After we started dating, these included dire threats that he would have to eliminate me.

A former Army ranger during the 1950s, after Korea and before Vietnam, he stopped me one day outside a meeting and warned me to cease and desist dating Nancy, his predestined true love. He informed me that he had tracked my movements, that there were numerable opportunities where he could kill me and escape detection with impunity. We took this information to the New York Police precinct in her neighborhood, showing them the reams of materials and diagrams he had left for her. These included a primitive stick figure of me with a slit throat bleeding profusely. They told us that until he actually attacked one of us, there was nothing they could do. The following Saturday night, as Nancy and I were leaving a meeting on Madison Avenue, Tommy stepped out of the shadows and hit me with two quick body punches to my torso, severely bruising me and fracturing a rib. After I was released from the emergency room, we went to the precinct and reported the assault. I wanted to press charges. I was told that due to the "minor" injuries I had sustained this would not be possible. The best the police could offer was for us to see a mediator for a binding mediation process.

After I moved to Albany, the relationship with Nancy became estranged. It turned out I had been a rebound affair after the ending of an affair she had been having with a married man, whom she informed me was her true love. We had a disastrous and very unpleasant weekend at a house she rented on Block Island. On the way to the ferry in Connecticut, I got lost and barely got to the ferry on time. Mine was the last car to be loaded and secured on the ferry. It would perhaps have been better had I missed the ferry !~!~!

Here's a journal entry from late May, 1979, about the ending of this one other "romantic relationship":

> *Another relationship splintered. One other myth dissolved, fractured on the painful road through loneliness to myself again. Just letting the deep welling fear that I'm forever unlovable and incapable of loving, resigned to accepting I'll never change, that I'll go through life butterflying and being butterflied from, an endless cycle of women's faces landing, lightly touching, then catapulting away at any sustained intimacy breaking through the make-nice, in-love-with-love, superficial masks, feeling my vulnerability, raw, open, insatiably thwarted, deprived, can't escape from the compulsion to be drawn like a lemming to the cliffs to non-nurturing, non-sustaining women in endless, repetitive cycles of self-defeating, premature ejaculating ruts. Yet, I choose to know, to believe, I Am All Right. My despairing, hopeless, dissociative feelings, though very real, very undeniable, very present, I choose to affirm these feelings are not all of me. Through this period of transition through the alienation, the isolation, the fear, the struggles, I continue to trust explicitly the process of transcending change by NOT drinking, NOT smoking, by accepting, by surrendering. Very grateful I am just now able to accept the dried, stuffed up, act-as-if belief, this moment now brings, to reflect remembering there is great hope for me a day at a time sober in AA.*

Almost thirty years later, in 2008, when I was living on Long Beach, NY, I saw Tommy at an AA meeting in the city. He was dressed most dapperly. I was a bit wary when he approached me with his right hand outstretched, but I needn't to have been. As we shook hands, he made an amend for the assault three decades previously. He coyly smiled and quipped he had been off his meds. As it turned out, he had been awarded a sizable lifelong income for designing a popular toy. I told him I was most pleased for him. I asked him if he had had any further contact with Nancy. He replied that the last he knew of her from twenty or so years ago she was somewhere out on the west coast.

With each of these romantic relationships, I came to see that I had repeated a variation of the earlier pattern that I had begun in high school. I would capture a hostage around which I would spin a one-and-one-only romantic love fantasy. I would deluge my love object with gifts, poems, flowers, love cards, etc. As it turned out, Tommy and I shared a similar modus operandi with women. The difference was that his fantasies and delusions of starting a new master race were just more bizarre and extreme than mine. It was a humbling, but gratifying, realization. I was able to discern that smothering and chafing under my incessant demand that "more is never enough," my love objects would either cleanly break off with me, or they would insist on seeing other people, which was unacceptable to me. This caused me much jealous resentment and rage, as I had experienced with Debbie.

After similar episodes with each of the women above, I began to suspect that I was cleverly conning myself to believe that I really wanted a committed relationship. It became clear to me that I kept choosing women who were most incapable of giving me what I insisted I wanted. Something was indeed rotten in the state of Brinsondom. When the relationship inevitably didn't work out, then I could play a favorite role, that of the jilted, unrequited lover until the next hostage entered from stage life. See, dear lady love-object-hostage, if I kept the focus on you who was withdrawing your love from me, then I didn't have to focus on what was perhaps my deepest fear: Not that you would not love me, but that *I* could not love *you*. I never gave myself a chance to test out my ability to stay committed in a longterm, love relationship. I unconsciously made sure the woman always left first.

This pattern radically changed, when in October of 1979, I met and fell in love with the woman who became my third wife. I'll relate this 22-year relationship in the next chapter.

The Two Most Significant Relationships

Without a doubt, however, the two most significant relationships I had during my first decade of recovery during the 1970s were the relationships I reestablished with the two daughters from my first marriage to Kathy, Rebecca and Jennifer. During the last two years of my using, and the first year of recovery, while married to Debbie, I had been estranged from them and had no contact with them at all. I just disappeared. Debbie was jealous and felt threatened by them. One of the most shameful afternoons I ever spent was when Debbie and I, rather methodically, went through a trunk of memorabilia and tore up all the pictures I had of Rebecca during the first three years of her life. I readily attest that this was the height of my rampant co-dependency upon a love object.

After Debbie and I separated and divorced in 1974, I reestablished contact with Kathy, making amends to her by sending her, more or less regularly, child support money. This enabled me to have periodic visits with my daughters. Several times each year during the 1970s, I would either visit them at their home in Maryland, or they would come and visit me in New York City. One summer, we took a week-long trip, driving to Mississippi to visit my family.

I have a picture that is emblematic of the difference between the two sisters. The oldest, Rebecca, was three when I disappeared from her life and remembered me. Jennifer was an infant and had no memories of me. Rebecca is hurt and angry as she glares into the camera. Jennifer is just sitting there, hanging out with this guy called Dad. I am most grateful to have a close on-going relationship with them and their children.

Chapter 14: Third Marriage – Sara

In the fall of 1979 I met Sara, the woman who was to became my third wife. In many, many ways, the story of the 22-year relationship with Sara exceeded my wildest expectations of a forever relationship with a bersherta, the yiddish term for soul mate, or the one person with whom you are fated and destined to be with forever. On the other hand, the long relationship with Sara was the cause of incredible rage, resentment and suffering. This chapter is the story of our 22-year relationship, which like everything else "came to pass, not to stay."

In many ways, this relationship was incredible, absolutely wonderful, but it was fatally flawed from the start. Through this marriage, I disproved the primary fear I sometimes had, while bouncing from one serially monogamous relationship to another, that I was incapable of sustaining a longterm, committed, one-and-one-only romantic relationship.

Sara is the mother of my now 36 year-old son, Tommy, with whom I share recovery. In June of 2015, I presented him with his 10th year coin of being clean and sober, one of the happiest, most fulfilling days of my long life in recovery.

Shortly after I moved to Albany, NY, in 1979, as the Coordinator of Alcoholism Counselor Credentialing with the New York State Division of Alcoholism Services, I experienced the rather ugly ending the relationship with Nancy that I described in the previous chapter. It was just as devastating as any I had previously experienced. I found myself desolate and alone again in a world filled with pairs at a Doobie Brothers concert at the Saratoga Performing Arts Center. There, grieving mightily, I let go of my need for "the" one and one only soulmate forever and ever and ever. It was like a bloody psychic birth!

I accepted and became at peace with the reality that perhaps I was only capable of having serially monogamous relationships, the fashionable psychobabble term at the time. I let go, and let the good orderly direction of my life in the AA Fellowship guide me to my highest good. I didn't drink, I went to meetings, and I sometimes talked to Peter and others in my AA support community about how awful I felt.

One weekend I attended a conference on counselor burnout at a conference center near Albany. There, I was strongly attracted to one of the participants, a petite blond who happened to sit next to the spot where I had put my stuff down, including a man-bag I carried at the time. The next morning I sat next to her in a workshop by the noted addictions author, Lee M. Silverstein. He played what became one of our signature songs by Harry Chapin, "A Better Place To Be."

We were both aware of the strong attraction between us. I was also hyper aware that she was being pursued by every available male at the conference. At lunch, we took a walk with several others, including an especially aggressive suitor, to a nearby waterfall. By that evening, we had made a connection that became a tornado of pheromonal activity.

We cut the rest of the conference after lunch and spent the afternoon together either heavily making out or cramming our life histories into each other. Both of us had been unhappily married twice previously. Both of us had experienced a number of jilted love affairs. Both of us had two daughters.

BAM—I was hopelessly, madly, totally head-over-heels in one-and-one-only love again !~!~!

A rather sticky wicket in this relationshipal bliss was that she had recently separated from her husband of twelve years, Dave, the father of her two daughters. She and Dave were engaged in a most contentious custody battle. In fact, a couple of weeks earlier, he had kid-snatched her eldest daughter, Dawn, and taken off for places mostly unknown between Michigan and Florida, where his parents had homes.

By the end of the Conference on Sunday afternoon, we had made a lasting commitment to each other. The following weekend I went down to New York City to run in the New York City Marathon. I left a day early to spend it with her. We fully consummated our relationship in a motel near her Long Island apartment that evening. I ran my best time ever for a marathon the next day, floating on a blissful cloud nine of new romantic and sexual love.

I should perhaps interject here that I addictively got caught up in the New York City Marathon running boom during the 1970s. I've quipped at meetings that my higher powers—who or whatever they may be that I neither know nor understand—got me sober, so that I would quit smoking, so that I would kill myself running. The first time I ran, I ran for five miles and gave myself shin splints, likely due to me wearing Adidas track shoes for short sprints and not running shoes. I bought the track shoes because they were a cool blue color. The first race I ran was the Westchester half-marathon, which I ran in a sub 7-minute mile after four months of training —crazy !~!~!

The next weekend she visited me in Albany, which was wonderful. The following weekend I visited her in Bay Shore. On October 27th, just two weeks into our relationship, I made this journal entry while she was away at a mandatory weekend workshop for her work as an alcoholism counselor:

> *Sitting on the floor of Sara's bedroom, now made partially mine, scared to life ... Just finished huddling in the kitchen, wracked with sobbing tears, crouched against the refrigerator, feelings, thoughts tumbling, cascading upwards from so deep inside where so carefully I have compacted them, just letting my deepest fear feel itself. It's not a game anymore, I'm too old to "fall in love" again, but I am so afraid of loving and finding out I can't!*

Later that afternoon, committing myself to love her the best that I could a day at a time, I wrote her this poem:

Commitment

I smile inwardly
Remembering your smile

Unafraid not am I
Just wanting
To be held by you
Close, warm, soft
Though sometimes
When intimate with you
I feel scared to life
Moment by moment
I become more willing
To risk receiving
From
You
All

Can I learn just to let you give to me
Uncompelled to match your giving in kind?
YES, with utter joy I am willing to trust
Myself more to let you love me as you do

The memory last night
Of being touched by and touching you
Quickens this moment of anticipation
Again later tonight of having
Our twoness merge into oneness
Here and Now Forever

On the third weekend, the only time we had unprotected sex, I lost control. We both sensed she had become impregnated. We felt our son's strong spirit, whooshing in from the vastness of the wide Kosmos. In denial, I told her not to worry, that I had just read an article in *Runners World Magazine* that long-distance runners were likely to be infertile due to the heat generated around their genitals during long runs. I had just run a marathon the week before. No problem.

Ecccckkkkkk, choose once again, middle-aged runner. During the next week, I got word for the second time in my life that the rabbit had died. We discussed it, and made plans to do the sensible, "responsible," deed. We would abort the fetus, especially since Dave, her ex-husband-to-be, was in places unknown with her oldest daughter. Her being pregnant really put the custody battle with him at extreme risk.

We made an appointment for the next weekend with Planned Parenthood, so I could accompany her during this traumatic ordeal. Despite the Long Island Railroad being on strike, I got to Jamaica Queens by bus from Albany and subway. Rather bravely, since she'd only been driving less than a year, she drove to the Jamaica Long Island Railroad Station to pick me up. Amazingly in the teeming, chaotic, hustle-bustling crowds, we found each other—without the assistance of cell phones !~!~!

The next morning we drove out to Planned Parenthood in Patchogue, NY, for the abortion. Not to be. The doctor scheduled on duty was tied up with a family emergency, so it had to be rescheduled for the following weekend. When I came down the following weekend, I sensed immediately that something was radically different with her. It was. She firmly informed me that after a week of consultation with friends, she had made the decision that no matter the consequences, no matter how complicated it might be, no matter what difficulties that she might experience, she could not and would not abort our love child. It was ultimately her decision she told me, and whether I supported her or not, she had made an irrevocable decision to birth and raise our child. I assured her I would never leave her.

During the next week, I bought her an antique engagement ring at an Albany pawn shop, and gave it to her the next weekend. We began making plans for her and her youngest daughter, Jennifer, to move up to Albany to live with me.

The Albany Years

We began our new life in a rented duplex in the upscale Albany suburb of Delmar. Sara got a secretarial job with the New York State Department of Energy and filed for divorce with an attorney in Albany.

We were able to successfully re-kid-snatch Dawn, her oldest daughter, back from Dave, when he brought her back to live again on Long Island. In late July, her divorce from Dave came through a couple of days before our son, Tommy, was born on August 2nd. I was present in the delivery room when he was born. It was one of the most joyfully gratifying days I had ever experienced in recovery. We finalized our plans to get married at the same conference center on the upcoming one year anniversary of our meeting there the previous year. I don't think our parents ever forgave us for sending out our wedding invitations to our uptight southern New Jersey and Mississippi extended families. We certainly were not subtle, perhaps most improper even, when the invitations read:

> *Thomas Aaron Brinson cordially invites you to attend and celebrate the wedding of his parents.*

As it turned out, Dave became an integral part of our extended family. He would babysit for us when we went away on weekend trips, attending workshops or visiting romantic Bed & Breakfasts throughout New England, especially during fall seasons of blazing color. He sadly spent the last years of his life in the New York State Nursing home for veterans —he had a purple heart from Korea—due to intractable emphysema from his inveterate smoking. He died painfully, suffocating to death from lung failure in August of 2000 with all of us, including several of his adult children from other marriages, gathered around his hospital bed.

As wonderful in many respects as our first year was, there were a couple of flaws that manifested themselves early on in our relationship. Over the years, these grew, like a toxic virus, to poison and ultimately to destroy all of the bounteous good that our relationship had. We both, in our previous relationships and marriages, had struggled with jealousy and possessiveness. Soon these began to haunt us. One way I contributed to this destructive dynamic was that on my many business trips down to New York City, I maintained contact with previous lovers, whom I now considered dear platonic friends. I would on occasion schedule a lunch or dinner meeting with one of them. The significant rub, however, is that I would not inform Sara of these meetings beforehand. I would not include her in my plans. After the fact, she would always find out about them and be terribly hurt, feeling betrayed and jealous.

To this day, I don't understand why I couldn't simply be upfront and honest with her about seeing former lovers. We developed a destructive pattern, not only about me seeing ex-lovers, but about any subject that caused conflict or difficulty between us. These included issues about finances or my going away on business trips. I would avoid discussing something with her until the very last minute or she confronted me about whatever it was. An argument would ensue, during which I became very defensive, at times reacting resentfully and ragefully.

After a period of estrangement, I would always promise her that I would include her in my plans and not hide information from her. However, I continued the behavior of hiding things from her, out of fear that she would be upset, which would result in another argument. I always had the best of intentions to change my behavior, but I never did. Eventually, she came to lose whatever trust she had that I loved and cared for her.

I was also always very busy, not only with the demands of my job, which required me to travel often throughout New York State, but I also became actively involved with Vietnam Veteran issues, joining and becoming active in the Albany chapter of Vietnam Veterans of America. I served on its board of directors and did workshops on veterans issues throughout the Northeast. She couldn't understand my need to be so actively involved in activities outside of our home and soon came to resent them. She began to feel unappreciated and often left out, when I would choose—usually not telling her beforehand, or springing it upon her at the last moment—to take part in an activity away from the home.

She had no interest in joining me with these activities, especially after she started a very rigorous nursing school program. She developed a belief that my outside activities were more important to me than she and our family life were.

I also at times showed my hair-trigger anger/rage response. Though I now understand that much of this was due to undiagnosed PTSD, it doesn't mitigate the reality that Sara would be frightened by my outbursts. She also was often humiliated and embarrassed when I would "lose it" in public with a waiter, or a clerk in a store, or in a road rage incident when someone cut me off on the highway.

Despite these difficulties and the financial stress of blended families, those early years in Albany were perhaps the best of our 22-year relationship. We were both very active in 12-step recovery programs. We had a strong network of friends in recovery, and in our work, veterans and school environments.

For six months out of the year, the Albany area is absolutely gorgeous, being 45 minutes from Woodstock to the south, the Adirondacks to the north, the Berkshires to the east, and the finger lakes to the west. We hated, however, the other six months of the year with the brutally cold winters. Besides, we were both ocean people, not mountain people. We yearned to be back near the ocean. So, I quit my permanent civil service job with New York State government and took a job with a treatment center down in Garden City, NY, a 20-minute drive from Jones beach.

Slumming in Gaardan Cityae

During the summers, it was hot, it was humid, but our rented house on a tree-lined street was mostly in the shade, and often there was a cooling breeze. In Garden City, our expenses quintupled overnight. Sara, who had passed her Nursing boards, got a job at a nearby hospital, and I had a well-paying job in addiction treatment. It was pretty ironic, us renting a house and living in one of the most exclusive and upscale bedroom communities in AmeriKa, me being an ex-hippie, radical anarchist and her formerly having worked in public relations for the entertainment business in New York City, being chased around hotel rooms by rock 'n roll stars.

Our car, a 10-year old Chevette, was the oldest and most dilapidated on our block. We were probably one of the few "Gaardan Cityae" residents who were ever threatened with their electricity or phone service being turned off. It never was, but lots of the time, we were skirting along a razor-thin edge, especially during the second year of our three year lease, when I got fired from the job that had enabled us to move to Long Island from Albany. During this time, Sara was also out on disability from her nursing job at the hospital with a bad back.

Somehow, however, sober a day at a time, we always made our scant ends meet. After a few months of doing consulting work and starting a small private practice in the home, I got a full-time job directing a treatment center in Manhattan. This meant I was commuting four hours a day, whether driving or taking the Long Island Railroad.

During this time period we mutually agreed to begin exploring the old misguided 1960s ideal of an Open Marriage in an effort to confront and deal with our jealousy issues. We were following the theme of the 1971 hit song, "Love the One You're With." Since both of us had missed out on the "Free Love" swinging 60s, especially the Summer of Love in 1967, me being in Vietnam and mostly a drunk while married to Kathy, and she since she was in her first marriage with another violent Vietnam Veteran, we tried to make up for lost time. Following the utopian free-love ideals of Robert A. Heinlein, who wrote a number of novels, including *Stranger in a Strange Land,* we explored free love to the fullest extent, trying to discover our sexual freedom. Guess what? Though it might work for some, it didn't work for us.

In 1986, we were coming to the end of our lease agreement and had to make a decision to move out of our rented house in Gaardan Cityae. Since our credit had been substantially repaired with both of us earning fairly good salaries, we decided to join the American Dream and buy a house.

I went into a panic, absolutely sure that we would not qualify for a VA loan. Sara was much more certain and took charge, leading me, kicking and screaming all the while, into middle-class, upwardly mobile normalcy by becoming a landowner. Despite my prognostications of doom and gloom, we did eventually get a VA-backed mortgage. However, likely due to my negative energies, the loan application got lost not once, not twice, but thrice, between the loan broker way out in Suffolk County and the Veterans Regional Office in Manhattan.

In September of 1986, we moved into our very own Dutch Colonial house two blocks south of Montauk Highway in the lovely little south shore village of Islip, NY. There, we began a most fulfilling several year period, where our little family prospered and grew up, us included.

Early Years in Islip

Life in my very own castle with a Queen, two step-Princesses, two more distant Princesses and *the* Son was a somewhat daunting, but mostly happy and satisfying experience.

For the first couple of years, we were both commuting, me into Manhattan four hours a day, and Sara two hours a day to an evening shift nursing job in Nassau County. With the stress of commuting and being house poor, meeting a large overhead each month just for housing expenses, we sometimes struggled to keep our heads above water. It didn't help matters, when at the last moment in November of 1986, I made a unilateral decision to max out one of our credit cards to go by myself to my 25th high school reunion in Jackson, MS. Our first winter with a broken down 50-year old furnace was at times frigid in more ways than one.

In late February, my closest friend, another Vietnam Veteran, Vince, had a major depressive breakdown when his second wife was in the process of moving out of their recently purchased house in Woodstock, NY. Becoming very suicidal, he called me one early morning, asking me to come help him. After a screaming argument with Sara that included yelling at her daughters, I slammed out of our new castle and drove the old Chevette with slipping clutch, bald tires and failing brakes through a snowstorm up I-87 to Woodstock. There, I helped get Vince safely into a psyche ward in a Kingston, NY, hospital, while his then wife was skiing in Massachusetts with her two teen-age sons.

A couple of weeks later, I gave one of my co-workers, a short, dumpy woman from Brooklyn, a ride home after work. Her opened purse fell over as she was getting out, and a lipstick fell out on the floor mat. Later that evening, Sara found it and the usual jealousy-spurred argument ensued with me sleeping on the downstairs couch. Early the next morning, I slunk up the stairs to try and make up with her. She met me at the door to our bedroom with a serrated kitchen knife, telling me to leave, that she was scared of me. In a desperate moment of devastating alienation from her, as well as from myself, I grabbed the knife out of her hand and made two deep gashes in my left wrist. Quite ineptly, so I was later told by the German emergency room doctor, an ex-German POW from WW II, as he stitched me up with utmost disdain and contempt, muttering, "Dummkopf, Dummkopf, Dummkopf."

Sara was quite supportive, participating along with her daughters and Tommy in all of the family support regimens. We experienced a very pleasant flight back into health, when I returned to our regular routine for the next couple of months. I started another round of individual therapy in New York City with a social worker with whom I was associated who was respected in the field of addiction. He had a psychiatrist associate who diagnosed me with Bipolar Disorder I, whereupon I was put first on lithium and over the next number of years on several different SSRI medications.

Then, BAM, I lost the job I had in Manhattan after an anger/rage incident. I chose to resign from the job with a four-month full-pay severance package, rather than being fired for cause, which would have meant I could not qualify for unemployment benefits. So, there I was again, gainfully unemployed. As with all such devastating episodes in my recovery, after the shock and the panic, it turned out to be a very good thing. It resulted in starting my own private practice LLC corporation, initially as an addiction agency, with two associates. I'll deal with this in more detail in the chapter that relates my career in the field of addiction treatment. With Sara's excellent salary as a registered detox nurse at a nearby hospital, which also provided the family with excellent health benefits, we prospered and enjoyed several good years.

It Was the Best of Times, It Was the Worse of Times

The next several years could be characterized by this iconic Charles Dickens quote. Sara and our little family in many ways prospered, experiencing the best of an upwardly mobile family living the "American Dream" during the 80s and 90s. We also struggled through some very difficult times as well.

On the positive side, we travelled quite a bit, making two trips out to San Diego to visit my sponsor, Peter, and his wife. On many weekends, particularly in the Fall, we would travel around New England, notably in the Berkshires and upstate New York, antiquing and bed & breakfasting. One weekend we took a short cruise on a sailing ship from Mystic, CT to Block Island, RI. With both of us having good incomes, we repaired our credit and got a second mortgage to transform our Dutch Colonial cedar shake home in to a faux Victorian doll house with new roof, vinyl siding and a refurbished porch, complete with a wicker swing. Inside, our furniture was a mixture of antiques and Thomasville Georgian, accented with many framed pictures, *objects d'art* and plants. I built two floor-to-ceiling walls of bookcases for our large library of books.

We also had two "new" cars—Sara got one of the first Miata's on Long Island, a classy blue lady, very dainty, who was wonderful during the spring, summer and fall. She balked, however, at dealing with rain on the oil-slicked Long Island highways, much less snow during the winters. I drove about in a snazzy little Subaru Justy, a three-cylinder go-cart with an enclosed body that got some 60 miles a gallon—most practical. When I traded it in for a fully-equipped Honda Accord in late 1992, it had over 113,000 miles on it. Tommy and I began traveling all over the eastern part of the US, when he started inline skating competitively. I joined him and became a 50 year-old competitive inline skater for several years, finishing last overall in the Northeast Region. I fell down a lot and crashed a couple of times into the scoring table in the middle of the rink, but I finished every race I started, most often dead last, a lap or two behind everyone else.

One of the highlights of our relationship was that at Sara's urging we applied for and were accepted to be trained as Imago Relationship Therapists. We were trained by Harville and Helen Hendrix, the founders of this innovative couples treatment process based on their best-selling book, *Getting the Love You Want*. Throughout the several month training regimen, we continued to experience our power struggles with jealousy and possessiveness. We understood the process, believing deeply in its effectiveness, and after our training, we were quite effective in teaching it to others, both to couples with whom we jointly worked in our private practice, and teaching a class on Relationships in Recovery for several summers at the Rutgers University Summer School of Addiction Studies. Today, on Long Island there are several couples I'm still occasionally in contact with, whose relationships were "saved" by the work we did with them.

However, we had difficulty applying it to our own relationship, whenever we would get hooked into one of our power struggles. We had one of our worse, most volatile arguments while attending an Imago Relationship Conference in Chicago.

I remained quite active in veterans issues. Vince and I did seminal writing and training throughout the US on the correlation of alcohol/drug addiction and PTSD. A major theme of our difficulties, which kept plaguing our relationship, was that whenever I pursued my own activities, especially in regard to veterans activism, Sara felt that I was abandoning her and our family. Her high school sweetheart and first husband had both been Vietnam Veterans, and Dave, her second husband, the father of her two daughters, had been a decorated Korean Vet. Once, I chose to go down to VA Headquarters in Washington, DC with Vince to present testimony concerning the correlation of addiction with PTSD to an advisory group, while Sara was undergoing minor surgery to remove polyps from her cervix. Even though they turned out to be benign, I don't think she ever forgave me for abandoning her during that scary time for her.

On the other hand, I was able to be fully available for her when her Dad became terminally ill. An only child, her mother had died from alcohol-related causes in the early 70s before we met. The relationship between her and her Dad had always been strained. Despite the power struggles between us, I was able to be of caring support and solace to her, using the Imago process, to just hear and contain her upset and sadness about the difficult relationship she had always experienced with her father. For that, I am most grateful.

On another occasion, she totally surprised me with a party celebrating the 20th Anniversary of my recovery in October of 1992. Completely unbeknownst to me, she had organized some fifty friends and family, including my parents from Mississippi and daughters from Maryland, as well as members of a men's therapy group that I had been facilitating for over five years, to gather in our home while Tommy and I were away at skating practice. In that two-hour period, she had everyone assemble inside the house, parking their cars a couple of blocks away. She set up a vast banquet of catered food and decorated the living room. Tommy and I walked up the front steps, opened the front door, and were confronted by the crowd yelling, "Surprise!" We were both flabbergasted, since Sara had not told Tommy out of fear he would spill the beans to his best buddy. I stood in the middle of our living room, sweaty and smelly, jaw dropped, not really able to believe the crowd of dear friends and family gathered in our home. When I saw Mother and Dad sitting demurely in the living room, I not too adroitly queried, "What the fuck are you doing here?" I was absolutely blown away!

During 1993 and 1994, we had settled into a fairly easy and mostly comfortable routine. We had plans to do some traveling overseas and to visit the wide expanses of the US, as well as making our little faux Victorian castle even grander, but fate had other plans. Due to financial pressures with managed care aggressively coming into the New York healthcare market, I was in a constant state of panic, sleepless most nights, filled with dread, doom and gloom. In addition, Tommy began getting into serious trouble with rave-scene drugs. He dropped out of both skating and cross-country running, in which he also had excelled, running a sub-five-minute cross-country mile. For the next ten years he was in and out of rehabs, psyche wards, barely escaping prison, and sometimes surviving on the mean streets of New York City. Early one morning in the late spring of 1994, on a jog together along Main Street in the neighboring town of East Islip, NY, Sara tried to engage me in conversation about the bills, about the precarious state of our financial situation. When I run, I don't like to talk, having been influenced by the Tom Courtenay movie, *Loneliness of the Long Distance Runner*. I snapped, yelling at her to stop trying to talk to me, to just let me be alone in the misery of my black-ass mood. This incident turned out to be one of the final straws that broke the back of her love for me.

The Beginning of the Long End

To say that Sara was upset is an understatement. She was traumatized. Not only had I yelled at her, but I had done it in public. She felt humiliated. One of her deepest childhood wounds was that she had been loudly scolded in public by her mother, who worked in the school system where she grew up. She often chastised her in front of her schoolmates. Another particularly humiliating incident was when her mother dragged her out of the Junior-Senior prom, because she had snuck out and gone with a boy whom her mother disapproved of. My yelling at her in public triggered these old grievances.

We were somewhat estranged during much of another typically beautiful Long Island spring, but as time passed, we evolved again to some semblance of normality. We shared deep conversation; we laughed at ourselves and the silliness of much of life; we made passionate love again. My fifty-first birthday came and went. We prepared for an Imago Relationship Course at the Rutgers Summer School of Addiction Studies, and a series of workshops for recovering couples on Long Island. I don't remember now exactly what happened, what the specific incident was, whether we had an argument, whether I hid something from her about money or an outside activity, but by the end of the summer, during the hot, dog-days of August, we were very estranged again.

At her request I was sleeping down on the couch in the living room because my turning, tossing and snoring disturbed her sleep, so she said. If we made love, it was perfunctory and uninspired. On mornings before she went to work, I would go up to what had been our bedroom, watching her put on her make-up and get dressed, telling her over and over again how much I loved her. Mostly, she ignored me. Sometime in the fall she announced that she needed a break, that she was going to be staying nights with one of her best friends in a nearby town. She wasn't moving out, she claimed, just taking some time for herself to be in an environment where she could fully relax and not feel like she was under the microscope of my smothering attentions, always professing my undying love for her. In the mornings she would come home and get dressed for work, but she asked that I respect her need for privacy. Crestfallen, I accepted it. What choice did I have? It made sense to me.

For a couple of weeks, forlorn, desperately missing her, I fitfully dozed on the couch down in the living room. Early one morning I was startled wide awake by a vivid dream of her making passionate love to someone. Restless, unable to go back to sleep, I decided to go for a drive. Driving towards Robert Moses Park to watch the sunrise, I realized I was going through the town where her friend lived, the one with whom she was staying. On impulse, I decided to drive by her friend's house. I think I intuited before I got there that her Miata would not be there. Nevertheless, it was a devastating shock just the same, a deep, icy cold sinking from the pit of my stomach down deep beneath my loins when in the driveway there was only her friend's car.

I wanted so much to be able to trust her. I didn't want to believe that she would do to me what she had done in her other marriages and relationships. This was especially ironic, since we had an open relationship, meaning she was free to "love the one she's with," whoever and wherever it may happen. I went back home and made coffee for us, waiting for her to come home to get dressed for work. When she did, I simply and quietly confronted her with what I had done, telling her that I had driven by her friend's house and hadn't seem the Miata, that I suspected she had been with someone else.

She was silent for a long while and then she quietly admitted that, yes, she was having an affair with a co-worker, Joe. I didn't rant; I didn't angrily rave; I didn't make a scene. I told her that though it was most difficult for me, I would accept the reality of her having the affair. I told her, again, that I would always love her and that I would never leave her. As I got up to leave, she rushed over to me, clinging to me, telling me she still loved me and the life we had made, but that she also loved Joe. She related she was very confused, that she hoped I would give her some time to sort things out. I reiterated again that I loved her, that I always would, and that I would never leave her. I was determined to prove to myself that I had overcome my deepest fear, my inability to stay in a committed love relationship for better or for worse. We made plans to meet with her lover, Joe, to discuss the situation. In my heart I felt that I was in the stronger position, that she had much more of a life with me, the kids, the house, our long history together, than she had with Joe. I placed my bet on the premise that if I was cool and didn't react with anger or rage, that if I practiced my program of spiritual recovery, focusing on changing myself, living and letting her live, that eventually I would win her back full time.

We met later that night with Joe. It was not pleasant. Sara was totally different with him present than she had been with me that morning. He accused me of exerting a Svengali-like evil influence over her and demanded that I release her to him, who truly loved her. I read a favorite ee cummings poem about unrequited love to them, relishing the glory of being back once again in one of my favorite roles, that of the unrequited lover. For the next several days we dialogued, we trialogued, we remained stuck in the impasse of Sara being unable and unwilling to make a sole commitment to either Joe or myself. I remained steadfast in my position that I would never leave her. Joe likewise remained committed to waiting for her to shake off my Svengalian influence over her.

She decided she needed time alone from both of us, so she moved into an apartment by herself. She continued to see both of us. I accepted it, feeling in my codependent heart that having some of her was better than having none of her. I vowed again to her, and to myself, that I would never leave her, believing in my heart that if I just hung tough and was patient, didn't push her, didn't do a nut number and force the issue, that she would eventually come back to me.

The days passed and this impasse turned into weeks, into months, into a couple of years. My private practice was smaller, but it still provided enough income for me to handle all of the expenses of the house and most of our joint expenses. I was convinced that if I allowed her to have her freedom, she would eventually choose to come back to be only with me again. A favorite song of ours was the Gladys Knight and the Pips version of "Neither One of Us Wants To Be the First to Say Goodbye."

During this period we dealt with Tommy's rampant addiction. When he went to his first of many rehab programs, the Hazelden Youth Program in Minnesota, we each separately attended the family program. He relapsed a number of times, ending up in psych hospitals, other rehab programs and a long-term treatment program for disturbed youth in Pennsylvania. I bought my first computer, an Apple Performa, and slowly taught myself to become computer literate, something I had always wanted to do. I kept copious journals, both handwritten and on the computer. I began writing more poetry, working a lot of my angst, hurt and betrayal out through the written word, such as this poem expresses:

Knick-Knacks

*Looking around the house-space
where once we shared dreams
and other ghosts of memories now gone
one or two items pique
my curiosity darkly*

*Are they mementos
of our glorious past
once so vibrantly alive*

*Or, have you stolen moments
of your times with him
like a virus to toxify from within
our former hallowed space*

*For example, did you pluck
the fat pine-cone from some pine-matted place
lain on with him gazing skyward through pine-green haze*

I know we did not

*It puckishly plops itself
in the middle of the guest toilet bowl top*

*Upstairs is the small, delicate, perfectly shaped
conch shell on your bedroom bureau*

*Was it from one of our many
splendid jaunts to the shining sea*

*Or, did you, or him, or both of you soul-locked
espy it on Montauk Beach while resting up
for more love-making in the cheap motel*

*Such musings
I need not dwell upon*

*So, with quiet desperation
I will deepen a hardened
closing of my heart
bricking it block
by slamming block
with claymores of the mind*

For the first time since the late 1960s, when I lived in Washington, DC, I began submitting my poetry for publication. I also began to attend the various open mic poetry venues throughout Long Island and New York City, reading my poetry in public for the first time. I loved it, being able to utilize my thespian skills from Xavier and Catholic University. Both my poetry and myself were well accepted within the poetry crowd.

I transformed Sara's and my house into my house, where Tommy, when he wasn't in rehab, jail or longterm treatment, and Jennifer, Sara's youngest daughter, lived with our lovely Old English sheep dog, Offie, and several cats, including Shashu. I existed in this state of limbo for a couple of years, waiting for Sara to come back.

Making the Best of a Bad Situation

So, there I was, still very much committed to maintaining a relationship with Sara, even though she was still actively involved with Joe. In the spring of 1995, I became lovers with a delightful, extremely talented poetess, Fran, who was in a mostly dead 25-year marriage with a much older man. Through our relationship, she got the courage to leave the emptiness of her marriage to make a life on her own. We had a pleasant spring and summer, traveling around Long Island to poetry readings. This included getting stuck out in East Hampton, when we couldn't get back to our homes during one of the weekends of the huge Pine Barrens fire in August and September. Here's a long, prose poem I wrote about what happened during one of our first dates at a poetry reading:

Hormones

Teenage boys ... have only a brief season of exhilarating liberty between control by their mothers and control by their wives. The agony of male identity springs from men's humiliating sense of dependence upon women. It is women who control the emotional and sexual realms and men know it.

Camille Paglia

I don't remember what phase the moon shone through that evening at the first reading of Live Poets at McGuire's Grill in Bohemia. Whether a new sliver, a supine winking night half-eye, or a voluptuous ripe full circle. Nor do I know if it had any tidal influences upon our gathering of quiet poet folk, pacifists, Wiccans, Buddhists, Gandhinistas. All I know now in retrospect is that ominous primal waves of wispy violence sluiced from hidden corners of the darkened side room, where we gathered to share our gentle poesy. Slowly it seeped and swirled encircling us, so stark one could cut it with a K-bar.

Yes, I was protein deficient. Yes, the service was atrociously slow. Yes, I was nervous about my first public reading. But for the life, and/or death, of me I can't fathom in any god's realm what possessed me to challenge the pompous, pretentious owner with insults, casting verbal gauntlets to spark in the tight space between us. By Sweet Jesus, he towered over me by a head-and-a-half at least, was muscularly broad compared to my short Buddha-belly stature. What in the wide Kosmos did I imagine I would do "outside" with or to him? Me, a 52-year old pretend warrior in the would-be war of my generation, who never has drawn nor spilt blood in barroom brawl nor engaged in any duel of animus blood-letting. At first the gentle women looked aghast, then demurely turned away eyes downcast, seeking intuitively within their communal presence joined, some solution through delicate inaction while engaging in quiet contemplation. Thanking all goddesses the viciousness between us passed, as subtly evoked estrogen soothed boiling blood.

It is now several spins of time since, and in this bright day's sunlight amid a profusion of asexual nudity upon the wide nude beach underneath Fire Island Lighthouse, I contemplate in awe how effectively those like myself, the male of the species, are mastered by those we strive so peacockishly to suppress.

I broke her heart, when I told her later that fall I was still in love with Sara and hoped to get back with her. Nevertheless, I was the bridge which enabled her to free her life from a marriage that wasn't working, so that she could be available to find a more suitable love relationship with another extremely talented poet, John, whom she married a year or so later. It was another lesson that mysteriously the Kosmos works itself out for the best, as painfully difficult as sometimes that process is. Today she and her husband live very happily in retirement in Florida and we maintain an email and FaceBook friendship.

In the spring of 1996, Sara and I were faced with a rather onerous financial situation, which forced us to declare bankruptcy to protect our major investment, the house we owned in Islip. Tommy had accumulated some $250,000 worth of managed-care approved psychiatric and longterm rehabilitation treatment services for his virulent addiction to

Special K and other rave-scene drugs. The right hand of Sara's health insurance company had pre-approved all of his admissions, even recommending specific facilities. However, when the left-hand of the Accounts Payable Department received the bills from the facilities several months later, out of hand they denied them as being medically unnecessary. After about six months of providing additional documentation, including documentation that all admissions had been pre-approved by the insurance company itself, the facilities began initiating court orders to place liens against the house and property in Islip. Not nice. Luckily we knew how to deal with this. We contacted a friendly bankruptcy attorney who protected us from financial ruin and lifelong indebtedness, providing us with the same protections, then available to "we the people", that corporations have always had when they need to financially restructure themselves.

All throughout 1996, Sara, Joe and I stayed in contact, all of us struggling with what was increasingly becoming more and more unsatisfactory for each of us. None of us were having much fun. One of the strangest episodes Sara and I had during this period was once we had to sneak away from her jealous lover to have a moonlight tryst as legal man and wife out on the North Fork of Long Island. Of course, he found out and threw a hissy fit. We proved to ourselves beyond any shadow of a reasonable doubt that though "Open Relationships" may read nice and dandy on paper as an ideal, in practice they suck, at least our open relationships did for us, for each of us.

As the days of 1996 wound down to a close, Sara and I recommitted to our relationship. She ended her affair with Joe, and we made plans for her to move back into our home. I had waited the situation out. I had proved to myself that I could sustain a longterm, committed relationship. I had won. It was a Pyrrhic victory.

The Calm before the Final Perfect Storm

For several years, Sara and I had a renewed honeymoon period. We traveled for a week to California, visiting Esalen for a weekend workshop and rented a convertible to drive down the Big Sur along the Pacific coast Highway, stopping for a wonderful meal and evening in Pismo Beach, CA. We visited again my sponsor Peter and his now ex-wife, Camilla, for several days in San Diego. We had a marvelous visit to the San Diego Zoo. We remodeled the second floor of our faux Victorian house, combining two small bedrooms into a large master bedroom with a large, walk-in closet for her and remodeled the bathroom with wainscoting, lovely wallpaper and new fixtures. We bought two Maine Coon cats, Luci and Chelsea.

By 1999, however, Sara and I were mostly living separate lives, as we settled into a very comfortable co-existence within our property. She spent most of the time living in our home while I spent most of the time living and working out in my office behind the garage where I also slept since my snoring continued to disturb her. We often went to the nude beach in front of the Fire Island Lighthouse where I wrote this poem about a woman beside us, while Sara slept:

voyeur

the woman
serenely at ease
all body exposed
sat beside me
several feet away
on the nude beach
a young mother-to-be
buddha-bellied
ripe with child
so full

I could not restrain
my eyes from randomly wandering
over the flowing caress of her long wind-swept hair
to linger upon the melloned breasts with large aureole
pierced with taut nipples primed for suckling
when she lay back falling into deep slumber

knees widely spread and bent for birthing   for loving
the rounded curve of her near full-term midriff
rose and slowly fell in undulations
mirroring the rhythmic pounding
of white-frothed surf against
sand-slicked shore

looking closer I contemplated with considerable envy
a subtle almost imperceptible motion
across the wide expanse of her upthrust abdomen
her fetus child's movements soft within

who soon shall painfully slide
be compressed by ruthless nature
down her birth canal
through her orifice of life
to be shock-startled
into unconnected being

then carefully nestled
within the soothing
comfort of her
warm bountiful
bosom

Due to continuing episodic incidents of anger/rage, difficulties with intimacy with Sara, and increasing occurrences of Intrusive Recollections from Vietnam, I began seeing a psychiatrist, Dr. Krish, at the Northport, Long Island VA Hospital. After a couple of sessions, Dr. Krish suggested I apply for a PTSD disability rating. I related to him that I was a REMF, a rear echelon mother fucker, the derisive term used by combat troops for support troops, and that I hadn't really experienced that much combat. Vince, my close friend and work associate, who was also in recovery from alcoholism, had severe PTSD from Vietnam. As an infantry platoon officer, he had experienced six months of heavy combat, losing several men in his platoon. He had a purple heart and nearly died on the battlefield from a severe wound.

For years, even after I was diagnosed with PTSD in 2001, I always compared my PTSD with Vince's. Dr. Krish gave me an analogy that helped me resolve this dilemma. He told me to imagine a one-pint container and a one-gallon container, both of which were full of liquid. Whether it is a one-pint container or a one-gallon container, when a container is full, it is full. My PTSD, though not nearly as severe as was Vince's, was still debilitating and disabling. He again urged me to apply for PTSD. One afternoon, driving home from my office in Lynbrook, I experienced an especially strong and powerful intrusive recollection described in this poem:

Intrusive Recollection

Cool of early evening
Sharp edges of day meld together
Grooving to groovy sounds from 60s

I speed North on Wantaugh Parkway
Veer sharply right onto that long sweet arc of ramp
Merging into Southern State

Tease myself with virtual G-forces
In the imagined cockpit of a P-51 Mustang
Rolling into steep dive to strafe Okinawa beachhead

Damn! As I top the rise
A flurry of brake lights quickly test the limits
Of my real-time skills and my Honda's ABS

Pissed! My plan thwarted to be on time
While traffic assumes normal conditions:
Clogged-backed-up stop-and-slow-go creep

Flashing lights of state trooper
Squeeze traffic from three lanes to one
Around cars helter-skelter in roadway

Several people hold back
A tearful woman who strains against them
With a scream frozen on her face

On ground beside open-doored car
Lies a pot-bellied figure
One knee awkwardly bent

Three persons cluster about--frantic CPR motions
The other leg spasmodically flops
As despite my horror I stare

A police helicopter
Crazily tilts out of rose-tinted clouds
Thump-whump whirling debris

My heart pounds
Sweat pours off face
Breathing short and shallow

And for a spell
I am caught again
In that other place

When
Lush green was jungle

Not late blooming Spring

*When
Blood and dust commingled
Not tar and exhaust*

*When
Terror rode each pulsebeat
When
Screechings of incoming*

Last

For

Ever

It convinced me that perhaps Dr. Krish was right, so I did apply and was awarded a 30% PTSD disability in 2001. While examining the files of my company in Vietnam at the National Archives in Maryland for corroborative evidence of incidents indicating I had been exposed to the trauma of war, I came across a Unit History document I had written in 1967 and completely forgotten about. It was most strange to see my signature on a document 34 years later that I didn't remember having written. I've kept a copy of it in my records at home.

———

During 2000, besides my private practice, I was also unsuccessfully trying to initiate with several others an online virtual enterprise, eVanta, a website of interconnected websites for B and C list actors and actresses from television series and soaps. It became one of the earliest casualties of the dot.com bubble bust in mid-2000. I have some 35,000 shares of this virtual company whose value is exactly $0.00.

In October of 2000, "our" business, Brinson & Associates, took another disastrous hit when one of the managed care health insurance companies arbitrarily changed their rules. This resulted in them retroactively disallowing some $7000 worth of previously approved billing for client sessions during the previous three months. This occurred after I had again maxed out another of our credit cards to take another trip to my hometown in Jackson, MS for a mini-reunion with the family. As it turned out this was the last chance I had to be with my father before he died in the summer of 2001. Here is a prose poem I wrote about our last conversation, one of the most intimate we ever exchanged as men, as father and son:

One Cluster of Precious Moments

Dad and I are sitting in the den. Mother and the grown girls are in the kitchen cooking our Sunday dinner.

Our relationship as his first born and only son has always been strained, even estranged for most of our 57 years together. For many reasons, which I understand, but am still emotionally vulnerable to, he never wanted children, did not want to share "Bobby," his lover/sweetheart/hostage, our mother, with anyone.

I ask him what he does with his time at St. Catherine's, the Alzheimer's facility where he spends his long days, endless nights.

He pauses for a moment and slowly replies, "I think about all the friends I've had, all the family members I've known, each of you children, your friends and children, my grandchildren. I think how grateful I am to have known so many wonderful people. It fills me with such gratitude."

"That's really nice, Dad."

We sit in silence for a while, each listening to the slow tick-tock of the mantle clock.

"That's a really nice sound. The mantle clock tick-tocking," I say.

"Yes," he replies.

"I was with you, oh I guess around 10 or 11, when we bought it as a birthday present for Mom up in Fondren Place."

"I remember," he says.

The tock-ticking seems to slow, focusing all reality into each passing beat.

"Yes, each tick, each tock is so soothing, so comforting," he says. "Such a nice sound."

"Yes, Daddy, it is."

Sara was not pleased when I came back and told her about the insurance company snafu, which put us in a bit of a cash-flow squeeze for the next couple of months. We were still financially in as good a shape as any two-income, middle-class family. The business income was still sufficient enough to pay for most of our combined household expenses. Sara's income was mostly hers to use for herself and the kids, who were now more or less on their own, beginning their young adult lives. We made it through the holiday season, buying Chutney, a wonderful English Standard Poodle puppy, and taking a holiday weekend jaunt up to Woodstock, NY. There we watched the Y2K celebrations in awe as a new Millennium appeared across the globe, starting in the South Pacific at Christmas Island and steadily wending its way westward without any of the drastic prognostications of doomsday destruction for computer systems.

As a typical long and cold and stormy Long Island winter lumbered toward the new spring of a new era, we were stuck in a comfortable, but mostly dead, relationship of 22 years. Slowly, we became more and more estranged. We began bickering about money issues, dealing with the stress of Tommy's continuing struggle with addiction, and that also of Jennifer, her youngest daughter, who I was able to get admitted to a treatment center I was associated with at a greatly reduced rate. I don't recall precisely what our last argument was about, probably something to do with how I was not safe for her or didn't meet her security needs. It resulted in a couple of uncomfortable days of estrangement.

In response to this estrangement, on the morning of Sunday, April 1st—yup, April Fool's day—of 2001, I lost it and had a rage attack against myself, a major blow out, upstairs in the new bathroom. As I recall, I had a banana that I smashed into my face as I yelled and screamed at myself in the mirror. This was the final straw that broke the back of Sara's camel.

From then until she moved out of the house during the summer, the perfect storm of the end of our relationship crashed and swirled around us, as destructive as any Tsunami. She would not reconsider any kind of a reconciliation, refusing to continue seeing Ted, our gentle Imago Relationship therapist.

I decided that this time I would not manage the household expenses by myself. We put the house on the market in May and sold it at our price to the first buyer within the first week it was listed. The relationship with Sara was done, kaput, over, although I held on to the illusion that she was the only true love relationship for me for much too long a time. I was living by myself on the property waiting for it to close when the horror of 911 happened.

Thus ended the 22-year relationship with Sara, with whom I had been so certain I would spend the rest of my life. It wasn't meant to be. In retrospect, I can see, however, that it helped heal me of the fear I had that I was incapable of being able to sustain a committed love relationship. The years I spent with her, which included the years when she was with her lover, Joe, convinced me that I could, after all, remain committed in a longterm love relationship.

A number of years later, in 2011, I read an obituary that Joe, at age 62, had died. I was one of three people who signed his *Newsday* legacy page.

Chapter 15: Relationships Redux

I had a second period of "relationships du jour" during the first decade of the 21st century at the very beginning of the 3rd Millennium. After third wife, Sara, and I separated and were divorced early in 2002, I repeated the pattern of my first decade of recovery: I became involved again in a number of serially monogamous relationships.

Jane

I took my half of the money from the sale of Sara's and my home on Long Island and bought an upscale Rialta RV. For several months, I travelled around the US, visiting friends and exploring the wonders of the western USA. There was a rather ironic moment in mid-January of 2002, when I was traveling north on I-65 through Kentucky as light snow was falling in my new Rialta. All other RVs on the road were traveling south to warmer climes. This is perhaps a most fitting metaphor for what much of my life has been.

I visited the Grand Canyon, Chaco Culture National Historical Park and other national park areas, as well as visiting friends. This included visiting Don in Oklahoma City, my machine gunner in Vietnam, who took a picture of me dancing with the two Australian strippers that got me one of my several letters of reprimand. The ultimate destination was Tucson, the home of TOP, Tours of Peace, Vietnam Veterans. With TOP, I took my first trip back to Vietnam in February of 2002. Here is one of the most memorable events of the first day back in-country:

Hello GI

One of the most significant of many wonderful gifts I've experienced during the first decade of the 3rd Millennium is that I have been able to return twice to Vietnam, where I fought in the American War during 1967–1968. My first return trip occurred in February of 2002, when I was a member of a TOP Tours of Peace led by founder, former US Marine, Jess DeVaney. We landed at the former Tan Son Nhat US Air Force/Army base fairly early in the morning, seeing some of the same berms built by US Forces in the 60's, now protecting MIG fighter-bombers instead of Phantom F-4s. After being processed through customs, a rather daunting affair confronting again under much different circumstances the uniforms of our former enemy, we checked into the Rex hotel in downtown Ho Chi Minh City. During the American War, the Rex Hotel had been one of several BOQs for American officers in what shall always be for me Saigon. I had stayed in the Rex Hotel in January of 1968 on TDY duty just before the Tet Offensive that proved to be the turning point of the ill-conceived long invasion and occupation of Vietnam by US armed forces. It was, indeed, most moving to be returning to the Rex Hotel as a veteran civilian, where I had stayed as a young citizen soldier officer.

Later that afternoon, we went to see the Presidential Palace. During the war, this is where Ngo Dinh Diem and Nguyễn Văn Thiệu, the two major Presidents, ruled the Republic of South Vietnam and lived with their families. Today, it is a memorial to Ho Chi Minh and the victorious North Vietnamese Communist forces. The tour was somewhat interesting, but after awhile the party spiel of the guide about the corruption of the past and the purity of the present regime began wearing somewhat thin, so I broke away from the formal tour and went outside onto the vast palace grounds. Here was the NVA Soviet T-54 tank that knocked down the Palace gates and came roaring into the Palace grounds on April 30, 1975, signaling the end of the long American War, as helicopters airlifted the last remaining Americans from Saigon to aircraft carriers out in the South China Sea. I had watched this momentous event in sobbing horror on television in then girlfriend Barbara's W. 71st Street apartment in New York City. Almost 27 years later, I went down to take a picture of the famous T-34 Tank.

Taking pictures of the tank with me was a young Amerasian man in his mid-30s with an older Vietnamese woman, near my age, nicely dressed in Western clothes with short hair. The man in halting English told me that his mother wanted a picture with me standing in front of the T-54 tank. Would it be okay for him to take our picture. "Sure," I said, and put my arm naturally around her. It struck me, as the young man was focusing his camera, that he was old enough to be my son, that perhaps his father had been an American like me. The picture was taken, and the woman turned to me with a sad smile and said: "Hello GI. Nice to see you again."

I was speechless, dumbstruck with emotion, and before I could recover and say something back to them, thank them, thank her, they had disappeared. I do so wish that I had taken a picture of them. I also wish I had had someone take a picture of the three of us.

It was a most healing and beneficial trip, during which I was able to visit again the An Nhon Orphanage and be reunited with two of the orphans who were children when I was Civil Affairs Officer for my battalion. The orphanage was still in operation, now run by the Vietnamese government instead of the order of French Vietnamese nuns. It was a most joyous occasion to be reunited with two of the orphans, now adults working at the orphanage, who had survived the terrible time of the Tet Offensive.

But the trip also included a visit to My Lai, a most daunting but ultimately healing experience. There was no way I could prepare for the visit to the My Lai Memorial Park. I fully expected it to be one of the lowlights of my return trip to Vietnam after 34 years even though I accepted the rationale that it was a requisite ordeal for healing from the war. Nevertheless it was an experience I anticipated with considerable dread, especially since I was still in the warm afterglow of having had such a most positive experience the day before at the Ah Nhon orphanage, the scene of the most traumatic episode I experienced during my tour of duty in Vietnam.

The tour bus pulled into the parking lot and the first impression I had, seeing the refreshment and souvenir stand, was that it was like a theme park, a Vietnamese Disneyland. I made a smart-ass remark to this effect to fellow tour member, Wally, who was not amused. Silly, cynical me, trying to use the denial of foxhole humor to shield me from fully facing the belly of the beast of what my war was, of what any war just awfully is.

Being the loner that essentially I am, I detached myself from others in the group and went off on my own. I walked through the front entrance and was immediately aware of how un-Disneyland a place it actually is. Beautifully landscaped gardens surround stone walkways lined with hedges and row upon row of somber monuments, attesting to the brutal reality of My Lai: "Here Mr. Nguyen and his family were killed." "Here died Mme. Ahn and her three children." "Here Mr. Phan died alone." The profusely blooming flowers offered some solace. In the center of the park I gazed up for a seeming eternity at the large, rough-hewn stone memorial statute, fashioned in a Soviet-heroic-style. It portrayed women and children, one or two old men, in grotesque poses of unutterably unbearable suffering, pleading with outstretched arms for some merciful god or goddess to intervene on their behalf. There were, unfortunately I suppose, no gods or goddesses on duty to hear their desperate pleas on that awful day.

I walked into the Museum on the south side of the park. It was filled with stark, blown-up photographs of the massacre, with voluminous commentary in English, French and Vietnamese. Slowly I read through the account of the terrible events with their vile pictorial testimony of what had happened that infamous day in American History. I was surprised to read what I had previously been unaware of, that I was still in-country on that fateful day, March 16, 1968. Further, that Task Force Barker, to which Calley's unit was attached, was one of my primary customers for resupply from the Qui Nhon depot, about a hundred kilometers to the south. With a horrible chill down my spine, I recalled that I had accompanied a small convoy of a couple of trucks in my gun-jeep to the forward operating supply base of Task Force Barker, during the frenetic days after the devastating Tet Offensive. I hadn't shot a civilian, nor torched a hootch, but I had directly supplied those who had. I sometimes refer to myself as a combat support war criminal.

I stood for a long while before an almost life-sized photograph taken during his trial of Lt. William Calley in a suit with a silly grin on his Alfred E. Newman face. I stared into what I interpreted were his hollow, vacuous eyes, trying to get some sense of who this man was. At first I was filled with revulsion, scorching condemnation, self-righteous indignation, which mirrored the rhetoric of the Vietnamese government's official account of that black day, not too much different from a typical American government official's depiction of the awful horror of another notorious day in America's history, September 11, 2001. Reading that Calley was a 90-day OCS wonder, I reflected upon my own inadequate preparation as an ROTC-trained junior officer to be a platoon commander in charge of a group of rowdy teenagers armed to the teeth in the brutal insanity of guerrilla warfare in Vietnam.

In truth, it was only the grace of some allegedly beneficent Higher Power, or good karma, that prevented me from being ensnared in a similar incident. With a command voraciously hungry for body counts; with the unwritten rules of engagement we had, especially during the reactive days following Tet, when we were trying so desperately to convince ourselves we were winning the war along with the hearts and minds of the Vietnamese people; with the callow prejudice so prevalent toward Vietnamese civilians, whom we derisely referred to as gooks, slope heads or dinks, whose freedom we were supposedly risking our lives to protect; with the awesomeness of superior American firepower from the land, air and sea, the reality on the ground was that many small unit leaders, such as Lt. Calley and I had been, were faced with making inexorable decisions that often resulted in the ruthless death of untold thousands of innocent civilians.

I was able to extend a bit of forgiving compassion towards Calley, surely a karmic victim of the insanity of war, just as the innocent civilians who died as a result of his horrendous orders were that tragic day. I was also able to experience a modicum of forgiving compassion for myself. In addition, I had the opportunity to do Tonglen Buddhist practice to forgive my judgmental derision that only Calley was scapegoated with a Court Martial. His company commander, Captain Medina, and battalion higher ups, faced no negative consequences to their careers as a result of that appalling day. Medina, LTC Barker, who was later killed, and other Battalion officers were not the only ones exonerated of the My Lai massacre. Colin Powell, then a major in the operations office of the Americal Division, was also certainly aware of what had happened. His report on the matter was part of the cover-up. Who knows what today may still haunt Powell and others in their sleeping and waking nightmares?

I also stood for a long while in front of the photograph of Hugh Thompson and his helicopter crew, reading of his valor, his integrity, his dedication to honor and ethical rules of engagement, wishing that we had more true heroes of his caliber all throughout the ranks of our military might. Thompson's heroic actions, doing what he could to deter the senseless slaughter of civilians, were the flip-side of the same coin of what Calley did. As well, possibly what I would have done in a similar situation.

After a long while, I left the museum and walked through the rest of the park. We were supposed to meet with a survivor from My Lai, and I certainly didn't want to miss that. Toward the extreme western boundary of what once had been the series of interconnected hamlets known as My Lai, also known among GIs as Pinkville, I came upon the infamous ditch, into which scores of civilians, mostly women and children, a scattering of elderly men, had been herded. Calley ordered them to be mercilessly gunned down by the young troops of Charlie Company. There it just starkly was, covered in the shade of thick foliage from the encroaching jungle, through which dappled sunlight streamed, creating surreal contrasts of shadow and light. In the ditch was a couple of inches of brackish water, filled with rotting leaves and brown palm fronds. It was eerily quiet, the profound silence interrupted from time to time by the hoots of a distant jungle creature or the buzzing of a nearby insect. It was very difficult to imagine in the quiet tranquility of that mid-afternoon of March 5, 2002, a week-and-a-half shy of the 34th anniversary of the massacre, that this serene jungle scene could have been the site of such ineffable horror. Ominously, as if to remind me of the reality of what had in truth taken place on that long ago day, one shiny, red high-heeled shoe lay on its side, half-submerged in the water of the ditch.

On a grassy knoll about 50 meters away from the ditch, I could see the rest of our group gathering around a petite, frail-looking, elderly woman, dressed in the typical peasant dress of white blouse and black pajama bottoms, holding a conical hat. No doubt she was the My Lai survivor. Gathered with us around Ha Thi Quy were several Vietnamese that included some of her grandchildren. Her story was incredibly moving, and she told it simply with matter-of-fact, quiet dignity in a soft and steady voice. Spellbound, in rapt attention we listened to her words, mesmerized by her methodical weeding of the earth in front of her, each phrase slowly translated by our Vietnamese guide and interpreter.

She was 42 years old in 1968. She had been shot in the thigh and side. She survived by hiding motionless underneath the body of her 14 year-old daughter until the American soldiers left. She told us that she was very grateful, not only to have survived that terrible morning, but that she was still alive in good health. She was so privileged to be able to spend her days tending to the My Lai memorial. She was especially grateful to be of some comfort to the many American soldiers that visited, who needed so much forgiveness. It made her very happy and satisfied to be of service.

What an incredible lesson in forgiveness and compassion! If only our leaders and politicians were as wise, as sensible. With unutterable grace, she thanked us, got up and left. I got up and walked back down by the ditch. Following her lucid example of simple service I did what I could do – I started policing the area, picking up refuse and sticks, finding here and there a cigarette butt that I carefully, slowly and methodically, field-stripped for the first time in almost four decades, like a ritual tea ceremony.

When I left the Memorial Park, I saw the two women members of our tour, Jane, a VA psychologist and former wife of a 100 per cent disabled vet, and Heather, the daughter of a Marine officer, who had prematurely died the year before from Agent Orange. They were sitting out in the refreshment/souvenir area, playing with several Vietnamese children. One bright-faced little girl, wearing a Mickey mouse-like hat, was a granddaughter of Ha Thi Quy. It was a hopeful and up-lifting way to end the visit to My Lai. The horror was long gone. But, it should never be fully forgotten. It doesn't have to be stared at either. We – I – can choose to move beyond it. The expectant future belongs to the young, and they deserve the best that we can fashion for them.

During this return trip to Vietnam, I also fell in lust with Jane. We consummated our relationship in a hotel that had been built on Red Beach, the Army R & R center in Qui Nhon, where I used to watch C-123 and C-130 cargo planes making their final approach to land at the Army Airfield. After we returned to Tucson, she persuaded me, against my better judgement, to move into her lovely home with her. Before I did, however, I drove to San Diego and picked up my longtime sponsor Peter. We took a wonderful two week drive up the amazing Pacific Coast Highway all the way to Seattle to visit a cousin of his.

When I returned to Tucson, I sold the Rialta RV for enough cash to buy a used Miata with several thousand dollars left over. It was certainly more sensible to drive the Miata around town, finding parking for it instead of the RV. Several weeks later, however, Jane began to doubt whether or not she truly loved me. It turned out that I was a rebound lover from a recent break-up she had before the Vietnam trip with another Vietnam Vet, a retired colonel in Army Intelligence, who was also named Tom. She was confused as to which of us she really loved. It was a repeat of what I had experienced with several other serial non-monogamous affairs, as well as what I lived through for several years with Sara and Joe.

One of the more daunting moments I've ever experienced occurred one early afternoon when I was sitting in Jane's living room, concentrating on writing an article about the necessity of forgiveness in the healing process of Vietnam Veterans. I heard nothing, but was startled to feel the cold steel of a pistol barrel pressed against the back of my brainstem. A deep voice, queried:

"Would you prefer the Colt. 45 or the Beretta 9 millimeter for your demise?'

"You must be Tom, I surmise."

"Yes," he replied. "I am."

"Can we perhaps discuss the situation?" I asked.

We ended up chatting for a couple of hours, vet to vet, man to man. I deeply identified with his pain, relating to him what I had recently gone through with Sara. We commiserated about how difficult it was to be in love with women like Jane and Sara. The following week, Jane asked me to move out, which I did.

Despite the ending of our relationship, I decided to stay in Tucson, where I got a job as director of an outpatient mental health clinic. I got an apartment and with the savings was able to furnish it to my liking with another set of golden oak victorian furniture. I joined the Tucson chapter of Veterans for Peace. I trained for and ran in another New York City marathon. I read poetry at open mikes and competed in Poetry Slams throughout Arizona and the Southwest. Here's a poem for which I won third place at a Tucson slam:

burnings

an angry orange ball of rising sun
burnishes a dull-bright glow
through the dirty gray plume of smoke
spreading across the whole horizon of morning sky
detritus from the raging fire that engulfs Mt. Lemon

it casts an ominous purple pallor about me
as low-flung smokey mists enshroud
the sharp ridges and ragged peaks
all along the Catalina Highway
like mountains in Vietnam after napalm

too keenly it reminds me of my present life
crashing and burning around me
as the woman with whom I committed
and settled down in this desert Tucson town
reverses field for her previous lover
like a screaming F-4 Phantom jet
whoop-banging the sound barrier
after raining fiery veils of death
or the suddenly disappearing Twin Towers
now only real in memory
except for a very large ragged hole
many blocks wide and many blocks long
deep within the tip of Manhattan Island

I also moved son Tommy from Long Island to live with me, hopefully to break his repeated pattern of relapse. It worked—he's made a good life for himself with his wife, Mica, from a prominent Arizona pioneer family.

In retrospect, I can discern that I was more in love with the story of me, a Vietnam Vet, finding true love on his return healing trip to Vietnam near where he served, than I was actually in love with Jane, the person. Nevertheless, I'm forever grateful to her for being the reason for me to live in Tucson for a couple of years, during which son Tommy was able to find a new, productive and creative life in recovery.

Bonnie

I had another relationship with a woman named Bonnie before I left Tucson to live in Sri Lanka for a couple of years as an unarmed peacekeeper with Nonviolent Peaceforce. I'll relate this adventure in a subsequent chapter. Bonnie was a delightful woman, somewhat of a heavy drinker at times, who worked as a meter reader for the gas and electric company. We knew each other from a Universalist Church I sometimes attended. One weekend I mentioned I was going camping, and she asked if I would like some company to which I replied, "Sure, why not?"

Early the next morning, instead of taking my Miata with the camping equipment in a large bag on the trunk luggage rack, we took her Toyota pickup truck, which had a camper shell. We made love the first night we camped under towering conifer trees beside a mountain stream in Cleveland National Forest. The next two nights, we camped in South Carlsbad California State Park overlooking the Pacific Ocean. It was most pleasant to watch her doing yoga on the beach as the sun sunk brilliantly orange-red-purple into the sunset glimmering across the ocean.

We dated for the next several months, while I was applying for duty as an unarmed peacekeeper in Sri Lanka. After a three-week training trip in Thailand, when I was accepted as a member of the first peacekeeping Team of Nonviolent Peaceforce, she agreed to store pictures, books, and knick-knacks during the two years I was deployed to Sri Lanka.

During August of 2004, we spent two weeks together in Great Britain. She flew to London from the US and I flew from Sri Lanka. After two days in a Piccadilly Circus hotel while visiting London, we rented a car and drove throughout the British Isles, visiting Stonehenge, Tor, Avebury and other sacred sites, steeped in Celtic lore. It was a delight to drive into the town square of a village and stop at the Tourist Office to find suitable lodging for the night in guest houses and cottages, so much more civilized and reasonable than the American system of overpriced and usually dreary motel rooms. A highlight of the trip for me was visiting Scotland, from which my Henry ancestors hail, near Glasgow. When I stood at the border crossing between England and Scotland, it may have been my sometimes overactive imagination, but I swear I felt my corpuscles deep within me celebrating joyfully, "We're home! We're home! We're HOME!" I was most impressed with Rosslyn Chapel, home of the intricate carvings of Green Men, the Apprentice Pillar, mythically related to Free Masonry, and reputed to be the seat of descendants of Jesus Christ, the Holy Grail and the Knights Templar, as promulgated by Dan Brown's novel, *The Da Vinci Code.* Our last day and night in England was spent in a lovely cottage near Windsor Castle. The next day she departed Heathrow for a return flight to the US a few hours before my return flight to Sri Lanka.

Lynn

While serving in Sri Lanka with Nonviolent Peaceforce, I survived the devastating Tsunami that struck on December 26, 2004. I escaped harm because a half-hour before the 40-foot high wave demolished the French Garden, a seaside guest house where I stayed for a two-day Christmas holiday, I took a bike ride inland to visit the 2200 year-old Vilgram Vihara, a temple complex where vedda, the indigenous people of Sri Lanka, Hindus and Buddhists have worshipped throughout the centuries. Through an amazing series of coincidences, I connected online with Lynn, a recently divorced woman from Deer Park, NY, near where I had lived for so many years with Sara. She'd read an article in *Newsday,* about my surviving the Tsunami, written by a former client. The article had a picture of me along with my email address.

On impulse, she emailed me, and we established a long-distance relationship via the Internet through email and chat. A school nurse, she visited me in Sri Lanka for a week during her spring vacation. Her therapist was a woman I had known from AA meetings on Long Island, who assured her I was a decent sort of a fella. We made plans for me to move into her Deer Park home upon my return from Sri Lanka in July of 2005.

Our relationship, as most do, began wondrously with us traveling to Arizona to give Tommy his 90-day chip of being clean and sober and to transport my paintings, books and knick knacks back to New York from

Bonnie's house in Tucson. We also took camping trips to Cape Cod and to North Carolina, visiting the Outer Banks near where her father lived. I had a wonderful Thanksgiving, Christmas and New Year's holiday season with a family, hers, for the first time since Sara and I parted ways. I was able to be very supportive of her during both the death of her father, from whom she had been mostly estranged for many years, as well her brother, Gary, who suffered a massive heart attack. I helped convince her sister-in-law, Dee, that it would be more merciful to let him die naturally, rather than artificially keeping him alive indefinitely in an ICU. Here's a poem I wrote about his death scene:

Blond hair, Blond eyebrows, Blond eyelashes

I look down upon your smooth face, Gary,
under the harsh light of the death room
in Good Sam's ER. I stroke your downy brow
while little Nigerian priest prays his prayers.
I hold tight, close, your devoted sister, Lynn,
as she smoothes your blanket and affirms the truth
you are without sin.

Blond hair, blond eyebrows, blond eyelashes.
You look so innocent, so at peace
even with the awkward angle of the tube
jutting sharp out of your mouth lax.
I am not haunted by dead VC boy faces
when likewise I looked down upon Daddy's stoic face
so prim so proper in his casket that awful summer of 2001
nor bruised, bloodied, burnt faces of Ah Nhon orphans.

Just you, blond hair, blond eyebrows, blond eyelashes
and the priest and Dee, your wife, and beloved Lynn.
We repeat the Buddhist Medicine Prayer for healing.
We avow Buddha's truth that we have two deaths,
once when the body fades to dust and twice
when the last person who remembers you
passes into the vast unknown.

Gary, long shall you live.
Blond hair, blond eyebrows, blond eyelashes,
like a white stone skipping over blackened waters
you easily shall sail through Bardo home.

Blond hair, blond eyebrows, blond eye lashes.
No more suffering, no more broken heart.
You are at peace.
We are at peace.

In early 2006, I became very active with Veterans for Peace, establishing the Long Island Chapter 138, and participating in peace actions throughout the Eastern Seaboard. During the summer of 2006, Lynn and I took a several week camping trip around the US, visiting family and national parks out west en route to the Veterans for Peace convention in Seattle.

However, by late fall, like Sara before her, she began to resent my ardent peace activism. In the fall of 2006, severe PTSD symptoms also began to manifest. I had several rage attacks and again began seeing the VA psychiatrist, Dr. Krishamourti, with whom I had initiated my PTSD claim in 2001. Dr. Krish was quite surprised I had only received a 30% disability rating and urged me to appeal for an increased rate. This was what caused us to become estranged after several contentious arguments. I began experiencing insomnia and night terrors. When I would leave our bed, due to her snoring and restlessness that awoke me, to try to get back to sleep on the futon in my office, Lynn was wounded to the core. She became convinced I didn't truly love her, since I couldn't sleep through the night with her.

Shortly thereafter I had a yelling altercation with her youngest son. She told me to leave her house, or else she would call the police. I knew this would be a lose-lose situation, so I spent a couple of days at a friend's house. After a couple of days she left a suitcase of clothes and my computer on the front porch for me to pick up. She would not let me back into the house to pack up the rest of my belongings.

Instead, one afternoon, she and her sons moved my stuff onto her front yard. I borrowed a friend's van and loaded all of my stuff in it, taking it to a storage space I rented. Thank goodness it didn't rain! Thus ended another most strange and doomed romantic relationship. As with previous crazy, contentious, cataclysmic relationships I'd experienced, I didn't drink, went to meetings, and communed with people in my AA support groups.

In March of 2007, I was awarded a 100% permanent disability. I used much of the money from the lump sum back payment to buy a Honda Insight, the first battery assisted hybrid automobile marketed in the US that got upwards of 45 mpg, and to furnish a lovely studio apartment on the Boardwalk of Long Beach, NY.

Michele

The last lady I had a serial monogamous relationship with was a woman named Michele, who I met one cold winter night in December of 2006 at a peace rally in New York City, where I was one of the featured speakers. We spoke after the rally and walked across town to her apartment in Greenwich Village where she cooked the first of many meals for me. That night, she told me she had been living as a vestal virgin for years after several bad relationships with ex-convicts who stole money from her. She hadn't been in a romantic relationship with anyone for several years, after her mother had died.

Like a lemming over the cliff, I became determined to rescue her from her loneliness and alienation. That night we also discussed the possibility of forming some kind of commune for young Iraq and Afghanistan vets to help them recover from PTSD and their war experiences. Since I was actively involved with Veterans for Peace and Iraq Veterans Against the War, we began attending peace gatherings throughout the eastern seaboard.

Similar to what I had experienced years previously with Barbara, she was also involved in a long, devoted, mostly platonic relationship with an older man. Bill had severe PTSD from being the only survivor of his tank crew as a young soldier during the Battle of the Bulge towards the end of WW II. A member of a Boston Brahmin family, he had homes in Boston and on Martha's Vineyard, as well as owning the Greenwich Village apartment where Michele lived. An ironic quirk was that the apartment was directly across the street from the building where Debbie's psychotherapist lived and practiced when I first got sober in 1972, where we had met on the evening I decided to stay sober and get involved in AA.

For a couple of years, Michele and I had a mostly platonic relationship during which she and Bill sold their Greenwich Village apartment. They took the money from selling the apartment to buy her a house near Woodstock, New York. I helped Michele move into their new house, and helped her start a large organic garden. Since this was during the financial meltdown of 2007 and 2008, I decided to move upstate to the Woodstock area rather than to stay stuck on Long Island, where several million people were dependent on trucks to bring in food and supplies. If the worse happened, I would have food from Michele's organic garden, and we could defend the compound on her property. The worse didn't happen, and I was able to rent a comfortable apartment on the main street of Woodstock.

Once more, I began to reinvent myself, making a life writing, taking long bike rides throughout the Catskill mountains and attending poetry readings throughout the Hudson River Valley. The relationship with Michele devolved into a low-intensity disagreement about just what the relationship was about. She saw it as primarily a platonic relationship, and I kept trying to force it into a one-and-one-only romantic relationship. Here's part of a journal entry from April 5, 2008, where I describe the crux of the dilemma I experienced with Michele, so similar to what I had experienced with other relationships:

> *I hassle with myself over the limits of the relationship with Michele. Late now, so will go to bed so I can hopefully get up early enough to go to morning meeting, but I want to write of my confusion, my sadness about the limits of our relationship. Can I do this with Michele, have a mostly platonic relationship sans love-making, except when she determines it's okay to service me, as we deepen a friendship to maybe forge together a 7th Chakra work project with vets forming a community of what – vets who become revolutionaries instead of veterans for peace?*

This impasse continued for a couple of years until late November of 2009, when I began dating Jill, the woman who has become my fourth and final wife. Today, Michele and I still speak occasionally, but mostly we are estranged, as I am from all of the many ladies with whom I forged serially monogamous romantic relationships.

Nevertheless, it is most rewarding, during this time of the early winter of my life, to bask in the pleasant memories of the many extraordinary and gorgeous women whom I have been gifted to know and with whom I spent many wondrous intimate times. I am grateful to, and for, each and everyone of these women I've related about. From them, I learned some difficult lessons of self-acceptance, which have evolved me into who I am today. Through these relationships I learned about "love and tolerance" for myself and for others.

Chapter 16: Jill, My Fourth and Final Wife

I met Jill, the woman who became my fourth and final wife, in 12-step meetings during the late fall of 2009 after I moved to Woodstock, NY. I noticed her at AA meetings, but where I encountered her the most, and became attracted to her, was in meetings of ACOA, Adult Children of Alcoholics. Neither of my parents were blatantly alcoholic, although mother was certainly a heavy hitter, especially during her elder years. However, I had the realization that both my father and my mother were themselves adult children of alcoholics. As a result of being raised by them, I had infused within me many of the characteristics attributed to ACA's.

The 12-step recovery book that resonates most with me in describing the dynamics of my personality is the Red Book from the ACA Fellowship, published in 2006. I identify deeply as an Adult Child, whose whole life has been severely impacted by the family disease of addiction. Another book that was immensely helpful to me, especially when I was struggling throughout the relationship with Sara, was Earnie Larson's, *Stage II Recovery: Life Beyond Addiction.* Larson posits that using a 12-step process to achieve lasting abstinence from addictive behavior is Stage I of recovery. He proposes that Stage II Recovery is using a 12-step process to rebuild one's life that was saved from the addictive behavior in Stage I Recovery. This entails becoming aware of and changing self-defeating behavior patterns. A lasting result of this slow process of progress, never perfection, is achieving relationships that work. Most certainly this is what I have experienced during the relationship and marriage to Jill, my fourth wife.

But, I get ahead of myself ...

On Thanksgiving day of 2009, I went to the all day Alkathon for people in recovery at a large church in nearby Kingston, NY. There, I talked for an hour or so with Jill and a friend of hers. Towards the end of our conversation, Jill and I exchanged phone numbers. The next day I called her and asked her to go to a free-form dance event, also in Kingston, but she said she had other plans. I later found out that her plans were to watch a marathon showing of the TV comedy series, *Monk,* one of her favorite shows, about a brilliant San Francisco detective who is challenged with a virulent obsessive-compulsive disorder. Throughout our years together

I've enjoyed teasing her that on what would have been our first date, I was stood up so she could watch a favorite TV show.

We did have our first date on the following Saturday. I picked her up, and we had dinner at a sports bar with multiple TVs playing college football games. I noticed she was watching them and asked her if she liked football. "I adore football," she responded. "I've been a diehard Chicago Bears fan all of my life." This was a definite bonus in her favor, since I've been a diehard New York Giants fan since I played high school football when Charlie Conerly from Ole Miss was winning championships. None of my other relationships had any appreciation of my love of football, especially when I would become enraged and scream at the TV during games when my Giants became the gints they are so capable of being in crucial games.

She told me that for several years, while she was getting her PhD in Sociology from the University of Oregon, she had been coordinator of academic tutors for the athletic department, and she still had longterm friendships with former student athletes on both the football and women's basketball team.

She also related to me that she was bisexual and for the previous 20 years she had lived with a woman partner. Her partner had been severely abused and traumatized during childhood and had been treated for years for a dissociative identity disorder, also known as multiple personality disorder. Like me with Sara, she had vowed that she would never leave her former partner, but like I did with Sara, she had eventually broken off the relationship, when she discovered that her partner, an inveterate gambling addict, had once more squandered all of their money and ruined their credit.

Shortly after the holiday season, Jill moved from her tiny apartment a couple of blocks away into my larger Woodstock apartment. In February, we packed my 2-seat Honda Insight with camping equipment, suitcases, etc. Jill is an extremely accomplished and competent organizer, and ingeniously packed the Insight. We took a two-month camping drive-around to visit my daughters and grandchildren in Maryland, my sisters and Mother in Jackson, and son Tommy and his fiancé, Mica, in Tucson. Along the way, we camped and did sightseeing.

We enjoyed a magical couple of nights camping out under the starlight skies at Cochise Stronghold in the Dragoon Mountains west of Sunsites, AZ. After spending a couple of weeks with Tommy and Mica in Tucson, we drove over to San Diego, camping at Imperial Beach and visiting the

San Diego Zoo. We then drove to the Grand Canyon. At the Navaho Nation gift shop before the east entrance, my favorite approach to catch the first glimpse of the spectacular view of the Grand Canyon at sunset, I bought us silver rings to exchange with each other – we were officially engaged. We then drove, camping along the way to visit her brother, Brian, and his family in Bolder, CO. From Bolder we drove to Wichita, KS, where Jill had gotten sober, to spend a couple of days with her closest friend in recovery, Terie, and her husband, Dudley. We ended our first 2-month long, camping, drive-around trip, visiting her hometown in Wenona, IL, where I met her parents and best friend, Jan, from high school.

4th Marriage

When we returned to Woodstock, we had a session with an astrologer friend. Sue read our charts, telling us we were "fate-mates," destined to heal each other from our "deepest wounds that we experienced from our very first breaths." With this endorsement, we began to finalize plans to get married. We decided to keep the wedding small with friends in our 12-step recovery communities. Jill had a friend, Amy, who was director of the Woodstock Library. She gave us permission to get married under a huge, beautiful oak tree on the library grounds at 1:00 p.m. on June 27, 2010. Sue, a registered New York State nondenominational minister, officiated. After the wedding ceremony, we shared a pot-luck meal back at our apartment on the patio with rented tables and chairs. We honeymooned several days later in Washington, DC, spending leisurely time, exploring the Smithsonian Museums, the National Gallery of Art, and the Native American Museum.

We were well-integrated within the 12-step communities of Woodstock AA, Al-Anon and ACA. Thank goodness, the meetings in Woodstock were like the meetings in New York City and Long Island in not being overly dogmatic. Instead, they were inclusive meetings for anyone who wanted recovery with or without religious beliefs.

At least once or twice a month, I would participate in poetry readings throughout the Hudson Valley. My chapbook of poetry, *Love and War*, was published by a small press operated by fellow poet and Vietnam Veteran friend, Dayl Wise.

We were able to get a large HDTV set with accompanying Bose sound system. In the summer we had the nice patio in the backyard of the apartment, where we barbecued, and in the winter we had a fireplace, where we built roaring fires. We took care of our two long-haired cats, Lady Charlotte and Sir Gerry that I had adopted from the Kingston, NY Animal Shelter.

In the early December of 2010, I was awarded an additional 60% disability for Agent Orange related coronary disease. With the lump-sum back payment, we were able to buy a 2007 used Honda Element, so we became a two-car family. Jill took a healing trip by herself in the Element back to her hometown in Wenona, IL to reconcile with her fundamentalist Christian family. She had been mostly estranged from them due to her lesbian relationship.

In March of 2011, I had hip-replacement surgery. Jill was a most excellent and caring nurse, managing my pain medications and helping me with the physical therapy rehab exercises. By early summer, I was riding my bike again and taking regular walks. We planned another long two-month, camping drive-about during July and August.

The Second Long Drive-About

We started by visiting the family in Maryland, and then drove to a campsite in the Blue Mountains near Thomas Jefferson's plantation in Monticello, Virginia. There, we celebrated our first wedding anniversary. Jill even packed a piece of our frozen wedding cake from the year before, which we shared before a roaring fire listening to the night sounds of the forest, most romantic. We awoke the next morning in an enchanted forest of mist and dew-dropped vegetation. Simply magical !~!~!

After visiting Monticello, we drove to Louisville, KY to visit my Aunt Mary. We then drove and camped through Oklahoma and Texas into New Mexico, where we stopped for two days of camping while exploring Chaco Canyon. Chaco Culture National Historical park is the largest site of Pre-Columbian pueblo culture north of Mexico. It's located way out in the San Juan basin of northwestern New Mexico, about a three-hour drive from Albuquerque. For years, I'd been fascinated by the ancient Anasazi Native American culture that spanned the four corners region of New Mexico, Colorado, Utah and Arizona.

After visiting Tommy and Mica in Tucson, we traveled to the Eastern slope of the Sierra Nevadas, visiting Lone Pine, CA after a horrible drive through Death Valley. The nearby Alabama Hills have frequently been used for filming western movies. We dodged a bullet—pun intended—when we nearly got stuck in an off-road gully into which I had foolishly driven. However, Jill was able to expertly drive our AWD Honda Element back up to the primitive road into Lone Pine. We camped for several days in the splendor of the Sierra Nevadas, underneath Mt. Whitney, the tallest mountain in the contiguous 48 United States.

A problem we encountered was heavy smoke from forest fires that severely aggravated my COPD. By the time we got to San Francisco bay area for a couple of days, I was suffering horribly, racked with coughing and had difficulty breathing. I didn't want to wait for hours in the San Francisco VA Hospital, so we cut our visit to California short to drive up to nearest VA hospital in Roseburg, OR. There, I got relief from a breathing treatment in the ER and new inhalers. We spent the next couple of weeks exploring Oregon, visiting Eugene, where Jill lived for 20 years as an undergraduate and graduate student while getting her sociology PhD. We also camped a couple of nights at Crater Lake and drove up the wild and wondrous Oregon seacoast highway US 101.

We got word, however, from the person we had paid to take care of our two long-haired cats, Charlotte and Jerry, that she couldn't do it anymore due to a flea infestation. We had to cut short our plans to visit the Badlands of South Dakota and Devils Tower, WY, so we could drive straight back to Woodstock. It took us two-and-a-half harrowing days of driving 12-plus-hour days to get back to rescue our beloved kitties, who had begun to go feral again. It took us a couple of days to clean up the apartment and debug the flea infestation.

Our First Major Move

Once we were settled more or less back into normalcy in Woodstock, we began to seriously discuss an idea we had hatched on the trip: to move across the country to Oregon. I had always been fascinated by the Oregon coast, since I first traveled up US Highway 101 in the Rialta RV in March of 2002 with Peter, my sponsor. Jill had lived for twenty years in Oregon and considered it more her home than where she grew up in Illinois. We went online and through Craig's List found a cottage built in 1934, whose rent was cheaper than what we were paying in Woodstock. One of the prime motivations for me to make the move was that with my somewhat declining health, I wanted to live in Oregon, which at the time had the most humane "right-to-die" laws. We were greatly influenced by the wonderful HBO documentary *How to Die in Oregon*.

Several days before the move, Jill had three abscessed teeth, which had to be removed, a $500 emergency dental expense for which we had not planned. At the same time, the porcelain upper bridge I had had installed at the Long Island VA dental clinic began disintegrating. With the titanium bar from which it hung exposed, I looked like something out of a cyborg horror movie. It was a karmically bad time for our teeth.

In late September, we hit the road in a caravan. Jill drove the Honda Insight with the two cats—now without fleas and domesticated again, and I pulled a U-Haul trailer with the fully packed Honda Element. It took us two days on the road for our first stop, Jackson, MS. There, we visited family, and I went to a 50th Class Reunion with some 26 members of my graduating class from St. Joseph High School. After the gala celebrations, it took us four-and-a-half days to drive to our new home on the southern coast of Oregon. We were adept and dedicated road warriors by then, for sure.

For the first several months, our life settled into a comfortable routine of exploring our new community. Though the winter months were chilly and damp with lots of rainstorms coming off the Pacific, we loved being so close to the ocean. At least two or three days a week, I took long walks along the rocky beach with waves crashing over the scattered rock formations out at sea.

During the spring and summer months I was able to take long bike rides. I was in the best shape I had been in a couple of years. At least once a month we would take the three-hour drive to Eugene, or visit other seacoast towns along the coast. Once or twice a year, either both of us, or I by myself, would take the long drive down to Tucson to visit son Tommy and his wife, Mica.

Initially, we enjoyed the southern Oregon AA meetings, which we attended several times a week. Over time, however, we found that much of southern Oregon AA was reminiscent of a white supremacist Christian cabal. Every meeting had a reading of How It Works and several also read the portion of Chapter 2 that explicitly defines "a real alcoholic," who can only get sober by the divine intervention of God, who the vast majority of AA members ardently interpreted as their Lord and savior, Jesus Christ. Most meetings were filled with a profusion of the-wonders-of-God talk by people who insisted they were recovered only by the grace of Jesus. Jill always left meetings a couple of minutes early, since they all ended with the Lord's Prayer, which was abhorrent to her due to her religious abuse from her mother as a child.

We met another New Yorker, Herb, who had worked successfully for years as an executive in the garment district of New York City. He was President of the Alano Club, where many of the 12-step meetings were held. Jill, Herb and I were rather outspoken about our non-Christian beliefs in AA. Jill also spoke very openly about her previous lesbian lifestyle. Ironically, one of the oldest oldtimers with over 50 years of recovery, Jack, was a gentle, but outspoken atheist Buddhist, who like us spoke openly about his non-Christian beliefs and his reliance upon eastern philosophy and meditation.

When Herb's term as president of the Alano Club was coming to an end, he, Jill and I spoke about Jill taking over as President of the Alano Club. We discussed initial plans to make it more than just a meeting hall, to have it function as an actual clubhouse for recovering people with workshops and opportunities to improve newcomers' lives. As a tutor in graduate school, Jill had wanted to start a program to help recovering high school dropouts get their GED.

However, a cabal of five of the more ardent Christian men began meeting and conspiring to insure that this heathen, lesbian bitch never got elected, mounting an effective smear campaign to prevent her from being elected. Jill and I were quite upset about this turn of events. Fortunately, during this time we found out about Roger C.'s *AA Agnostica* website. I began researching and writing articles for the website. To this day, I am most grateful for *AA Agnostica*, which certainly saved my serenity if not my sobriety.

We began to yearn for more access to the cultural delights of a larger, more metropolitan city. Whenever we would travel to Eugene, which was often, especially after we got season tickets to the Oregon Ducks home games during the 2012 football season, we would kid each other, "Look, there's a really tall building. Oh, and here is a real bus! Isn't it amazing?" We became willing to consider the possibility of making another move closer to a more metropolitan area, either Eugene or Portland.

———

I made this journal entry in the "Missive to Peter" on December 10, 2012:

> *I just had a deep awareness about the deep love connection with Jill, a realization which resonates with all I have experienced on this earth-time trip this time around: She is the alpha and omega of all the beloveds I have been graced*

to experience this time around. With her, through her, I experience to the deepest core of my being the ultimate of loving and being loved that I have striven and so desperately searched for so mightily throughout my now long life, as Sue healingly foretold, since the first breath. Perhaps this is the genesis of a poem I shall gift her with for Christmas.

Y E S !~!~!

And I did write the poem, on December 12, 2012, which I had framed and gave to Jill for a Christmas present. It had been a long time since I had experienced so much satisfaction and gratitude in creating for and giving a Christmas present to my beloved. Here it is:

For Jill at Christmastime, 2012

… and guiding me at every point, and enlightening me through and through, and forgiving me all along, and for being You-and-I.

– Ken Wilber

We both have had numerous lovers, several even
Whom we've married, all with whom we've suffered
Sometimes seeking oblivion by subtle suicidal gestures
Superficial marks upon flesh, soul and karma

Despite ourselves we continued ceaselessly to endure
Dragging each ragged breath into and out of ourselves
Only aware of the trillion pinpricks of slow torture
Baffled beyond any reasonable notion or rationale

Far and wide we wandered over high frozen mountains
Across arid plains stretching beyond each horizon
Through raging cities and listless country towns
Until once again we found each other in fabled Woodstock

We are the Alpha & Omega of all Beloveds
Who teach each other every passing day
Deeper and surer what most we yearn to live:
How better to learn, to love, to serve

Sage Wilber says it all so heart simply,
"Thank you deeply for coming on this journey with me"

In February of 2013, while up in Astoria for a writing workshop, Jill and I visited the seacoast town of Seaside. I instantly fell in love with it, since it reminded me so much of the seacoast resort town of Kismet on Fire Island, where I had summer shares while living in New York City during my first decade of recovery. Astoria, a 20 minute drive to the north, at the confluence of the Columbia River and the Pacific, had fine restaurants and shops, along with a Costco and other box stores for our shopping needs.

In May of 2013, we drove down to Tucson to take part in Tommy's wedding to his fiancé, Mica. For the first time in several years, I was able to spend time with all my biological and step children together, Rebecca, Jennifer, Dawn and Jennifer. Sara, who had survived a dire cancer scare requiring a double mastectomy, and I had a very poignant exchange, about which I was most grateful. However, I realized that I was also most grateful that she had Michael as her husband, who is so devoted to her and takes such good care of her, just as I am so grateful to have Jill who is so devoted to me and takes such good care of me.

June of 2013 was a most momentous month. On May 31st, Mother, then 91, finally gave up her ghost. She had lived on and on with failing health from a slow-growing cancer and gathering dementia for over two years, wailing at times that she just wanted to die, so she could join Carroll, her husband of almost 60 years, and several of our former pets. One of my sisters quipped, "For someone who wanted so desperately to die, she sure hung around for a very long while." I was able to get a direct flight from Portland to Louisville where I rented a car. I drove her sister, our Aunt Mary, to Jackson for the funeral and Memorial Service at St. Richards, where she and I had converted to Catholicism and were baptized.

The funeral Mass and memorial services at St. Richard's were most healing and appropriate, focusing on Vatican II principles of inclusivity and full participation from women, especially the lovely developmentally disabled altar girl, who assisted at the Mass so devotedly. In the receiving line, I was able to see some folks that I hadn't seen or been in touch with for over 50 years. The five of us siblings bonded and healed our differences immensely, with care and concern and mutual respect, communicating and laughing together, as we split up mother's remaining earthly belongings among ourselves to everyone's satisfaction.

Another Move Occurs

In late June, Jill and I went to Seaside, OR, to celebrate our third wedding anniversary. While there, we found and signed a year's lease for a marvelous, upscale four-bedroom house in Seaside with a backyard that had a koi pool and hot tub. The house also had a working fireplace and was two blocks from Seaside Cove, where I could take long walks and bike rides along the Pacific Ocean. We could regularly drive to Portland, a really sweet and kick-ass town, in less time than it took for me to drive into Manhattan from Long Island. To boot, it was a much prettier drive over the coastal mountains into Portland, than battling stop-and-go traffic on clogged Long Island highways. We loved being close again to a metropolitan area that we loved.

So, in August, when our lease in Coos Bay was up, we packed all of our stuff up into a large U-Haul truck. We paid sober friends to drive the truck and unload it in Seaside. We loved living in that house near the shining Pacific Sea and weird Portland for the next three years. When Mother and Dad's estate was probated, we got a windfall of almost $90,000 so we paid off some debts and bought ourselves two convertibles: a 2013 Mazda Miata M5 hardtop convertible for me and a 2008 VW Beetle convertible for Jill.

Struggles with a Happy Ending

At times Jill and I struggled with our core issues, especially when I would have a raging nut-number, yelling and screaming about one thing or the other, not necessarily having anything at all to do with Jill. Such raging behavior was a trigger for Jill's PTSD as a result of living with her raging mother, who would slap her and yell at her to "Honor your mother, goddammit!" Once during one of my nut numbers, Jill softly cried and said, "Why, Thomas, why does your PTSD always trump my PTSD?"

On March 3, 2014, I had another major melt down. When Jill went to leave the house during an argument, I grabbed her coat, pulling it off of her, so she wouldn't leave. She was traumatized, and so was I. For the next several months, we lived separate lives within the large and rambling Seaside house, while both of us focused on doing intensive individual healing.

Jill did an intensive 4th through 9th step process, using the ACA Red Book and Step Guide Workbook that included writing amends letters to many in her family. This included her parents, where she sought a reconciliation, but it wasn't reciprocated. I started regular sessions with a VA psychiatrist, who recommended I attend an 11-week Anger Management course for veterans with PTSD. It was quite humbling to be on the other side of the table, taking a course that during the 90s I had facilitated for veterans, but I recognized the truth of the proverb, "Social Worker, Heal Thyself!"

While Jill was doing her intensive work using the ACA Red Book, I delved deeply into and examined the root causes of a consistent pattern I had experienced throughout both my active addiction and my recovery. Here's an excerpt from a journal entry on March 7, 2014:

> *Want to write and explore more what it is that triggers me to such a panicked rage when a woman-love threatens to leave—it happened with Kathy, Debbie, Aneen, Sara, Lynn, Jane, Michele, and now again with Jill—I don't get it, but I must plumb the depth of this deep character trait/terror within me that renders me unable to sustain a love relationship. Maybe I need to accept that, as Bill W. notes on page 53 of The Twelve and Twelve, "What we fail to realize is our total inability to form a true partnership with another human being."*

Through the sessions with the psychiatrist, and another intensive inventory process, I was able to discern that, like Bill W., I have deep abandonment issues. I had always known that as her firstborn I had never bonded with Mother. I never felt safe with her, or trusted her, either as a child or later as a teenager and young adult. I recall, even as a young child, that whenever she hugged me the skin on the back of my neck would crawl, and I would feel smothered. I was able to discern that when a woman threatened to leave me, it would trigger a misplaced rage against Mother that I would project onto my partner. At any cost, I felt compelled to prevent the woman from leaving. Not nice, not pretty, but there it was.

The psychiatrist also suggested I drink only decaf coffee. For several years prior to the violence with Jill, I was drinking on average 10-15 triple-shot venti, or 20-ounce, cups of caffeinated lattes daily, which I made with my own Starbucks latte machine. The doctor explained that drinking that much caffeine was like giving myself a daily low-dose of crystal-meth! I switched to mostly drinking herbal tea.

Within a couple of weeks, Jill and I were able to respectfully and easily develop a comfortable routine of living separate lives within our home and AA communities. She focused on meetings in Seaside, and I focused on recovery in Portland. We were able to civilly communicate with each other, sharing household chores and caring for our animal friends, while enjoying movies and favorite TV shows together.

The estranged relationship with Jill lasted through the spring and summer, during which time she went through an incredible healing process, deeper than perhaps ever before. She was able to see that she needed the catalyst of my raging and violent behavior to break through her denial, so she could take action to heal herself. She was able to firmly establish her boundaries with me and to seek the help to assist her through the traumas I re-triggered. I also proved to myself, like I did with Sara, that despite my deepest fears I am, indeed, capable of sustaining a committed love relationship by focusing on changing what I can within myself and letting my partner have the freedom to explore whatever she needed to do for herself.

―――――――

From late August to October, 2014, I did another six-week camping and drive-around-the-US trip, visiting family and friends in my Miata. For the week I was in Maryland visiting my daughters and grandchildren, Jill flew out and spent the week with us. We had a splendid week with family, taking day-trips to visit Aberdeen Proving Ground and go sight-seeing in Washington, DC. In a very real sense, we experienced a second honeymoon visit to DC, much deeper and realer than our first honeymoon trip in 2010. Our time together in Maryland with family was a successful test-case to see if her PTSD from my PTSD had been alleviated to the point where she could trust being with me again. Also, during the first week of October several classmates and I from our 1961 high school class met for a couple of days down in New Orleans. Jill again flew to New Orleans for those couple of days, and we enjoyed some wonderful food and the Big Easy with my classmates.

―――――――

For the next couple of years, Jill and I focused our recovery efforts in Portland, rather than in the small-town environs of Seaside. We loved living in Seaside, but after a year we experienced that Seasiders were no more our tribe than had been the folks in Bandon and Coos Bay. They were not perhaps as egregiously cultish as we experienced AA members in southern Oregon to be, but they were shunning and shaming just the same. In subtle and not-so-subtle ways they made sure to let us know that we were outsiders. We were much more comfortable with the city folk in Portland.

At least two or three times a week, either myself, or both of us, would take the gorgeous drive over the coastal mountain range into Portland, either to attend meetings or to browse around Powell's bookstore, which we both loved. Sadly, during this period we had to put down both of our cats, Sir Gerry and Lady Charlotte, who had come with us from Woodstock, NY. To replace them, we got Savannah (an expensive mix of a domestic cat and a serval cat from the African plains) from a breeder, and Elsa from the Astoria Animal Shelter.

During March of 2015, driving back to Seaside after another drive-around, I visited friends in Bandon, OR, Jan and Ken, who had two lovely Afghan Hounds, with whom I fell totally in love. Jill and I were able to find on the Internet a full-blooded, black rescue Afghan Hound in a small town between Seaside and Portland, whom we adopted. Her name is Keira, which in Gaelic means dark-haired. After several weeks she became the fifth loving member of our family of two humans, two cats and her.

———

In October of 2015, Jill and I took a long trip back east. We flew into Chicago's Midway airport where we rented a car so we could visit friends and family throughout the northeast. After visiting friends in Toledo, we spent a couple of days visiting the AA sights in Akron and the National Football Hall of Fame in Canton. We then spent a lovely night in a bed and breakfast on the Canadian side of Niagara Falls on the way to visit friends and attend secular AA meetings in Toronto, where I celebrated my 43rd sober anniversary. Next, we drove to Maryland for several days to visit our daughters and grandchildren.

We then went to New York City for three days. On the first night there, I had what I thought was another COPD attack. I went to the Manhattan VA Hospital emergency room, where I got a breathing treatment. The next day, a warm Indian summer day, I walked around Manhattan some five or six miles and felt fine. The next day, however, it was rainy and colder. I got chilled and felt a cold coming on. The next morning just before we were to check out of our hotel, I had a panic attack and couldn't breath. A taxi rushed us back down to the VA emergency room. There, I was admitted to the cardiac unit with severe congestive heart failure. Over the next several days, I lost some 15 pounds of excess water. What I thought had been progressing COPD the previous several months was instead the slow build-up of excess fluid from congestive heart failure. The emergency room doctor told me that had I not gotten treatment within the next several hours, vital organs would have begun shutting down, leading ultimately to my demise.

For the next several days, I underwent all sorts of tests and procedures to rule out coronary blockages and to stabilize the atrial fibrillation I had experienced checking out of the hotel. I was discharged on the afternoon of Wednesday, November 5th, two days before the start of the 50th Anniversary celebration of my 1965 graduation class from Xavier University. I was successfully reunited with many members of my graduating class and shared cherished memories of our times together at Xavier 50 years earlier. I was most grateful and comfortable to be true to myself, wearing casual clothes instead of a suit and tie for all the festivities—no, I did *not* attend the celebratory Mass for the Class of 1965.

On Valentines Day of 2016, John Albert O'Brien died. He had been my oldest and dearest friend since the seventh grade, when I met him at St. Richard's school after I converted to Catholicism. He had suffered from cardiac, kidney and other problems, after surviving several strokes during the previous ten years. I was so grateful I had been able to spend a lovely afternoon with him the previous October when Jill and I were visiting family in Maryland. We sat out on his sunny patio and watched birds chirping and flying around a bird feeder, as we shared old memories from our long-gone youth.

I can no longer deny the reality that I am moving through the final laps of the winter of my long and most gifted life.

One Final Move

Due to severe childhood religious and physical abuse she experienced from her mother, Jill chose not go back to Illinois when her mother was dying from cancer in the spring of 2012. During the intensive inventory and amends making process with the ACA Red Book, however, she made peace with her mother's memory. She also re-established contact with her father, whom we planned to visit during our trip back east in the late fall of 2015. In September of 2015, however, Jill found out that her father had died the previous June, when her brother sent her legal documents to sign regarding the estate.

In March of 2016, Jill drove back to Wenona, IL to sign the requisite papers to probate the estate. We made a decision to take possession of her childhood home, which would require us to move two-thirds of the way back across the country. Though we both would miss the splendor of the Pacific Northwest, and the many friends in secular AA we had made in Oregon, it was worth it to be within a days drive of family and friends on the east coast and in Mississippi.

On May 24, 2016, Jill and her friend Terie started the four-day trip to Wenona in another U-Haul truck packed to the gills with most of our belongings. Guy, another dear, sober friend from Seaside, followed the truck in Jill's VW convertible with the two cats, Savannah and Elsa. Several weeks later, after I finished cleaning the house and turned it over to the landlord, I followed in my car with Keira, and the rest of our belongings. Here's a journal entry from July 4, 2016, after I had gotten settled into our new house.

> *Well, Pietro, a whole new life has begun, and I sit here at my new office space, looking out at the verdant green of grass, trees, and the ubiquitous cornfields of Illinois in the tiny 1,000 person town of Wenona with birds a-flying and the red water pump standing tall. I am quite content, quite grateful, quite fulfilled with all the mysterious ups and downs of my long, strange trip of a life that continues to be just what it is, sometimes awful, such as I've been experiencing with the respiratory condition the last several days, other times, quite simply marvelous and glorious, and I am so grateful for all of it.*
>
> *I can spend the rest of my days quite comfortably here, reading and writing, with the ability to visit New York, Toronto, Maryland, Cincinnati and Jackson so readily, all no more than a long day's drive away. It just feels right, and the move has fallen into place in ways we could not have imagined—the easiest one I've made of the some fifteen or so major moves I've made since 2001. And Jill is so excited about discovering the Lady Carpenter-Plumber-Electrician within to transform her childhood home, where she experienced so much terror, into her wildest dreams. I am so grateful to be able to support her in this endeavor.*

So, here we are in Wenona, IL, where I trust we'll live for the rest of our days …

Chapter 17: Sober Work

Sigmund Freud, one of the founders of modern psychology, is famously quoted to proclaim that "Love and work are the cornerstones of our humanity." In the previous four chapters, I've explicated, in perhaps way too much extraneous detail, the adventurous, at times most tortuous, endeavors I pursued while seeking Freud's factor of love in recovery. This chapter will delve into how I have experienced Freud's other factor, my work life throughout recovery.

I described in Part One how I flunked out of two graduate school programs: The first one in English at Xavier University and, secondly, the MFA directing program at Catholic University. Both failures were due to my virulent and self-destructive addiction to alcohol and drugs. For years, during my late 20s and early 30s, I would quip that I was a jack of several trades, master of none. I worked numerous odd jobs, on a mostly free lance or part time basis, in publishing, teaching English as a Second Language, public relations and advertising, as well as in the theatre. During a large portion of this time, my primary source of income was from extended New York State unemployment benefits as a result of the 1973 oil embargo.

Throughout my recovery, I've pursued two primary career paths, first the theatre and then working in the field of addiction treatment. In addition, I've devoted as much time and energy to being an activist for peace with justice, as if I were pursuing a third career path. In the next chapter, I'll relate my endeavors as an activist for peace with justice, which included being a paid volunteer, when I lived for two years as an ex-patriot in Sri Lanka.

The Theatre

For much of the first 33 years of my life, I was active in pursuing a life in the theatre. In Part One, I described the theatre experiences I pursued during high school, while attending college at Xavier University, and while studying for an MFA program in directing at Catholic University prior to getting sober. I also described the first theatre work I did after moving to New York City in May of 1972 during my last months of active addiction, designing a set for an Off-off Broadway workshop production.

This section will describe the theatre work I pursued during the first several years of recovery in New York City.

During my second year sober, I became acquainted with Jerry Brody, an acting teacher and Off-off Broadway director. Together with several other actors and actresses, who were also sober in AA, we started an Actor's Equity Showcase theatre company. It was named Walden Theatre, the name of the private high school on the Upper Westside where the theatre was located. Jerry was the Artistic Director, and I was Executive Director, reprising the role I had played at the Xavier Masque Society, serving as the company producer. Our first production was Eugene O'Neill's *Anna Christie*. It was during this production that I became romantically involved with Barbara. One of the benefits of producing a theatre company at the school was that we involved the students as apprentices in our productions. We mentored them, providing them with hands-on experience in all aspects of the theatre arts. As opening night approached, those of us in recovery became obsessively immersed in day and night rehearsing. We stopped going to meetings, and the result was that we all went on a dry drunk together. It's a wonder none of us relapsed!

I directed the second production, *Whispers on the Wind*, a whimsical musical with a cast of two women and three men about growing up in the suburbs and moving to the City to pursue successful careers. It was panned by the Village Voice as being a mere musical review, not really true *the-A-ta*, worthy of the noble profession of drama. During the third production, *Dark of the Moon*, the administration of the school fired Jerry and myself, replacing us with two younger people in the company who were in their mid-20s. The principle and his staff felt they were more appropriate to mentor and relate with high school students. Jerry was in his late-30s and I was in my early-30s—it was my first and only experience with ageism.

A month or two later, through a friend, Larry, I got involved with the Gene Frankel Theatre Workshop for several months. Frankel was one of the leading practitioners of experimental theatre, including the theatre of the absurd, and was one of the most renown founders of Off-Broadway theatre in New York during the 1950s and 1960s. He had several successful Broadway productions as well. Many of his productions had socially conscious themes of civil rights for African Americans, Native Americans and women. When Larry and I worked for him, he experimented with integrating video into stage productions. This was the basis of the last Broadway production he directed, *The Night That Made America Famous*, a musical review of the popular songs of Harry Chapin.

Chapin's songs were poignant character studies with socially conscious themes. Unfortunately this production was short-lived, closing a run of only 47 performances. Perhaps it too was not true *the-A-ta!*

Larry and I worked together as assistants to Mr. Frankel, helping him with the video equipment and stage-managing student video productions. Larry, his fiancée, a writer for the television soap, *Days of Our Lives*, and I spent a delightful Christmas Day of 1975 with Mr. Frankel and his family in their Washington Square Village apartment home. Shortly thereafter, however, in mid-January, I resigned from the Gene Frankel Theatre Workshop to take my first full-time job as an alcoholism counselor in what evolved to become a 30-year career in the field of addiction treatment.

Though my New York theatrical career was rather short-lived and not very commercially successful, I am immensely grateful for the experiences I had and the many talented theater people, some notable such as Gene Frankel, that I knew and with whom I worked.

A career in Addiction Treatment

In the fall of 1975, while working at the Gene Frankel Theatre, I took an orientation course in alcoholism counseling. I was following the seed that had been planted by a couple of AA qualifications I heard during the first year of recovery. The course was taught by the New York Federation of Addiction Counselors, which I was able to join upon successful completion of the several week course. Through NYFAC, I applied for and was hired as a "para-professional" counselor at the Beth Israel Hospital Alcoholism Outpatient clinic program at 50 Cooper Square, the same program where I had been a client during the first year of my recovery.

The Beth Israel Addiction program was one of the first programs established as a result of legislation promulgated in 1970 by Harold Hughes, a Senator from Iowa, who was in recovery from alcoholism. The legislation provided funding for treatment of alcohol and drug addicts. It established the federal authorities for managing addiction, the National Institute of Alcoholism and Alcohol Abuse and the National Institute of Drug Abuse.

At this time in New York, there was strict separation of treatment services for alcoholics and drug addicts. The alcoholism clinic was on the fifth floor and the drug clinic, where methadone was dispensed, was on the 2nd floor. There was no coordination between the two clinics. We were severely cautioned not to have any discussions with staff or clients of the drug clinic, and they were just as reticent to deal with those of us treating alcoholism. A major reason for this was that using alcohol was legal, whereas the use of drugs was not. The thinking at the time was also that addiction to alcoholism and addiction to drugs were two essentially separate and different diseases.

Since I've been in the field of addiction treatment, I've come to believe that addicts are not so much addicted to specific substances or behaviors. Instead, we are addicted to the state of getting high and escaping reality. Push comes to shove, we will use any substance, or behavior, to get high and to escape. Over the years, though sober from my primary drug of addiction, the liquid, legal drug, Colt .45, I have obsessively and compulsively used other substances, such as nicotine and caffeine, and other behaviors, such as exercise and browsing the Internet, meditation even, to escape and to get high. Around some recovery rooms, this is described as "switching seats on the Titanic."

There was a period during the late 1970s and early 1980s, when I would on occasion use marijuana recreationally. However, I never became addicted to it like I did with Colt .45 and other alcoholic beverages. Though perhaps this might sound like denial, I could always take it or leave it. Nevertheless, on one occasion in 1982 or 1983, after smoking a couple of joints, I got into as depressed and suicidal a state as ever I had experienced numerous times when drunk. I've never used marijuana again. I had not gotten sober from my primary drug of addiction, Colt. 45, to experience suicidal despair using another potentially addictive substance. I also was never tempted to snort or smoke cocaine, even though at times Sara and I went to night clubs where its use was prevalent.

Using marijuana and prescribed mood-altering pain medications was a fairly common practice among many New York City AA members in good standing, including staff members at the General Service Office. In 1987, AA's General Service Conference promulgated the "Blue Card," which makes definitive statements regarding AA's Singleness of Purpose. The Blue Card has a statement on one side for closed meetings and on the other side for open meetings. In essence, both statements reiterate that this is an AA meeting in which it is suggested that all discussion be confined to the discussion of the use of alcohol only.

I have always disagreed with the Blue Card statements, which discourage discussion during AA meetings of one's use of other other addictive substances, even at open meetings. After all, Dr. Bob, one of AA's two co-founders, extensively used self-prescribed sedative hypnotics. Further, on page 22 of the Big Book, there is this description of some alcoholics:

> *As matters grow worse, he begins to use a combination of high-powered sedative and liquor to quiet his nerves so he can work ... Perhaps he goes to a doctor who gives him morphine or some sedative with which to taper off.*

Research during the late 1980s indicated that during the process of metabolizing either alcohol or drugs there is created the same byproduct, THIQ, in the brain. This suggests that alcoholism and drug addiction derive from a common neurological process. Continuing research has demonstrated that there are considerably more commonalities than differences between those addicted to alcohol and those addicted to other drugs. A substantial number of addicts are polyaddicted. All addictive drugs, and for that matter any addictive behavior, share this identical essential experience—a pleasurable high brought about due to spiking dopamine in the brain's reward system. At times at meetings I've quipped that essentially I am a dopamine junkie. I can use any substance or behavior to get high and to escape.

In 2003, when I lived in Arizona, I was at a meeting where a crusty oldtimer rudely interrupted a young Native American woman, a newcomer, who was speaking about how terrible her use of alcohol and methamphetamine was. "Miss, this is a meeting of Alcoholics Anonymous. We don't talk about using drugs here." The woman broke down in sobs and quickly left the room. I was appalled and rushed outside to speak with her. She thanked me, but I never saw her again at an AA meeting. How many folks, especially younger persons, are shunned out of the rooms of AA by such prejudiced sentiments?

My belief about this is that many caucasian members of AA, by far the majority of AA's membership, have biased and prejudiced views about addicts who use illegal substances. White folks may have experienced horrible things due to their drinking, but at least they were not criminals! Of course, with current stringent impaired driving laws this has somewhat changed over the past twenty years, but overall caucasians are still less likely to be imprisoned than those of other races for drinking and drug-related criminal offenses. It's a reality that the vast majority of people in prison facilities are non-caucasian. African Americans, Hispanics, and

Native Americans are jailed at a much higher percentage than their fraction of the North American population. AA's own periodic membership surveys demonstrate that our Fellowship is underrepresented by non-caucasian people.

At the Beth Israel Alcoholism Clinic, there were two distinct classes of staff: First, there were "para-professionals," those such as myself, who were in 12-step recovery and who had, at a minimum, some kind of basic orientation training in treating addiction, such as the NYFAC course I had taken. Secondly, there were professionals, those with masters, PhD or MD levels of education and credentials in one of the mental health professions, such as social workers, psychologists, nurses, medical doctors, and psychiatrists. Most likely professionals during the 1970s were *not* members of a 12-step recovery program. One of the people who interviewed me for the "paraprofessional" job had known me when I was a client at the clinic during my first year of recovery. She was now the clinical director. After I got the job, I suggested to her that I had been hired primarily because it was good PR for the clinic to hire someone who had previously been a client. She vehemently denied this, but I always kidded her about it.

As an entry-level alcoholism counselor, I had a caseload of some 75 or so men and one woman, the alcoholic partner of one of the men on my caseload. They, like most of my clients, lived in substandard housing on the Bowery, until recently one of the most notorious and largest skid-rows in North America. Beth Israel Hospital also operated a large detox facility, the Bernstein Clinic, where there were several floors for detoxing patients addicted to drugs and two floors devoted to detoxing patients addicted to alcohol. Many of the clients on my caseload would have several admissions for week-long detox treatment during the year paid by Medicaid.

The job at 50 Cooper Square Beth Israel outpatient clinic was a most discouraging and disheartening job. It provided at best mere bandaid solutions to a population of the most needy and impoverished individuals in our society. Many of them were in the late stages of their addictive disease. One of my clients had had two open heart surgeries, but couldn't get Social Security Disability payments because he kept losing his medical files. He would also miss scheduled appointments with the Social

Security office due to his drinking. I sometimes quipped I worked for one of the most prestigious Medicaid Mills on the planet.

Most of my clients' primary source of income was welfare, or Home Relief as it was then called. Home Relief provided meager funds for housing in flop houses or substandard tenement apartments in public housing, like the one I lived in with Joe and John on E. 11th Street during my first year of getting sober. Arbitrarily, the city of New York would send out notices to ten percent of the persons on the welfare rolls. They would be informed that their checks would be stopped unless they made a scheduled appointment at the cavernous and highly disorganized Welfare Offices on 14th Street.

Often my clients, severely disabled from alcoholism and other mental disorders, as well as severe physical health conditions, would fail to keep these appointments. Consequently, they would lose their housing allowance. This resulted in them and their scant belongings being kicked out on the mean streets of the Bowery again. A good portion of my job entailed assisting them to get back on the Home Relief rolls, a daunting task that often required obtaining requisite documentation again, such as Social Security cards. I came to accept that though very few of my clients consistently remained sober, I was helping them and their quality of life immensely by getting them back on the rolls of Home Relief.

One very pleasant assignment I had at the clinic was escorting members of a "cultural group" to a local movie theatre to see a first-run movie. The clinic paid for tickets and popcorn. We would see a movie and afterwards have a group discussion about it back at the clinic. One of the movies I fondly recall having seen with the cultural group was Peter Sellers in the hilarious farce, *The Pink Panther Strikes Again*.

―――――

Let me describe my very first client at the clinic. Harry was a highly educated and most articulate gentleman with a photographic memory. He had grown up in one of the wealthiest, most privileged communities, Sands Point, on the North Shore of Long Island. His grandfather had founded one of Wall Street's most reputable bond trading houses and had built a mansion on what was known as the Gold Coast of Long Island. Harry had an MBA from Harvard and had been a successful stock broker before his alcohol addiction spiraled him down to living and working in the Bowery. He supported himself by doing basic bookkeeping work for temporary employment agencies. These agencies provided workers from the Bowery to the hotels and ski resorts in the Catskill Mountains. A number of my clients would dry out for a period of time, so they could go to the Catskills and work for a number of months to save up for their next bender. They would pick up the first drink, get drunk again, and return to the Bowery, repeating this cycle over and over again.

Often, whenever Harry drank, he would end up in an emergency room, getting stitches, or casts on his limbs, for falling off barstools, or from passing out drunk on the streets. During the year-and-a-half he was on my caseload, I visited him in the hospital on three different occasions. His face was a mishmash of scar tissue. On a wintry day in late December, I had my last counseling session with Harry. His left arm was in a cast, and he had a black eye and a broken nose that he had sustained from falling off another barstool. The next to last thing I said to him, after looking at him with a deep sigh, was, "Harry, it would be kinder if you put a bullet through your head."

With downcast eyes, he mumbled, "I know, Tom, I know."

The session over, we stood up, and I hugged him, whispering in his ear, "Harry, get sober, you deserve to get sober."

After several months working at the clinic, it was obvious that there was little opportunity for advancement as a "para-professional" alcoholism counselor. Aneen, another of my romantic relationships in early recovery, who had an internship at the clinic as part of her coursework for the Columbia School of Social Work, suggested I start taking courses for a social work degree, which I did in September of 1977. It was a most opportune time for me, a male and a Vietnam Veteran to boot, to be pursuing a typical woman's professional degree. I was advised by Columbia's admissions office to apply for a National Institutes of Mental Health fellowship to attend social work school full time. I applied and was awarded one, so I was able to begin full-time coursework at Columbia in January of 1977. I chose a concentration of studies in psychiatric social work. Like many of my fellow students, I wanted to pursue clinical work with an MSW, perhaps even start a private practice someday. The Fellowship paid for all tuition costs and books, and it provided me with a generous monthly stipend for a living allowance. Along with my veterans benefits, I was making more money than I had ever made previously.

At the time, Columbia had a reputation for being a traditional and conservative graduate school, whose clinical program was primarily based on the psychoanalytic theories of Freud. I was aware that I could have gotten a more progressive, holistically-oriented social work course at the Hunter College School of Social Work, which is part of the City University of New York. I was much more drawn to the thinking of Jung than I was to Freud. However, I rationalized that since Columbia was a renown Ivy league university that my prospects for employment would be considerably better going to Columbia than if I went to Hunter College, which was well known only within the New York City area. So, I continued at the Columbia University School of Social Work for my masters degree.

―――――

One of the worse days I ever experienced sober occurred when I was interviewed for my first field placement assignment for a social work clinical internship. Since I was a Vietnam Veteran and in recovery from addiction, I eagerly sought an interview with the Veterans Administration for a field placement with one of the several VA mental health clinics in the New York City area. The person who interviewed me was a thin, dark-haired gentleman with thick eye glasses, probably a psychologist, who chain-smoked, in his office in the VA Central Office Building, a tall monolithic building on 7th Avenue. It was most daunting inside, and I got lost several times, walking through the endless maze of grim and crowded hallways, brightly lit in bureaucratic fluorescent shine. Waiting rooms were crowded, filled with disgruntled veterans, who smoked and grumbled about the lousy services they were getting. I was about 10-minutes late for the interview.

The interviewer was not pleased and gruffly asked me why I wanted to work with Vets, especially Vietnam Vets, as I had answered on the Screening Form. I honestly answered him, relating that since I was a veteran from Vietnam, I could relate with them. Perhaps I could help them overcome their difficulties since I was familiar with what they had experienced. What a huge mistake this was, since he held a fervent classical psychoanalytic ideology that emphasizes transference and counter-transference during the therapeutic process.

The rest of the "interview" devolved into a stern and degrading tongue-lashing about how sick and naive I was. It was as severe as any I received in boot camp from a DI, a drill instructor. He screamed at me about what harm I might do to unsuspecting patients. He asserted that it was highly unethical for me to foist my delusions of god-given powers on mentally sick veteran patients. He strongly suggested I get into intensive, five-day a week psychoanalysis, so I could be cured of my self-centered, narcissistic and delusional neuroses before I tried to treat others. He threatened to call Columbia telling the school of social work that I was most unworthy to be in professional training.

Let me digress here to note that during the 1970s there was no recognized diagnostic category for Post Traumatic Stress Disorder (PTSD), only for an acute stress disorder, lasting no more than three months after one experienced a traumatic event. If stress-related symptoms occurred longer than this, it was presumed to be due to some underlying psychosis, most likely schizophrenia. In 1979, after a decade of advocacy by VVAW and their friendly mental health professional associates, DSM III recognized a very narrow diagnosis of PTSD. Up until then many veterans avoided VA mental health services like the plague. Otherwise, if they mentioned disturbing symptoms from their Vietnam experience, they would be misdiagnosed as schizophrenic and placed on thorazine or other major tranquilizers. Vets learned to assiduously avoid becoming heavily medicated zombies with the thorazine shuffle.

I was shaken to the core by this "interview" experience. When it was over, I stumbled through the halls of the VA in a fog and went across 7th Avenue to the nearest pay phone. There, I frantically called Gloria, a former lover, now one of my closest friends in recovery. She gave me sage advice: Don't drink and go to a meeting. I did, and like everything else, this acute stress episode, too, came to pass ...

Instead of a VA facility, my first field placement was at the US Public Health Hospital on Staten Island, which provided health services to merchant marines and hardship cases. One client, a sailor from WW II, had survived two ships being torpedoed out from under him while he was delivering supplies to Europe. Over several weeks I watched him slowly die from alcoholic cirrhosis of the liver, a horribly painful way to die.

Another client, a devoted family man with several young children, had ALS, Lou Gehrig's disease, but no health insurance. He also slowly and painfully died. He was severely depressed to the point of despair. He could not accept that the god of his devout Catholic faith had abandoned him to this fate. A successful self-employed business man in his early forties, I sat with him for several of his last hours while he was unconscious and experiencing episodes of Cheyenne-Stokes respiration during the final stages of his dying. He did not go gentle into that good night.

My second year field placement was at St. Luke's Hospital Psychiatric Emergency Room up in Morningside Heights near Columbia. There, I once tried to calm down a 14 year old who had been admitted in a severe delusional state from the powerful anesthetic, PCP, known on the streets as Angel Dust. He Had been strapped down to a hospital gurney. In a state of raging delirium and seizures, he turned the heavy gurney over on its side, breaking his arm. Strange, he's the only one of my clients during my second year of full-time study that I recall. Ah, the fickleness of memory.

During my two years of study at Columbia, I also had a couple of part-time counseling jobs to add to my more than sufficient income. One of them was in a hospital-based inpatient rehab unit for addiction in Manhattan that was directed by a woman in recovery. Several years later I would be hired to work for her full time on Long Island. A serendipitous thing happened while I was working for this program. One of the other part-time staff members was Glen, the individual who in November of 1972 had given me my first AA meeting list. I thanked him profusely for being an integral reason for me getting and staying sober.

I was very active on the Board of Directors for NYFAC helping to organize lobbying efforts up in the state capital of Albany. There we advocated for legislative support for increased money for addiction treatment services and for the creation of the NYS Office of Alcoholism and Substance Abuse Services to manage and oversee treatment services for addiction. This happened as a result of legislation promulgated by Governor Hugh Carey.

———

Due to my active involvement in NYFAC, I was offered an upper-mid-level management job in the newly formed agency as the coordinator for counselor credentialing. In May of 1979, after graduating with the MSW from Columbia, I gave up my New York City apartment and moved to Albany. For the next couple of years or so, I developed the New York standard for licensing addiction counselors. I travelled throughout New York State to coordinate the testing and credentialing process for some 300 addiction counselors, myself included. We were now fully recognized as integral "professional" members of the treatment team for the provision of addiction treatment services. We were no longer mere para-professional staff.

On occasion during my two years in social work school, I would think back upon the last session I had with Harry, about which I would critically judge and berate myself. What in the world kind of a treatment intervention had that been? Suggesting to a client that he kill himself? Within the first several weeks after moving to Albany, I went to a noon AA meeting. There, sitting across the room, was none other than my former client Harry. Dressed in a business suit and tie, he looked ten years younger than he had looked when we had our last session. We exchanged business cards and agreed to have lunch the following week.

When we met, he related that after our last session he realized he was on a fast downward track to nowhere good. He determined that he had to get out of New York City in order to get sober. He moved to Albany where he completed a longterm treatment program. After a year, he was able to get back into his profession as a financial adviser.

He also related something we had never previously discussed during our sessions together at the outpatient clinic. He was a 1963 graduate of the West Point Academy and served as a company commander with the 1st Calvary Division (Air Mobile) in Vietnam. He had survived the brutal battle in the Ia Drang valley, the first major engagement of US Armed Forces with regular army units of the North Vietnamese Army. A number of the men in his company had been killed when they were ambushed. He felt responsible for their deaths and suffered from survivor guilt. Instead of making a career in the Army, he resigned his commission in 1968 and got his MBA at Harvard instead.

Thereafter, his rapid descent into late-stage alcoholism was fueled by his self-medicating with alcohol so he could fall asleep and forget his traumatic battlefield experiences. His photographic memory flooded him with these memories in agonizing detail. When we spoke, he related he had chosen to focus upon the last thing I said to him, about how he deserved to get sober. He heartily thanked me for saying this to him. It had given him hope that he too could recover, not only from alcoholism, but from Vietnam.

I worked in Albany as a bureaucrat in the addiction field for the next three years, two of which I was the Coordinator of counselor credentialing.

During this time Sara and I had our son and got married. She graduated from a two-year degree program as a registered nurse. During my third year, despite having the highest score on a civil service exam for mid-level managers, I was demoted to a back office job with a significantly reduced salary. This happened as a result of the credentialing process being outsourced to NYFAC. I also had a negative reputation for not being a loyal team player.

As a bureaucrat, I learned that there are two sets of loyalties. The first set of loyalties is to the goals of the mission and the second set of loyalties are to the people who are in charge of carrying out the mission. Often these two sets of loyalties are in direct conflict with each other. As a recovering addict to alcohol, I always chose to advocate for and to act in accordance with the first set of loyalties, to the mission of helping alcohol and drug addicts.

During my final year in Albany, I essentially had a no-show job and became close friends with another Vietnam Veteran, Vince. We did some of the seminal research and initial writing about the strong correlation between PTSD among veterans from Vietnam and addiction. Knowing about Harry's story was instrumental in motivating me to write about this correlation.

―――――

Vince was hired by the Albany Vet Center. There he led a long term Sober Vets group for addicted veterans who experience difficulties adjusting after their service in Vietnam. He developed a two-phase group treatment model for Vietnam veterans who were addicted to alcohol and drugs. I called Harry and suggested he take part in the Sober Vets group but he told me he was moving back to his family estate on Long Island because he had gotten a lucrative job on Wall Street. Like so many others, clients as well as lovers, I lost touch with him.

One of the concepts we wrote about, knowing Harry's story and my own, was that we veterans had a form of denial that differed greatly from the usual addict's denial. Harry and I did not deny that we were addicted to alcohol. Quite the contrary, we readily accepted that whenever we drank, not only did our lives become unmanageable, they often also became unbearable. Nevertheless we continued to drink because it gave us some modicum of relief some of the time. If nothing else, we often passed out. Instead of denying that we were addicts, we denied the hope that we deserved and indeed could recover. The last thing I said to him gave Harry a sliver of hope that maybe he deserved to recover.

Throughout the 80s and 90s, Vince and I did workshops and seminars on the correlation of PTSD and addiction throughout the VA Vet Center program and with addiction treatment centers across the US. We presented workshops at a number of national conferences dealing with addiction. We were integrally involved with the New York State Commission for the Readjustment of Vietnam Veterans, me as a Commission member and Vince as a staff member. There, we organized the first national conference that specifically dealt with the correlation of addiction and PTSD.

We published two articles about this correlation, one in the monthly magazine of Vietnam Veterans of America and the other in the *Alcoholism Treatment* Quarterly, which included detailed discussion of the two-phase treatment group model. In addition, for a number of years we taught a course about the correlation at the Rutgers University School of Addiction Studies.

In the summer of 1983, partially due to our missing the ocean and hating the long and very frigid Albany winters, Sara and I decided to move back to Long Island. I gave up my permanent New York State civil service job, which would have given me a most comfortable retirement, and I took a job as the director for one of the first Intensive Outpatient Programs licensed in New York State, located in Garden City, NY.

Sara and I with our three children, our son and her two daughters from her marriage to Dave, moved to the upscale bedroom community of Garden City, where we rented a house. Sara, who was licensed as a registered nurse, got a job at a nearby hospital. After working in Garden City for a year, I was fired because I resisted a major marketing strategy of the co-owner. He had sold his very successful heating oil business on Long Island to bankroll the facility. He urged me to offer kickbacks to union representatives and companies for referring clients to the program. I believed this was unethical as well as being illegal, but it's the way much of business in New York is done.

After months of working several part-time jobs, I was hired as the director of a Hazelden-model Intensive Outpatient Program in New York City. In 1949 Hazelden had pioneered the establishment of 30-day inpatient rehabilitation programs for addiction in Center City, MN. It was started by two sober members of AA at the farmhouse of one of the founders. The first group sessions were held in the den of one of their wives, Hazel. Thus the name of their treatment facility became Hazelden.

The Hazelden program was so successful that it became the foundation of what came to be referred to as the Minnesota Model of Chemical Dependency Treatment throughout North America. The Minnesota-model of treatment was initially based on the following three basic principles:

1. That addiction, which they term chemical dependency, is a treatable disease,
2. That recovery requires total abstinence from all mood-altering drugs, and
3. That indoctrination in the 12 step process of AA is an integral part of treatment. To be discharged from treatment with staff approval, each patient had to complete written assignments on the first five steps.

In addition to providing addiction treatment services themselves and consulting with other treatment providers, Hazelden became one of the largest and most influential publishers in the addiction field. Though today there are many other successful approaches to addiction treatment, the Hazelden model of addiction treatment is still widely prevalent throughout North America.

In the early 1980s Hazelden pioneered the development of Intensive Outpatient Programs (IOP), since they were much more cost effective than inpatient programs. Early managed care programs for health insurance companies, which sought to cut escalating costs for addiction treatment, were an influential factor in the evolution of IOP treatment regimens. In 1984 Hazelden consulted with ICD, the International Center for Disabilities in New York City, to open a Hazelden-model IOP at it's facility on E. 24th Street across from the Manhattan VA Hospital. A major organization in the treatment of disabilities, ICD was originally founded in 1917 to assist returning veterans from WW I who were disabled after being wounded in combat. By the 1980s it had expanded its mission to provide services to any person with a disabling condition, including those with chemical dependency or addiction.

The primary consultant and the first director of the program was Larry Barnett who previously had been instrumental in developing the intensive outpatient model to treat addicts while employed by Hazelden in Minnesota. He hired me to succeed him as director of the program in 1984. Besides managing the program, I had a small caseload of clients I counseled. One was John, an atheist, who had strong objections to the god-He language of the Big Book and the Steps. I helped him understand the history of the red-underlined portion of the 12-step shade, God *as we understand him*, introducing him to Jim Burwell's story of successful recovery as an atheist. I helped him accept that the "god-bit" could be interpreted to have a number of different meanings, including group of drunk/druggies, good orderly direction, gift of desperation, or gratitude over drama. I shared with him that I was a devout agnostic with atheist leanings, who was determinedly non-religious with a particular aversion to the Christian god-He language of the Big Book. Nevertheless I had experienced many years of successful recovery in AA and suggested that, a day at a time, he could too.

My sponsor, Peter, was one of the founders of an "After Eight" group up near Lincoln Center. This group was an open AA meeting which read a preliminary statement before the AA Preamble. It stated that the speaker had to have at least eight years of recovery and that the focus of the meeting was on problems experienced during longer-term recovery. Peter and other founders were concerned about the negative impact upon newcomers if they shared honestly about continuing problems and difficulties they still encountered with several years of sobriety. They wanted a meeting where they could be open in expressing their upsets, frustrations, and difficulties living life on life's terms without being concerned on how it would affect others.

One evening I attended the Thursday meeting of After Eight where the speaker at the meeting was "Elevator Tom," the same person who had been instrumental in changing my mind about drinking again when I was coffee maker at the Young People's meeting. I hadn't seen him in fifteen or so years. After the meeting, I went up to him and thanked him profusely, relating to him the story of how he had saved me from a relapse.

As I approached the downtown subway station to Penn Station to return home to Long Island, none other than John, the atheist, whom I had counseled the year before at ICD, was coming out of the station. We chatted for several minutes; he told me that he was on the way to his home group in the neighborhood. He also profusely thanked me for helping him to accept that he could stay actively involved in AA, even though he was an atheist. It was a most serendipitous full rounding of the circle of recovery for anyone, anywhere, whether one is a believer or not.

———

After three years on the ICD job I resigned. This was partially due to the arduous commute from Long Island and also because I had severe philosophical differences with ICD management. This led to an anger/rage incident with a staff member who supervised me. I was given a deal I could not refuse: Resign with a severance package, or be fired.

For several months we lived on the severance package from ICD, plus several part-time jobs I had, and a small private practice. After several months with two partners, one being Larry who hired me at ICD, we started two Intensive Outpatient Clinics, one in Manhattan that he directed and another on the South Shore of Long Island that I directed. We treated employees of Pam Am, TWA, NY Telephone Company, NY Police Department and other Employee Assistance Programs (EAPs). In addition, we opened, or consulted with other organizations to open, thirteen additional intensive outpatient treatment programs for addicts throughout metropolitan New York City. For several years these provided us with a most comfortable income.

Sara and I evolved a private practice in an office behind the garage of our home on Long Island in Islip. I provided addiction treatment services to individuals, a sizable number of whom were also Vietnam Veterans with PTSD. As discussed in Chapter 14, Sara and I had been trained as Imago Relationship counselors, and we worked together as a couple with couples, the majority of whom were in recovery. We also presented a number of Imago relationship workshops on Long Island for recovering couples and taught a course for several years at the Rutgers Summer School for Addiction.

With the encroachment of HMOs and managed care in the New York healthcare market, we soon experienced a significant downturn in business. Whereas in 1991 I had seven or eight groups averaging 8-10 clients each, by 1994 I had just one longterm men's group. I closed an office in Lynbrook, NY and just saw individuals and couples with Sara in Islip. Regardless, for a number of years, Sara and I had a successful private practice which, along with her nursing salary, provided us with an above average middle-class income until we separated and divorced in

2001. I marketed ourselves as psych-E-therapists, not as psych-O-therapists —we dealt with healing psyches, not treating psychos!

September 11, 2001

2001 was an awful year. September 11th a most awful day.

It began like so many of that dreadful year. I awoke somewhat stiff and cramped on the futon out in what had formerly been Sara's and my consulting office. I was still quite tired and emotionally hung-over as usual, since I had stayed up until the wee hours of the morning mindlessly browsing the Internet because I couldn't sleep. For most of the past year I had been sleeping out in the office, especially since Sara's and my desperate estrangement. Our house was mostly empty. She had moved out several weeks before, taking all of her personal belongings and most of our furniture and knick knacks. The remainder I had given away or sold at a tag sale the previous weekend. The detritus of our fully separated life was scattered throughout the empty rooms. Our 22-year, mostly wonderful relationship had crashed on the shallow shoals of my unrelenting resentment, anger and rage, a pernicious holdover from war trauma I experienced in Vietnam.

The lovely faux-Victorian house wherein we had placed so many of our dreams – and most of our meager capital – had been sold. I was waiting for it to close, so I could take my half of the proceeds to pay cash for the Rialta RV I had ordered. My plan was to hit the road so I could somehow reinvent myself somewhere, at least find some way to survive a radically different way of life.

Chutney, our English standard poodle, now in my sole custody, was out doing his morning constitutional in the fenced backyard, and I had just made my first cup of latte when the phone rang. I picked it up with a flurry of hope it might be Sara. Nope, it was one of my clients, who worked for TWA airlines. He was yelling excitedly into the phone for me to turn on the TV, that a plane had just crashed into one of the tall World Trade Center towers. I turned the TV on. MSNBC came up on the screen. It wasn't the usual Don Imus show that I watched many mornings. Instead, an excited correspondent breathlessly described the chaos as a handheld camera jerkily panned horrified faces, necks craned back, looking upwards. A thick, black smudge of smoke was spewing out of one of the towers, along with flickering orange-yellow flames. In the background was a hubbub of noise and confusion and the hallmark sound of that awful day, the wailing of incessant sirens. I switched to CNN. Different commentators, same scenes. Back to MSNBC. No change. A quick scan of CBS, CNBC, ABC, local New York Stations – no different, all the same. Every channel depicted a Hollywood special effects nightmare, except it wasn't fake, it was real, way too real.

Could I pinch myself hard enough to make it go away? No, I could not, god damn it !~!~!

Suddenly a huge, horrifying, psyche-tearing roar muted the screams of frantic people, blurred their faces covered in ash, running in panic. I watched the second plane hit the other Tower. Mesmerized in terror, in a trance, I mutely switched from channel to channel for the next couple of hours, as one terror piled upon another: the strike at the Pentagon; the downing of Flight 93; the President flying all around the country in Air Force One; the collapse of one tower, then the other huge tower; the demolition-like collapse of building seven. The confusion, dismay and babbling conjecture from a plethora of talking heads and so-called experts about everything—but the truth—was appalling.

By late morning I had resoundingly driven myself crazy, flipping from one speculative, self-important suit to another, each carefully groomed for primetime to cover the biggest story of the new, now no longer idealistically hopeful, Millennium. The world was inexorably changed; history would never be the same.

I had spent much of my professional clinical life dealing with trauma. I had also been been trained in Critical Incident Stress Debriefing, so I thought I might be of some service. I had to do something. I called the Suffolk County Red Cross to volunteer. They suggested I contact nearby Nassau County Red Cross, who was mobilizing Mental Health Volunteers for Manhattan. I got copies of my New York State Social Worker license and other credentials to include with a copy of my resume.

On the 45-minute drive to the Nassau county Red Cross office in Mineola, I switched back and forth between several radio news stations— no real new news, just more talk, talk, talk. The Southern State Parkway at noontime had little traffic going in towards the City but already a near rush-hour stream of traffic was heading east. Eventually I pulled up in front of the Nassau County Red Cross building in Mineola. By late afternoon I was registered with the Red Cross as a Mental Health Volunteer and was issued a Red Cross ID badge. Someone was needed to go to LaGuardia Airport to offer support to American Airlines staff and passengers who were stranded at the terminal.

I volunteered to go. I was given instructions to contact an EAP colleague, and an additional Red Cross pass, which would authorize me to be on the Parkways and Expressways going towards Manhattan. They had been closed to the general public at the Queens border since early in the afternoon. By the time I left the Red Cross office, dusk was slowly gathering. I stopped at a Seven Eleven to get a large cup of coffee and a sandwich. Everything had a specter of daunting unreality. It was like being in an endless fog while simultaneously everything glimmered in sharp detail. It was the end of a beautiful early fall day, radiantly gorgeous, with bright, cloudless blue skies and just a hint of fall crispness in the air.

The Red Cross ID got me onto the Long Island Expressway without too much hassle. The older Nassau County policeman, however, was extremely nervous and didn't take his hand off of his service revolver, while he methodically examined my Red Cross IDs and driver's license. It was most eerie driving toward the City on the empty expressway. On the other side all lanes were packed with people escaping Manhattan. During normal rush-hour traffic, all lanes in both directions would be stop-and-creep-forward, full of traffic going home.

I was shocked to see the huge, dark plume of brownish-black smoke, silhouetted against the Manhattan skyline and leaning East over Brooklyn from far downtown. As I merged onto the Grand Central Parkway, I became aware of the screaming wail of sirens from scores of emergency vehicles—fire trucks, ambulances, military vehicles, the ugly, squat bomb squad trucks. They were speeding along the Parkway in both directions. I carefully stayed in the slow lane, hugging the shoulder as much as I could.

It was dark when I turned off the exit into LaGuardia Airport at 97th Street. I could still see the darker splotch of smoke pouring out from where the Twin Towers had been. The dark cloud now glowed ominously, a deep orange-red that cast an uncanny sheen all along the skyline from Lower Manhattan far up past Midtown. There were no stars. I was stopped by two regular City highway patrol cops at the entrance to LaGuardia. They carefully scrutinized my ID and radioed their commander for instructions. After a static-filled conversation, most of which I missed, I was brusquely motioned onto the LaGuardia Airport premises.

I was struck with how eerily strange and similar it was to the Twilight Zone movie episode about Vietnam, during which the actor, Vic Morrow, had been killed. It was like I was driving through jello in an alien time warp, but this wasn't a movie. It was all too real, just like Vietnam had been, especially during the Tet Offensive. Images from that horrible time also flitted through my consciousness. There was not a plane in the sky nor on the runways of LaGuardia. One of the busiest of our nation's airports, with planes landing or taking off every 30 or so seconds, it was completely shut down. All commercial airline traffic everywhere had been grounded indefinitely. No commercial planes were flying anywhere, since four had been hijacked that morning, which now seemed like another lifetime ago.

Overhead, I could hear the distinctive whump-whump-whump of helicopters and the screeching roar of F-16s, who were providing cover overhead. I came to a roadblock manned by National Guard troops in full battle gear. They wouldn't let me further into the main airport artery. A Captain suggested for me to try going around a back way to the American Airlines terminal.

Within a quarter of a mile of the terminal, I encountered two members, a Mutt and Jeff, of an NYPD SWAT Team, both wearing combat boots, flak jackets over khakis and dark blue NYPD baseball caps. The large, burly, silent one kept his sawed-off double-barreled shotgun aimed straight at my head during the entire ensuing encounter. The other, a diminutive, high-strung, extremely nervous fellow, like Dustin Hoffman's Ratso Rizzo character in *Midnight Cowboy*, threatened me with a truly ugly assault rifle, which I desperately hoped was loaded *and* locked.

He couldn't understand what I was doing at LaGuardia, being not at all impressed by my Red Cross ID. He was obsessed with my car, which was an old, gray '88 Pontiac clunker that had my mountain bike on the trunk bike rack. I guess, in retrospect, it makes sense that my driving around in a 13 year-old, rattletrap of a car with a bike on the back mightily concerned him. I mean, after all, what better tactic, than to pack an old car with explosives, park it somewhere, then ride off to safety on the bike and detonate the bomb by remote control.

He ordered me to step outside and carefully searched me. It was the first, and only, time I assumed the position, feet straddled with my hands on the car roof. Then he searched the car, including the trunk, finding nothing suspicious underneath the piles of trash. Nevertheless, in a loud, squeaky voice, he informed me, "No, you cannot go into the terminal, because everyone has gone home." I asked him if I could call the EAP and Nassau County Red Cross for instructions. After he carefully examined my cell phone, he allowed as I could, muttering all the while about what a royal cluster-fuck this was. The EAP didn't answer, but I got through to the Red Cross office. They told me that yes, American Airlines had moved everyone into a nearby hotel and that there was no need now for me to provide any services that night. They suggested I go home and get some rest, asking me to come back in the morning. I thanked the officers, carefully got back into the car, and headed for the entrance to the Grand Central Parkway going East.

As I approached the Parkway, another sound punctuated the steady stream of screeching sirens. It was the roar of jet engines from a large aircraft. I looked up and saw over Shea Stadium, making its final approach into La Guardia, a large four-engine aircraft heading straight towards me. I hoped it was military or some other government aircraft. Apparently it was, because I wasn't crashed into.

I made the long, lonely trip back to the empty shell of a home in Islip unscathed with no further incident, stopping to get some Chinese take-out. After feeding and walking Chutney, bone-achingly tired, I collapsed onto the futon where I had begun that awful day, at least an eon or so previously it seemed.

Little did I suspect just how much my life and all earthly existence had been changed by that awful day. Chutney cuddled up beside me on the futon, offering me some whimpering comfort, as I finally sobbed myself to fitful sleep, to end a perfectly horrible day.

The following year, when I lived in Tucson and was on an early morning run, training for another New York City marathon, I had an intrusive memory of that awful day, that I describe in this poem:

Sirens

Near the start of my long Saturday morning run
through downtown late summer Tucson
the wail of a siren splits the quiet early daylight
Another follows sharply thereafter
Yet one other adds a discordant shriek
as several fire engines screech through nearby intersection

I crumple against the Unisource Energy Tower
air collapsed from lungs
as if I had been thumped soundly in solar plexus
Keening sobs catch in throat
as I am catapulted into that dark night of 911
when the sirens wailed and wailed and wailed and wailed and wailed
and wailed and wailed and wailed and wailed and wailed
and wailed and wailed and wailed and wailed and wailed
and wailed and wailed and wailed and wailed
lights red-streaking speeding all along
both directions of Grand Central Parkway
as the blackened downtown Manhattan skyline
glowed ominously burnt orange

A Red Cross volunteer, frantically I had been dispatched
to comfort frantic relatives passengers and employees stranded in the
American Airlines Terminal of La Guardia Airport

Later as I left the airport to return home I watched mesmerized
one large four-engine military plane I had to trustingly suppose
make its final sweeping approach over darkened Shea Stadium
a darker shadow against this dark dark dark night
looming larger and larger
to aim itself straight at me

For the next three weeks, I continued serving in Lower Manhattan as a Red Cross Mental Health Volunteer. Several days I was down in the hole, the still burning, smoldering pit where the World Trade Center had been. One day I took DNA samples from the mouths of relatives of persons who were still missing. On another day I answered phones from relatives and other concerned people about missing persons, recording information about them. One of the days I spent several hours at the New York City Red Cross headquarters building talking with a distressed Vietnam Veteran who was experiencing difficulties dealing with 911. It reminded him of what mostly he had repressed for the past 35 or so years.

I also spent a couple of days out at the United Airlines terminal at Newark International Airport, the homeport of high-jacked Flight 93 that crashed in a field near Shanksville, PA. United Airlines personnel were in a state of shock, having known all of the dead members of the flight crew, realizing that fate had spared them from being on that flight. I was especially moved by one young Bronx Irish Catholic stewardess with whom I spoke. With an astonished face, lips quivering, she told me that some 20 or so members of her large extended Irish family—policemen, firefighters, EMTs, nurses, etc.—had either been killed or seriously injured during 911 and its aftermath.

The house sale finally closed on September 29th. At the closing I had a check cut for me to purchase the upscale Rialta RV waiting for me. I also booked my first return trip to Vietnam where I began the affair with Jane that I related in Chapter 15. After we returned, she persuaded me to settle down with her in Tucson, AZ. There I got my last job in the field of addictions. I was hired as the program director for a year-and-a-half at an outpatient clinic located in South Tucson that served street addicts and the severely mentally disabled. In a sense, I had returned full circle to again be providing services to the neediest, the most severely underprivileged, and the most disabled cohort of our North American society.

I supervised a clinical staff of some 20 entry-level counselors, like I had done at the Beth Israel Clinic. The staff included two nurses, two psychiatrists and ancillary support staff, including another social worker. During the first year I had two anger/rage episodes with staff members. I was put on a final warning probationary period. As a result, I began weekly counseling with a psychologist at the Tucson Vet Center program and went back on another SSRI medication.

His assessment was that I was much more severed disabled from PTSD from Vietnam than the 30 per cent rating I had been awarded in 2001. He urged me to take a leave of absence from my job so I could be admitted to an intensive, several week PTSD program at the Tucson VA Hospital. I was seriously considering this option when I was offered a job as a civilian unarmed peacekeeper. That meant moving overseas to Sri Lanka, to work for Nonviolent Peaceforce.

Chapter 18: Activism for Peace with Justice

Throughout my entire life I've been actively involved with issues of peace and social justice. I was very taken with JFK's inaugural exhortation "to ask not what your country can do for you, but what you can do for your country." An early career goal during high school was to attend Georgetown University School of Foreign Service and to serve in the US State Department. In high school my parents and I were involved actively in the civil rights struggle in Jackson, MS, which I described in Part One. I received academic scholarships to both Georgetown and Xavier, but chose to go to Xavier because its costs for room and board were considerably cheaper than that at Georgetown in Washington, DC. How different my life would have been had I attended Georgetown, eh?

I described in Chapter 3 of Part One my activism while a student at Xavier on the student council. I was an early member of SDS and organized one of the earliest Teach-Ins against the American War in Vietnam. In Chapter 7 of Part One I discussed at length my protest activities while living in Washington, DC, after I returned from Vietnam, even when I was still on active duty in the Army at Aberdeen Proving Ground.

Though I unfortunately missed out on the Dewey Canyon II protests in 1971 against the American war in Vietnam, which were organized by Vietnam Veterans Against the War (VVAW), I've been an on and off member of VVAW since the mid-1980s. In 1992, I had the following poem accepted for VVAW's 25th Anniversary Memorial publication:

25th Anniversary

Tears slowly dry
On greybearded cheeks
I feel faintly in memory again
The white-shimmering heat
Rising from the barren, barrack-pocked
Sand dunes of Cam Rahn Bay
While walking along the slatted-wood sidewalk
Back from the foul-smelling, shit-burning latrine
To the O Club with the large reel-to-reel Sony
Playing groovy sounds from across the wide sea

Already such a far time and place away
As I await the slow number-crunching
Of the 90th Replacement Battalion
To decide my assignment fate
On my very first exhausting afternoon
Twenty-five years ago yesterday
In sunny South Vietnam
Land of wonder, land of woe

All at once while daffodils ply the shadows
Of this early spring late afternoon
It's like it barely ever happened
And never can be forgotten enough

> *For those who died*
> *For all who still survive*
> *May some god somewhere*
> *Grant us much peace*

I've been an active member of Veterans for Peace since 1986, the year after it was founded, when I attended its second national convention in Portland, ME. Since then I've attended several other VFP national conventions, participated in numerous demonstrations for peace with justice wearing VFP colors and for two years served on the National Board of Directors. With a couple of other VFP members in recovery, I was instrumental in initiating a policy for there to be non-alcoholic beverages available at all VFP functions and 12-step recovery meetings at conventions.

Throughout the 1980s and 1990s, during the presidential administrations of Ronald Reagan, George H. Bush and Bill Clinton, as a member of both VVAW and VFP, I participated in numerous peaceful protests against brutal wars supported by the US government throughout Central America, during the First Persian Gulf War, and the Balkan wars. While living in Tucson during 2002 and 2003, I was actively involved in the local VFP chapter and participated in weekly protests with the progressive pro-peace community during the time after 911, leading up to and after the illegal invasion of Iraq. To my mind, the US was replicating the travesty of the Vietnam War that I had experienced as a young man with one in the Middle East during my late middle age.

Following the invasion, I became most disenchanted with USA USA USA. The initially victorious shock and awe campaign with its captivating images of massive bombing, Marines storming Baghdad's Diyala Bridge, toppling the Saddam Hussein statue, devolved into a chaotic hit and run guerrilla insurgency, replete with suicide bombers and IEDs, the signature weapon of the growing Iraqi resistance. I began to feel more and more like an alien, like a man without a country. When early news reports disclosed that Amnesty International had accused the US and its coalition partners of grievous abuses and torture of Iraqi civilians at Abu Ghraib, Muslims at Guantanamo Bay and other secret rendition sites around the world, I made a decision to become an ex-patriot. I applied for and was accepted to become one of the initial members of international Nonviolent Peaceforce, consisting of 13 civilians from some eight countries. After three weeks of training for unarmed civilian peacekeepers in a jungle monastery north of Chang Mai, Thailand, I deployed with thirteen comrades to Colombo, Sri Lanka in September of 2003.

Serving as an Unarmed Peacemaker in Sri Lanka

As a 60 year-old elder I served in a second vicious combat zone for 20 months during the vicious Sri Lankan civil war. The opposing combatants were the military forces of the majority Buddhist Sinhala government and the Hindu Tamil rebel forces of the Liberation Tigers of Tamil Eelam, the brutally notorious and vicious LTTE. As an unarmed, paid volunteer member of the civilian protection force, we fostered dialogue among parties in conflict and provided a protective presence for threatened civilians. Experience had demonstrated that opposing armed factions would cease and desist attacking civilian areas where unarmed peacekeepers from First World countries were located to avoid negative international press if any of the peacekeepers were killed or wounded.

How did I stay sober in such a hostile and stressful environment? As it turned out my boss, a Brit, was 24 years sober. At least once a month I would share an AA dinner meeting with him and a sober Aussie friend of his in Colombo, the capital of Sri Lanka. I had a monthly subscription to the AA meeting in print, the *Grapevine*. Each month I devoured the current issue, translating every mention of the G-O-D word into one of the acronyms I substituted for god or just simply Good, about which Bill was so pleased, when Buddhists asked him if this translation of God would be acceptable for them in AA during the mid-1950s.

The LTTE, founded and led by Prabhakaran, pursued a deadly civil war to establish a separate state for the minority Hindu Tamil population. The civil war began in 1983 and continued until the LTTE were eradicated in 2009. Under his leadership, the ferocious LTTE set up a rebel government that controlled vast tracts of territory along the sea coast of Eastern and Northern Sri Lanka including the predominantly Tamil cities of Batticalola, Trincomale, and Jaffna. The LTTE pioneered the use of lone suicide bombers against their Buddhist enemies. The Sri Lankan civil war was very deadly, killing an estimated 80,000-100,000 Sri Lankans between 1983 and 2009.

To complicate an already most complicated situation, the LTTE itself fragmented into two warring factions, a larger force under Prabhakaran in the northeast of Sri Lanka and a breakaway Army in the southern Batticalola Province under the command of Colonel Karuna. Karuna claimed his troops were not getting sufficient recognition and support from Prabhakaran. There are speculations that he may have been handsomely paid by the Sri Lankan government to split off his forces.

On several occasions I had to cross the Verugal River, the border between Trincomalee Province and Batticalola Province. When I did, I encountered members of the two opposing Tamil armies, consisting mostly of teenagers armed to the teeth, warily eyeing each other from bunkers along both sides of the river. The following poem describes one such river crossing, always a somewhat daunting experience:

entrenching tool

from the primitive ferry
crossing the Verugal River
the concertina-wired boundary
between two teeny-bopper armies
teeth-deep in heavy weapons

i look back at the bunker
being relentlessly hardened

i see an entrenching tool
lying in the freshly dug mud
on the verdant river bank

how quaint, been about 36 years
since i've seen one

i wonder if their bunker
will be any more effective
than ours – probably not

just so sad
so pitiful so
maddening
the always
waste of
soldiers
mostly
children

The Nonviolent Peaceforce team I was a member of was stationed in Mutur, a predominant Muslim fishing and trading village on the south shore of Trincomalee Bay. Nearby were major check-points between the Sri Lankan government forces and the LTTE government territory and a major LTTE naval facility, the home base of the Sea Tigers who smuggled weapons to the LTTE army. In addition to several Buddhist families who worked for the Sri Lankan government, Mutur also had a small community of Catholic and Protestant Christians who warily shared a small Christian community near the house where we lived.

The nearest city, Trincomalee, was a lovely 45-minute ferry ride away across the large Trincomalee Bay, one of the world's largest natural harbors. The only alternative to get to Trincomalee was a grueling six-hour trip along primitive roads around Trincomalee Bay. During World War II, invading Imperial Japanese forces were prevented to occupy the deep harbor by British, Indian and Sri Lankan military forces. They protected the strategic Trincomalee Bay from heavily fortified positions around the coast.

Team Trinco consisted of myself, a Palestinian woman with family in Israel but who lived in Brazil with her father, and a woman from Germany who got sick and was replaced by a woman from Portugal. We also had a Catholic Tamil from Mutur who served as our interpreter. During daylight hours we would take long peace walks and bicycle rides throughout the town and surrounding areas, letting our presence be known.

Much of the work we performed in Sri Lanka was helping both Buddhist and Hindu families become reunited with their young sons and daughters. Both the Sri Lankan armed forces and both LTTE factions kidnapped children, forcing them into service as child soldiers. Working in close collaboration with the United Nations High Commissioner for Refugees and Save the Children Foundation, we escorted escaped child soldiers safely back to their families.

Muslim traders in the town gladly supplied the Sri Lankan army and the two opposing factions of LTTE with contraband weapons and supplies. Despite my being an American, the Muslims in Mutur treated me with utmost courtesy and respect since I was an elder. They warmly welcomed me into their community even though the United States was invading and bombing Muslim countries throughout the Middle East and Africa.

The Mutur District experienced the most violations during the tenuous cease-fire that had been negotiated in early 2002 by the international community under a United Nations mandate. Nonviolent Peaceforce worked closely with the Sri Lanka Monitoring Mission, mostly comprised of citizens from Scandinavia, the majority, like myself, who had previously served in the military. Almost every night we would hear sporadic exchanges of small arms fire. Occasionally one side or the other would lob a random rocket or mortar shell into the other's territory.

On December 26, 2004, I survived the devastating tsunami that destroyed the coastal areas of Sri Lanka. I survived because fifteen minutes before the devastating wave destroyed the guest house where I stayed, I went for a bike ride inland to visit a 2200 year-old temple. For the rest of my tour I reverted to doing what I had done as a young US Army lieutenant during Vietnam—I escorted convoys of supplies through Sri Lankan Army and LTTE checkpoints to fishing villages deep within LTTE rebel territory. Civilians used these materials to rebuild their destroyed homes and villages. A major difference was that this time, instead of being in a gun jeep, I was unarmed.

Shortly after the tsunami, many well-meaning volunteers from the United States traveled to Sri Lanka to assist in the rebuilding efforts of devastated communities. One day, I got a frantic call from a Muslim associate in the nearby village of Kinniya. Several southern Baptists from Texas were brandishing their New Testaments in the town square, exhorting Muslims to convert to Christianity. An angry mob had formed and was threatening to stone them. Fortunately I was able to ride my motorcycle, taking a ferry across a flooded river, to get to Kinniya in time to defuse the situation. I convinced the Texans that this was not an appropriate activity for them to pursue in helping Muslim civilians to recover from the recent tsunami.

I remain most perplexed by my experiences in Sri Lanka which deepened my abhorrence for any organized religion. In Sri Lanka, as an elder, I daily lived with the vicious conflict between adherents of two of humanity's oldest religious traditions, Buddhism and Hinduism. Both traditions stretch back thousands of years through recorded history. A central tenet of both religions decrees that one be unconditionally compassionate towards all living beings. Despite this belief, however, Buddhists and Hindus have been brutally killing each other throughout recorded history.

In Colombo, I encountered a sect of Buddhist monks who dressed in camouflaged robes and brandished AK-47s. Marching through the streets of Columbo they were cheerfully devoted to killing as many Hindu Tamils as they could for Buddha. They reminded me of ardent Americans I've known, who were just as devoted to killing Commies for Christ.

Whether conversing with Catholics, Protestants, Muslims, Sinhala Buddhists or Tamil Hindus, I've never encountered such virulent extremes of prejudice and bigotry against "the other". This is somewhat surprising since I grew up in Mississippi and lived in New York City, where Irish and Italians and Hispanics and Blacks have been segregated from each other, at times viciously battling each other in gang warfare, as depicted in *Westside Story*. I am convinced that all extreme fundamentalist religious devotion, which includes hardcore atheism, manifests a major obstacle to achieving any kind of lasting peace in the world.

When I returned to the US in 2005, settling in Deer Park, NY with Lynn, I re-engaged and became very active with Veterans for Peace. During the fall of 2006, I helped organize a benefit in New York City for Lt. Ehren Watada, an Army 1st Lieutenant at Ft. Lewis, WA, who refused to deploy for combat duty in the Iraq War. His refusal was based on his strong belief that the invasion and occupation of Iraq had been illegal.

In early 2007, I was the primary facilitator for the Raheen Tyson Heighter Memorial Chapter 138 of Veterans for Peace. It was named for the first Long Island resident who was killed during the 2003 invasion of Iraq. Here's a prose poem I wrote following one of the Memorial Day demonstrations the Chapter organized and participated in with other peace activists, during the 2007 Jones Beach Air Show, one of the biggest annual events on Long Island:

The Bone

The festive crowd, underneath a sea of umbrellas, filled the beach and lined up all along the mile-wide boardwalk for the 2007 Memorial Day, Jones Beach Air Show. Vendors hawked their genocidal wares, Army, Navy, Marines, National Guard, the Coast Guard even, and of course the mighty Air Force in the midst of an extravaganza of dazzling corporate displays, GE, Northrop Grumman, United Technologies, Boeing, Raytheon, etc. etc. etc.

In giddy exaltation roars of approval catapulted skyward from the crowd of 443,000 or so souls. Manly cheers, womanly cheers, even kidly cheers greeted each display of martial skill: Army Golden Knights parachuting, Navy Seals scuba diving, National Guard Special Ops repelling from black-black Blackhawks. BUT, the most solemn, neck-craning, mouth-open-slack, vacant-eyed adulation was reserved for a huge Air Force air-e-o-plane that thunderously roared by not once nor twice but thrice to the fevered commentary of the announcer, which blared from mega-decibel loudspeakers, accompanied by a rousing, bass-pounding rendition of "Ba-a-a-ad to the Bone":

"Yessiree, Ladies and Gentlemen, the B1B Bomber, aka the Bone. The backbone of America's nuclear arsenal. Carries the largest payload of guided and unguided nuclear weaponry ever. More firepower than 200 WW II bombers. Look at that baby. Here it comes. Aren't you proud to be an American on Memorial Day? There it goes. Doesn't the sight of that thrill you? Listen to that roar. That's the sound of freedom."

Marching with a solemn little band of 40 or so Peacemakers, who commemorate the true meaning of Memorial Day, carrying a string of Code Pink ribbons, one for each fallen American soldier, some 3,452, ever mounting and thinking of the hundreds of thousands of Iraqi and Afghan civilians casually snuffed out as "collateral damage," I was disgusted and saddened by stark memories of my quagmire forty years ago in jungle.

For comic relief, to ward off a plunge into keening despair, I visualized scores, nay thousands of Raging Grannies, Code Pink ladies, Pax Christi nuns, Cindy Sheehanistas, and us aging, gray-haired, pot-

bellied Veterans for Peace, all of us falling down, writhing on the Boardwalk, gleefully moaning in frenzied ecstasies of simultaneous orgasms.

In September of 2007, I participated in a large protest on the grounds of the US Capitol in Washington, DC. Thousands of veterans from all eras attended. Some four hundred of us along with supporters were arrested, painfully flex-cuffed, and detained by the Capitol Police for fifteen or so hours with only water and stale bologna sandwiches for sustenance. After we were released, a number of us gathered at The Wall, the Vietnam Veterans Memorial, to have an impromptu memorial service for David Cline. David, who had passed the night before from Agent Orange related health conditions, was a leading Vietnam Veteran activist for some forty years, ever since his return from Vietnam, and was a former national president of VFP. He was also prominently featured in *Sir! No Sir!*, the award-winning documentary about the GI resistance movement during the latter years of the Vietnam War.

Another major protest was held a month later during the Presidential debate between McCain and Obama at Hofstra University. I wrote a deposition for a civil lawsuit that was pursued by Iraq Vet Nick Morgan, who was injured during the protest. It describes what I judged to be egregious and illegal violence perpetrated against peaceful veteran protestors and their supporters by members of the Nassau County police department.

> The mounted police charged a group of peaceful protestors who were following orders to disperse to the sidewalk opposite the entrance to Hofstra University. During the melée, Nick was trampled by one of the horses. Struck in the head, sustaining a severe cut under his right eye and a broken cheek bone, he lay unconscious on the pavement for several minutes before being revived by another Iraq Vet, Jabbar Magruder. Instead of being offered medical assistance, he was arrested and harassed with some fifteen other protestors during the long booking process. For hours he received no medical attention, despite having been knocked unconscious with a profusely bleeding head wound. He later required extensive follow-up medical treatment by the VA that required surgery to repair his broken cheekbone.

In the deposition, I included this observation:

> *The history of the United States is fraught with incidents where heavily armed police violence is used against citizens, whether to disperse protesting students and veterans, to break unions and other labor groups from seeking redress for grievances from corporations, or to prevent peacefully assembled citizens from obtaining civil and human rights.*

In March of 2008, I participated as a VFP mentor for three days during the Winter Soldier: Iraq and Afghanistan event in Washington, DC. Like had been done by Vietnam Veterans in 1971, veterans of the recent wars throughout the Middle East testified to war crimes they had witnessed and/or in which they participated.

When I moved from Long Island to Woodstock in 2009, I cut back on my activism for peace with justice. Though I still participated in the local Woodstock Chapter of VFP, I chose not to run for reelection to the national board, nor did I attend other major, nationally organized protest gatherings. In truth, I began to question whether the strategies and tactics of the peace movement were effective in the 21st Century. The National Security State had radically changed their tactics. Foremost was the creation of an all-volunteer military which eliminated the draft. With no draft, young people were not nearly as motivated as was my generation to resist the war. Less than two percent of the American population are currently directly impacted by having a son or daughter on duty with the US military.

The peace movement, on the other hand, had not changed. Essentially, we continue doing the same protest activities that in the mid-20th century had to some considerable extent worked to bring about the end of the long war in Southeast Asia, as well as improving civil rights with congressional legislation. In 2010, I marched in my last major peace protest at the White House on a cold, snowy December day and was arrested for the last time.

I focused my endeavors for peace with justice by writing poetry and participating in Warrior Writers readings in New York City, New Jersey and throughout the Hudson Valley. Here's a poem written about my never-ending experience with war:

Pleiku Jacket

Once you've experienced the horrors of war, it seems you never can escape it. "There's Always Something There to Remind Me," as the early 60s song by Burt Bacharach and Hal David goes. Yesterday morning, for example, I was dumbstruck by an unexpected sharp reminder of what I experienced in the Central Highlands of Vietnam almost 42 years ago during the brutal Tet Offensive. There I was in Bread Alone, one of the tonier of tourist-filled establishments on the main street of my new hometown in Woodstock, NY, with a bagel and a latte. As I stirred raw sugar into the latte, I glanced back at an elegant 40-something woman placing her order.

BAM-POW – the air swooshed out of me as if I had been punched in the solar plexus. She was wearing a faded-green satin jacket emblazoned with the words, "Pleiku, Vietnam." One of the typical GI slogans of the day, "When I die I'll go to heaven because I've spent my time in hell!" encircled the colored embroidered image of South Vietnam.

I approached her, "Excuse me, but I ran supplies to Pleikiu in late 67, early 68. Are you the daughter of a Vet?"

"Oh, I'm sorry," she replied. "No, I went to high school in Manhattan in the early 80s, and there was a thrift store near the school that had lots of these jackets. A bunch of us bought them and wore them. We thought they were cool. I've kept mine after all these years and wear it from time to time."

Cool??? What could I say? Nothing really. So I wished her a good day and went out into the bright sunlight of a beautiful morning, deeply breathing away the dark images from that faraway place that never is too far away in memory.

In addition, I published some 15 articles on a blog, *In the Mind Field*, from 2011 until 2015 that I operated with four other Vietnam Veterans, all of us members of VVAW and VFP. Though maintaining my membership in VFP, for most of the past several years, since Jill and I moved to Oregon in 2011, and recently back to her home in Illinois, I've chosen not to be actively involved planning or attending protests for peace with justice. I've chosen instead to focus my energies upon advocating for the inclusion of agnostic, atheist and free-thinking addicts within traditional AA. This has included writing some twenty-two articles for *AA Agnostica* and *AA Beyond Belief*, as well as writing this memoir.

Veterans Stand for Standing Rock

There has been one exception, however. In December of 2016, I joined some 4,000 other war veterans at the Standing Rock Reservation in North Dakota to protest the Dakota Access Pipe Line. I was most privileged to assist the Standing Rock and the Cheyenne River tribes of the Sioux Nation in trying to halt the construction of this pipeline through sacred tribal lands and underneath the Missouri River near Cannon Ball, ND, thereby threatening the water source for millions of people.

Mni Miconi—Water is life !~!~!

During the week I was there, I helped load and unload trucks of supplies and firewood for the sprawling camp of some 7,000 or more persons who had gathered in peaceful protest against the pipeline's construction. The gathering included representatives from a majority of indigenous tribes in North and South America. With some irony, I observed that once more I was engaged in humping boxes like I had initially done in Vietnam and later in Sri Lanka.

In a traditional Native American ceremony with smudge, chanting, and tasting salts of the earth, I was inducted into the Cheyenne River tribe as a peace warrior and awarded a feather from the Red-tail Hawk as a talisman to join a dreamcatcher of other feathers and objects in my car to protect me on my travels. I am most privileged to be an honorary member of the Lakota Sioux Nation. They are, indeed, my relatives. I echo the belief that I heard from many of my veteran peers that week. The experience at Standing Rock felt like for the first time I was truly serving my country.

I had wanted very much to return to Standing Rock during rhe last week of February, when militarized police forces forced the evacuation of the main camp. It broke my heart to see the military might of the US once again threatening Native Americans and their supporters that included veterans of all races. This is one other repetition of the dark legacy of continued colonial repression and egregious violations of the many treaties agreed to between the US government and the Sioux Nation. Later in the spring, I plan to return to Eagle Butte, SD, to join the Cheyenne River Tribe of which I am an honorary member to join my Native American relatives in continued resistance to protect their land and our water.

Chapter 19: Challenges to Recovery

Throughout my longterm recovery process, I've experienced a number of daunting challenges to staying sober. I survived a brutal second combat zone; I endured the sad endings of significant romantic relationships, including two divorces; I lost a number of jobs; I was arrested numerous times protesting for peace with justice; I lived through the devastation of 911 and the Tsunami in Sri Lanka.

By not picking up, staying connected to AA meetings and helping others, I have continued to successfully stay sober a day at a time, despite experiencing Muggings, Resentment and Rage, and Deaths:

Muggings

During my first decade of recovery, while living in Manhattan during the 1970s, I was mugged three times. The first mugging was rather comical. I was rushing downtown to speak at a Perry Street Workshop meeting, when I got lost in Penn Station. I found myself at the dead end of a cul-de-sac. I could see the tracks for the downtown subway through a barrier, but I didn't know how to get to them. When I turned around, I was confronted by a middle-aged man with a handgun and an unlit cigarette hanging between his lips. He demanded I give him my money. I started maniacally talking to him, telling him I was lost and late for an AA meeting in the Village. I didn't know how to get to the downtown train. Could he please help me?

Looking at me with amazement, he queried, "Are you crazy? Don't you see my pistol? I said give me your money!"

I gave him the few, crumpled dollar bills I had with me and got my Zippo cigarette lighter from Vietnam, "Geez, I'm sorry that I have so little money. Here's a light for your cigarette."

He shook his head in disgust, accepted my light for his cigarette, put his weapon away, and thrust the crumpled bills back into my hands, "Here, I don't want your money, Man." He then proceeded to show me how to get to the downtown express train.

The second time I was mugged was considerably more unsettling. Late one evening after rehearsals at Walden Theatre, I was accosted by two addicts on E. 87th Street. While one loudly bantered about how good it was to see me again, the other put a knife to my ribcage, saying, "Be cool, Man, be cool!"

They escorted me into the barely lit basement entrance of a brownstone building. There, one of them removed the Seiko watch that I had bought while on R&R in Hong Kong. However, he couldn't reach my money clip with $20-30 dollars in the bottom of my bluejeans pocket. The other mugger pressed his knife against my throat. Bleary-eyed, breath reeking of alcohol, he told me, "I want to stick you like a pig and make you slowly bleed to death all over the fucking floor." I froze, making sure I didn't make eye contact with him. After a moment, which felt like an eternity, he threw me to the floor, saying, "Fuck you. You're not worth it." To his partner, he said, "C'mon, let's boogie." They quickly left, running up the entrance stairs and down the street.

I reported the crime to the police and several days later was interviewed by a couple of detectives. They informed me that I was one extremely fortunate feller, because an hour or so later two persons with similar descriptions and the same MO had killed a man several blocks away.

The third mugging occurred downtown on Lexington Avenue, when I was walking to the Midnight Meeting at the Moravian Church on E. 30th Street. I got hustled by two street prostitutes. While one sweet-talked me, the other stealthily picked my pocket, this time finding my money clip.

Resentment and Rage

Perhaps nothing, however, has been more of a threat to continued sobriety than incidents I've experienced as a result of resentment and rageful behavior during both brief and longer periods of being in a "dry drunk" state. AA orthodoxy depicts an especially dire portrayal of the negative consequences that result from resentment and rage for those of us in AA recovery. Bill Wilson, who was primarily responsible for AA's canon of beliefs about alcoholism and recovery, doesn't mince words regarding the negative impact of resentment for alcoholics in recovery:

> *Resentment is the number one offender. It destroys more alcoholics than anything else. (Alcoholics Anonymous, p. 64)*

In Part Two, I described the first person with whom I identified, Stanley Stancage, a resentful and raging alcoholic. Stanley resentfully raged both during periods of sobriety and while drunk. He died of alcohol poisoning, after chug-a-lugging a quart of 100 proof vodka in an alcoholic rage. Thus, he paid the ultimate price for our alcoholic malady.

Resentment and anger, at times exploding into apoplectic rage, have likewise dogged me all throughout my longterm recovery. I've been known to proclaim at meetings that I am "constitutionally incapable of pausing when agitated."

Here, I must interject that I am one who "How It Works" describes as "suffering from grave emotional and mental disorders." In addition to being addicted to alcohol and drugs, I have been diagnosed with several other psychiatric conditions. These include post traumatic stress disorder, bi-polar I disorder, attention deficit hyperactive disorder, and generalized anxiety disorder. Consequently, I've also been known to assert that though I have been gifted to remain sober, I still suffer immensely from the mental and spiritual aspects of addictive disease. In other words, at times I am batshit crazy.

Resentment and raging behavior have caused me to experience abundant negative consequences—lost friendships, lost jobs, lost wives and lovers, lost esteem and lost reputation. I've often been as powerless over resentments and raging anger, as I know I would be over my addiction were I to take that first drink or drug. According to the opinion of Bill Wilson, I am likely doomed to die a horrible death from addiction. However, unlike Stanley, I have yet to be tempted to take a first drink or drug while raging in a state of resentment. I have never experienced the thought, much less an urge or compulsion, to take that first fatal drink. I attribute this to the following three significantly influential factors:

1. The period of my active alcoholism was so awful, so horrible, so unmanageable and unbearable, that I know and accept this stark reality: No matter how bad a situation sober might seem to be, even during my worst ravings, taking the first drink would inevitably make the dire situation a hundredfold or more worse.

2. In my first decade of getting sober in Manhattan during the 1970s, I had this dictum reiterated over and over at most meetings: "No matter what, whether your ass falls off or turns to gold, no matter what, do not pick up that first drink or drug!"

3. During the mid-'70s as an alcoholism counselor in the alcoholism program on the Bowery, I had a number of clients on my caseload who lived the down and out, in the gutter existence of a skid-row alcohol addict. They lived an awful life, pan-handling, washing windshields, living in flop houses, being preyed upon and beaten up, eating maybe one meal a day, becoming lice-infected, and worse. Some had lived this kind of a brutal life on the streets for

decades and did not die. I'm convinced were I to pick up that first drink or drug this would likely be my destiny. At age 74, I'm way too creature-comfort-oriented and cowardly to live this kind of desperado lifestyle.

Throughout recovery I've always been acutely aware of the intractable and negative consequences associated with resentment and rage. I've done a number of thorough 4th and 5th Steps dealing specifically about them. I've written reams of musings in journals about the negative consequences they cause. I've seen a number of excellent therapists, whose focus was to help me deal better with resentment and rage. I've taken part in anger management workshops, several times as the facilitator and once as a participant.

I've been inordinately fortunate never to have been arrested for becoming verbally abusive with strangers or with partners in the public arena. I've also never had an accident nor gotten a ticket due to at times uncontrollable and reckless road rage. As obnoxious as I sometimes behaved, I've never, not once, ever been in a fist-fight. On several occasions, much larger individuals backed away, because I was so deranged they didn't want to risk dealing with me—they saw "the crazy" and chose not to mess with it. Be that as it may, I've never picked up the first drink again despite often sometimes being resentful and rageful. I'm not the only one. During the 1970s, I was acquainted with the "angriest sober person in New York City AA."

In addition to Stanley, the raging alcoholic who died drunk, I knew another raging alcoholic, Marty O'Farrell. Marty was a successful public relations and commercial film producer in New York City, who had a horrid family background. Marty married a nurse with a small son, and they had two children. The step-son died at age 11 in a freak accident, when their cat jumped on the lid of a hope chest in which he was hiding. It slammed close, locked tight, and he suffocated. Marty and his wife, the mother of his two biological children, were divorced shortly thereafter.

Marty would often rant and rave apoplectically at meetings in mid-town Manhattan. Nevertheless, he never drank again. People accepted him with compassionate love and tolerance. I hadn't seen Marty for ten, maybe fifteen years, when I ran into him at a mid-town Manhattan meeting in the mid 1990s. He was as cool and calm as a gentle sea breeze over Hawaii. I barely recognized him due to the deep smile lines upon his aging, serene face.

"Marty," I queried, "What happened to the angriest sober person in AA?"

He smiled, holding up two fingers, "Two open-heart surgeries!"

We chatted. He related he was in full retirement, writing poetry, spending time with his grandchildren. Marty's story is extremely powerful for me—sometimes destiny plays hardball. We either change or we suffer the consequences.

―――

I've meditated, more off than on, throughout my recovery, but for the last year or so I have made a concerted effort to meditate twice daily. I can readily attribute progress regarding resentment and rage to consistently practicing mindful meditation. Amazingly, "It Works, If You Work It".

Though far from perfection, I'm aware of appreciable and steady progress. I'm profoundly aware that the duration, intensity, and the number of resentment and rage incidents have lessened considerably. I'm increasingly able to "pause when agitated." Another practice I do, when I become aware of mounting frustration or irritation, is to pause and take several deep breaths, during which I say to myself a phrase that was ubiquitous among soldiers in Vietnam, "Don't Mean Nothing!" "Don't Mean Nothing!" "Don't Mean Nothing!" over and over and over again, like a mantra.

I could be like Stanley, choosing to drink behind my resentment and rage. On the other hand, I can choose to remember Marty and stay sober despite my resentment and rage. It is my sincere hope that, like Marty, I die sober, satisfied that I have broken the chain of addiction in my family.

Deaths

Like taxes, death is an inevitable occurrence that each of us mortals must endure, not only our own, but of loved ones and friends. In both Vietnam and while in Sri Lanka, I encountered people dying or being devastated by the dying of loved ones. In my long life, I too have experienced the death of loved ones and friends.

Both of my parents have passed, Dad in July of 2001, and Mother in May of 2012. Here is a prose poem I wrote to memorialize the passing of them both:

Death Quartet

In July of 2001, 87 year-old father died, which resulted in the following two stanzas:

1.

At the funeral home, I walk up to your casket, Daddy, with Mother on my arm. The flag is folded at your head, its neat triangle of stars swimming in a sea of dark blue. I squelch down the hot flash of rage -- my stuff, not yours, not Mother's. Your face is pancaked peaceful, gray hair stiff, except for one frizzed piece on the left. Your hands look real good though, Daddy, almost like they could reach up and touch me with a smile, like I hardly remember they ever did.

Bam! Pow!! Kaboom!!!

Three quick flashes of dead young boy VC faces bombard my consciousness, blood drooling from one mouth, dust caking on an eyebrow, a quizzical, shocked stare on another visage. They hit me like body blows to the midriff. I reel, feel myself staggering, going down for a final count. Quell myself again and again: "Don't mean nuttin'!" "Don't mean nuttin'!" "Don't mean nuttin'!"

2.

Next day, Daddy, I sit next to your casket in St. James church, while everyone's getting Communion. I'm just sitting there in the pew, just breathing, just listening to the beautiful duet of Pie Jesu, just beginning to really let the tears flow.

Bam! Pow!! KABAM kaboom !~!~!

Same dead young VC boy faces bombard me again along with several dead orphans, "Don't mean nuttin'," Daddy, "Right? But the babies, Daddy, those poor burnt and bloody bruised babies, the orphans killed, horribly wounded at the orphanage. Daddy??? Are you sure that they "Don't mean nuttin'???"

On May 31, 2013, 91 year-old mother finally died, resulting in these two stanzas:

3.

Sisters Meg and Beth assured me, Momma, you were beautiful, looking better, more yourself than ever these last harrowing months, as slowly you let loose this mortal coil. I walk up to the casket, look down. Finally your face is relaxed, no more startled terror, no more frantic, perplexed, open-mouthed stare. Just peaceful rest, your hands carefully folded on the tasteful blazer the girls picked out for your final viewing. Relief floods through me.

St. Richard's Church, your beloved parish, Msgr. Chatham's legacy, is pristinely simple, rooted deep within the mostly forgotten ecumenical precepts of Vatican II. The funeral rite was poignant, almost fully rainbowed: women prominent in the liturgy, the Hispanic priest, the developmentally-disabled altar girl. Would have been perfect if an African American had been a participant, but hey if not perfect, the progress made here in Jackson, Mississippi is astounding! You are proud I trust. Your activist life of service for racial justice and the arts here were memorialized with dignity and grace by the grateful gathering of celebrants.

4.

Sitting in the pew breathing deeply while others take communion, I fold my hands in meditative repose, let the Pie Jesu duet again sweetly overflow within me. A joyous vision flashes through me: You are with Daddy and Bambi, full of heavenly exuberance. You cavort and dance and gambol with the laughing VC boys and orphans, as Bambi runs around yapping. You all joyfully chortle and cheer and promenade-all with giggling glee.

A short time later, your simple wooden casket is loaded into the two-toned black and silver Cadillac hearse. Babs and I are first in line behind you in the funeral procession. As we drive away from St. Richard's in the black rented Mazda3, the Beatles harmonize "Here Comes the Sun." Just perfect! It is gloriously most fitting, another full circle revealed, spiraling up one other level: Everything means everything. Every moment means more, resonates deeper, than ever we shall fully realize.

I related in Part Two in Chapter 4 the death of my first and only sponsor, Peter, whom I knew and loved for 33 years. His death has impacted me perhaps most of all. There's rarely a day goes by that I don't think of him, forever fondly, always missing dearly the font of wisdom—which sometimes could be viciously dark and cynically humorous—that he consistently provided me. I know that somehow in the vast mystery of the

Kosmos that we are still connected through the "Missive to Peter" I have on my laptop.

The same goes for John Albert O'Brien, my oldest and longest friend from 7th grade who died on Valentine's Day of 2016. Throughout the years since we left high school, we stayed in periodic touch with each other. He's only the second member of our small class of 49 folks, at least that I know of, who have passed on—rather remarkable really. His Mass card is prominently displayed on my desk, a wry smile on his face, despite the suffering he endured during the last decade of his life due to several severe health conditions – cancer, kidney failure, a stroke and a broken jaw from radiation treatments. Here's a memorial poem with an explanation of the title following it:

Neirbo

*You've fled the coop of your
broken body, dear friend,
my oldest ever friend*

*rain falls hard outside
as a wave of deep grief
springs a flush of tears*

*too bad you didn't figure out
how to capture on a dynamo
the energy you ceaselessly jiggled*

*in Boy Scout tent in '56, so disappointed
were we when the Suez Canal crisis
sputtered to peace—no heroic war for us*

*we shared one of our first drunks
both getting so, so, so horribly sick
on the Pearl River behind your house*

*your trick shoulder prevented you
from being a mighty St. Joe Rebel,
but an excellent water boy you were*

*unrequitedly we lusted for
so many of the lush, nubile ladies
mostly terrified to approach any*

we spun reams of teen-age theology

*wondering how Jesus got out of
Mary's intact and virginal womb*

*also that THE god must be an
idiot-savant in a kindergarten
lab for the divinely-challenged*

*we holed up together mostly drunk
in a DC blizzard junior year as I
recall during Christmas vacation*

*you witnessed my first marriage
at Baltimore County courthouse
two days before I left for Vietnam*

*after I returned we sped along Atlantic
City Parkway in your proud shiny Corvette
on a visit from Aberdeen Proving Ground*

*through the years and decades we
kept in touch remembering our youth
as it slowly faded into now deep past*

*so dignified and stoic you were
dressed in black when we gathered
in Jackson for our 50th reunion*

*how disappointed we were your
treacherous health prevented you
from joining us in New Orleans*

*our last visit was at your home
on my trip back east in October you
fasting due to broken jaw from radiation*

*we spoke of old times, watched
sparrows hustle seeds, basked in
the glow of memories together*

*I last spoke to you in mid-December
so grateful you could eat again. I don't
recall much of which we spoke.*

*you are departed now, a whisper
on the wind, your molecules
joined with Kosmic stardust*

Au Revoir dear friend
John Albert is dead
Long live John Albert

[Nierbo is O'Brien spelled backwards. John Albert and I had primitive code names for each other in the 7th grade—mine was Nosnirb. Throughout the years, we greeted each other by sounding out these code names tor each other, a silly ritual that had very deep, symbolic, perhaps even sacred, meaning for us ...

From time to time, I shall continue to invoke him, communicating with him just like I do with Peter, my AA sponsor for 33 years, who passed in 2006. In the mystery of the Kosmos, I believe both shall hear me, and further that both shall continue to share with me their deep wisdom.]

With my current age just shy of 74, it's only reasonable to presume that John Albert's passing will be the first of the many friends with whom I'm still in contact from high school, college and throughout recovery. In Part Two, I related how a number of my earliest friends from the Midnight Meeting had relapsed and died as a result of their addiction. Subsequently, only a few other persons that I've known have passed on, which is truly rather remarkable.

One other significant death, however, was that of my theatre mentor and director from Xavier University, Otto Kvapil. He died in hospice after a long and horrible battle from throat and tongue cancer in November of 1985, which was perhaps a result of his years of alcohol and nicotine addictions. On a recent visit with his wife, Diane, she told me how much he suffered during his prolonged dying process and how awful it was due to his tongue grossly protruding out of his mouth.

I've never been that afraid of dying. After all, for many years I was actively suicidal. However, I've always been most fearful of the *process* of dying. That certainly was influenced by several of the deaths I witnessed during grad school at Colombia. To my mind, the quality of life has been considerably more important than mere longevity. I was greatly influenced by the Broadway play, and later Richard Dreyfus movie, *Whose Life Is It Anyway*.

Funny thing, though, in 2015 when I was being treated for congestive heart failure in the Manhattan VA Hospital, I developed, for me, a rather surprising new goal. I decided I wanted to live longer than either of my parents, Dad who passed at age 87 and Mother at 91. I even fantasized about being the oldest surviving Vietnam Veteran!

Another interesting dynamic I've become aware of is that the older I get, the further I proceed through the process of aging, the lower the bar becomes of what I consider constitutes a good quality of life. Today, I am much more comfortable with the vicissitudes of the aging process than ever I could have imagined I would be ten or fifteen years ago.

———

I remain ever so grateful for the solid grounding I received in New York City AA during the 1970s, where I was indoctrinated in what colleague and fellow secular AA writer, John Lauritsen from Boston, refers to as "The 24-hour Plan". It is amazingly simple and defies any magical or miraculous intervention. John describes it in an article he wrote on the secular AA website, *AA Beyond Belief* as follows: "If you don't pick up the first drink, you can't get drunk—you won't have to struggle against drinking the second, or third, or sixth, or tenth."

This simple formula was augmented by the following two corollary dictums, in which I was also most fortunate to be well grounded during my first decade of recovery in New York City AA:

1. "You don't drink if your ass turns to gold, nor do you drink if it falls off," and
2. "There's nothing so bad that picking up a drink won't make it incredibly worse,"

The result has been that so far I have been most fortunate never to have had to pick up the first drink again. Therefore, ever since, I have experienced continuous longterm recovery from addiction to alcohol and other drugs a day at a time. I am exceedingly grateful to be in my 45th year of day-at-a-time recovery.

Chapter 20: AA Service Work

Being active in AA service work has always been an integral part of my recovery. During the first decade of recovery, I held a number of service positions with AA groups. In Part Two, I related how important it was being coffee maker for the New York City Young Peoples group, my first elected service position in AA. It kept me sober when I was tempted to relapse. For several years, I was Thursday night chairperson for my first home group, the Midnight Meeting. I was also co-chairperson for the Step Meeting of one of my other favorite groups. In New York City during the 1970s, working the steps was considerably more generically spiritual, and not nearly as exclusively Christian as AA has become throughout much of North America during the past four decades.

Whenever I was asked to lead a meeting I did, and I often shared during discussion meetings. For months I volunteered to answer phones at the New York Intergroup Association, where I was also trained to man the Hospital Desk. This involved gathering information and referring callers who requested detox or treatment services for addiction.

Service work was important to me because it fulfilled the third factor in the formula I learned in New York City AA about how to stay sober: 1) Don't use, 2) Go to meetings, and 3) Help others. This formula made much more sense to me than the one offered by many religious members of AA: 1) Clean house, 2) Trust God, and 3) Help others.

Early on I got actively involved in the Young Peoples movement in AA., attending many young peoples conferences throughout the Northeast and Canada. I was most privileged to serve as the co-chair of the first New York City Young People's Conference held in the spring of 1978 in Stony Point, NY.

While working for 30 years in prominent positions as a professional in the field of addiction treatment, I felt it would be inappropriate for me to do General Service work in AA above the group level. However, I continued to be active in service work at the group level wherever I lived. While living in Albany, with colleague Vince, I helped organize a recovering community of Vietnam Veterans throughout the Capital District. On Long Island, I helped start a men's AA meeting and a meeting for couples in recovery. In Arizona, I helped start an AA group for those, like myself, with "grave emotional and mental disorders".

In 2011 my wife Jill and I moved from Woodstock, NY to a small town on the southern seacoast of Oregon. There we experienced AA to be a white supremacist Christian cabal. We were both shunned and shamed for our agnostic and non-Christian beliefs. Gratefully, we found Roger C.'s website, *AA Agnostica*, founded in Toronto after secular AA groups had been delisted by their Intergroup Office. There I became actively involved with the worldwide community of secular members active in Alcoholics Anonymous. I'm grateful to have had a number of articles published both on Roger's website and also on *AA Beyond Belief*, moderated by John S and edited by Doris A.

During the summer of 2013 I attended one of the initial planning meetings for the first biennial International Convention for Agnostics, Atheists and Freethinkers in Santa Monica, CA. I then worked online to help promote the convention. In November I was incredibly moved by attending the WAAFT Convention, where I facilitated a workshop, was a member of a panel on starting secular AA meetings and was one of several writers who reported on the conference for *AA Agnostica*. It strikes me that getting actively involved doing service work for the secular AA movement has been just as important for continued recovery as a longterm sober person as was becoming actively involved in the Young People's movement during my early recovery. Both movements influenced me immensely. They both motivated me to stay actively involved with AA as the core of my continuing recovery process.

After a couple of years Jill and I were able to move up the Oregon seacoast to Seaside, which is a reasonable commute to Portland, a most progressive and urbane city. On December 1, 2013, we held the first meeting of what evolved into the secular AA group, Beyond Belief, at the Portland Alano Club. Beyond Belief is a meeting for persons seeking recovery in AA as agnostics, atheists or freethinkers, but it is also inclusive of believers. We include members of many different beliefs, to include no beliefs at all. We stay sober by sharing our stories of experience, strength and hope with each other about how we don't use a day at a time.

After we had been meeting for three months with an average of 7 to 10 people attending, we decided that we were a viable enough group to be listed by the Portland Area Intergroup. I spoke with the manager of the Portland Area Intergroup about listing our group meeting.

Over the next several weeks, we had what he referred to as friendly "debates" as to whether or not we were truly an AA group. He contended that since we used different versions of the Twelve Steps, and read from non-conference-approved literature, we were not an AA group. He suggested we form a separate organization similar to what ardently devoted Christian members had done by forming *Alcoholics Victorious* and *Celebrate Recovery*. Many of his arguments were similar to those promoted by the infamous "White Paper" that had been used in Toronto and Vancouver to delist secular AA groups in these two Canadian cities.

It was the group conscience that we become active in AA General Service work. I was elected GSR and began attending District 9 monthly meetings in Portland. I was most gratified to receive strong support and encouragement from the DCM and other GSRs for our Beyond Belief secular AA group. They assured me that, contrary to the Intergroup Manager's opinion, we indeed did qualify to be a legitimate group of Alcoholics Anonymous by virtue of AA's history, traditions and concepts of service. They welcomed Beyond Belief group's participation.

In February of 2014, I attended my first Oregon Area 58 Assembly. Afterwards my assessment was that much of AA in Oregon was quite different from what I had experienced in New York. It was much more oriented to a strictly Christian orthodox interpretation and the use only of conference-approved materials, similar to what Jill and I had experienced when we moved to Coos Bay.

Most especially, there was an emphatic focus on the first 164 pages of the Big Book, which is revered by some as sacred text. I could sense from comments by a number of participants that a number of groups and persons in AA service work were adherents of the growing *Back to Basics* movement within AA. *Back to Basics* strives to replicate AA as it is alleged to have been practiced during the early years of AA history in Akron, OH, under the strong influence of the evangelical and pietistic Oxford Group. This impression was sadly reinforced when the final business meeting on Sunday ended with the Lord's Prayer.

At the next Assembly meeting I spoke with a former AA Delegate and Trustee about our difficulty getting listed by the Portland Intergroup. She told to me that this shouldn't be a problem, that she would speak with the Intergroup Manager. When next I communicated with him, a couple of weeks later, he informed me that our meeting had, indeed, finally been listed.

Throughout the following year-and a-half, the Beyond Belief group enjoyed rapid growth and evolution. This matched the growth of secular AA throughout North America, tremendously enhanced by the very successful international convention of agnostic, atheist and freethinking AA members during mid-November of 2014 in Santa Monica, CA. At that convention, both Phyllis H., then General Manager of GSO, and the Rev. Ward Ewing, former Chair of the AA Board of Trustees, gave keynote speeches, strongly endorsing secular AA meetings as being a legitimate part of AA.

By the end of our first year Beyond Belief moved into the largest room in the Alano Club, since our Sunday meeting had grown to average between 30-35 people. We also started a second meeting on Wednesdays in southwest Portland. On the last Wednesday of each month we hosted a city-wide meeting of Milestone Celebrations for all secular AA members in the Portland area who celebrated recovery anniversaries during the previous month. The group also worked with the Portland Intergroup to take secular AA meetings into two treatment centers each month.

Another secular AA group named Secular Sobriety was formed on the Eastside of Portland. They experienced no difficulty in having their three weekly meetings listed by the Portland Intergroup. Each of their meetings averages 25-30 people attending. A women's meeting, wittily called She Agnostics, was started at the Alano Club on Saturday mornings. So secular AA recovery has thrived in Portland.

In December of 2016, WACYPAA, the Western Area Conference of Young People in AA, was held in a Portland convention center. Some thousand young people in AA from throughout AA's Pacific Region attended the weekend conference of workshops, panels and speakers dealing with young people's experience of recovery in AA. The program included two panels of secular AA members from the Beyond Belief and Secular Sobriety groups who shared their experience of being successfully sober in AA as agnostics, atheists or freethinkers.

During our last year living in Seaside, Jill and I also started a secular AA meeting on Monday evenings at the Little Yellow House, the primary meeting location for Seaside meetings. This has been especially important for many of the young women who attend Awakenings Treatment Center in Seaside and are put off by the religious orientation of most traditional AA meetings in Seaside.

I continued actively participating in quarterly Assembly meetings of Oregon Area 58 where I shared experience, strength and hope as a secular member of AA with other GSRs, DCMs, Committee members and Area Officers performing vital AA General Service work throughout Oregon.

I became a member of the Area Hospital Committee where for a while I took monthly meetings into the Oregon State Mental Hospital. However, after several of these meetings another member brought his Bible to read from at the meeting, and I resigned from the Committee. I suggested to the Hospital Committee Chairperson that reading from the non-conference-approved Bible was perhaps not truly in accordance with the spirit of AA's tradition, as stated in the Preamble, of non-affiliation with "any sect, denomination, politics, organization or institution."

In March of 2015 I attended PRAASA, the Pacific Regional AA Service Assembly in Layton, UT. This was an incredibly rewarding experience, where I shared experience, strength and hope with AA members actively involved in AA General Service from all over the western third of the US. A highlight was hearing a panel presentation by Ashly M. from Idaho on the topic "Does our Fellowship make Agnostics, Buddhists, Spiritualists, etc., feel welcome in our recovery meetings?" Essentially her talk related how throughout wide areas of North America, especially in rural, small-town areas, AA members with different beliefs from the Christian language of the Big Book are often shunned and shamed. Certainly this was what Jill and I experienced when we first moved to Oregon.

By far the most rewarding experience of the two years service commitment as GSR for the Beyond Belief group was that I was able to facilitate the following motion to be approved by District 9:

> *Oregon Area 58 recommends that AA Grapevine, Inc. publish a collection of previously published stories written by members who are atheists, agnostics and free thinkers that share their experience successfully getting and staying sober in AA.*

Since 1962 some 45 or so stories by agnostics, atheists and freethinkers, describing how they have recovered in AA, have been published in the *Grapevine*. The intent of the motion is to have the *Grapevine*, which has published collections of stories for other special purpose groups, such as women, LGBTQ and young people, also publish a collection of the stories of secular AA members in recovery. District 24, where the Secular Sobriety Group in east Portland meets, joined with District 9 to successfully present this motion during the business meeting of the La Grange Area Assembly in September of 2015. We were most gratified that it received considerable commentary in support of the motion from the floor.

The motion was approved with substantial unanimity and tabled for final consideration at the next Oregon Area 58 Assembly in November at Clackamas. GSRs were instructed to take the motion back for consideration and discussion by their home groups for final consideration at the next Assembly. Prior to the Clackamas Assembly, I estimated that at best the motion had a 50/50 chance to achieve the requisite two-thirds majority of voting members to achieve substantial unanimity. However I was most pleasantly surprised and pleased when it received upwards of 90% affirmative votes. This is a testament to the effectiveness of AA's Twelve Concepts of Service. Though sometimes maddening, and at times onerously time-consuming, they do effectively reflect the group conscience consensus of the membership of AA through our inverted triangle of General Service in AA.

A final bonus occurred when we gathered in a huge circle around the large ballroom and were led in saying "The Responsibility Declaration" by the past Delegate, not the Lord's Prayer. What a nice cherry on top of the wonderful two-year experience I had serving as GSR of the Beyond Belief group.

In April of 2016, at the annual AA General Service Conference, the Oregon 58 motion that the Grapevine publish a book of our stories was passed by a substantial unanimity of conference delegates. A special purpose book of our stories is on the list of approved books to be published by the *Grapevine* in the near future. This is quite an achievement since the first such request for such a publication was made by a Trustee in 1976, over 40 years ago. Numerous times since then a motion to publish such a book has come before the General Service Conference and not achieved substantial unanimity.

I was later nominated and elected to fill a vacancy on the WAAFT board, which was planning for the second International AA Convention of agnostics, atheists and freethinkers scheduled to take place during November of 2016 in Austin, TX. However, after several months I chose to resign from this board, partially due to contentious disagreements with two of board members and a member of the Program Committee. They were deeply disturbed that at the Santa Monica convention in 2014, the General Manager of GSO, Phyllis H., had been invited to participate as a featured speaker. They were also most apoplectic that the Rev. Ward Ewing, an Episcopal priest no less, was also a featured speaker, even though he was a former Chairperson of the AA Board. It didn't matter that both speakers strongly offered their support for secular AA members being legitimate members of AA.

They were determined not to allow the Executive Editor of the *Grapevine*, Ami Brophy, be a featured speaker at the Austin Convention. This, despite the fact that there was a special issue of the *Grapevine* for agnostics, atheists and freethinkers in October of 2016 and a pending special purpose book of our stories to be published by the *Grapevine*. They further believed that secular AA members should distance themselves from traditional AA and not become at all involved in any AA General Service work. One of them wrote a scathing article suggesting that to do so, we secular AA members would be suffering from the Stockholm syndrome by identifying with the aggressors.

During the Austin convention I co-presented a workshop with John S. of *AA Beyond Belief* on the importance of secular AA members becoming actively involved in General Service work within AA. It's our strong belief that secular AA not be separate from traditional AA but instead be an integral part of it. We further strongly advocate that more of us in secular AA should actively become engaged at all levels of AA General Service to insure that our minority voice is included in all deliberations regarding AA's future. John and I with others strongly advocate that this is the best way to help ensure that the hand of AA will always be available for anyone, anywhere with a desire to stop drinking who reaches out for help, gets help from AA, regardless of belief or lack of belief.

———

At the Austin convention, I was elected to be a member of the board for the newly named International Conference of Secular AA (ICSAA). Much of my time for General Service work in AA will be devoted to serving on this board. ICSAA has incorporated a new organization named Secular AA in the State of Nevada, with the following two primary functions:

1. Organizing and facilitating periodic International Conferences of members of the secular AA Fellowship, formerly done by WAAFT IAAC, who facilitated the Santa Monica and Austin gatherings of secular AA members, and

2. Serving as the Intergroup, or General Service Office, for the secular AA Fellowship around the world. This function was formerly done by John S.'s WAAFT Central, which responded to queries and maintained listings of secular AA meetings around the world in consultation with Deirdre S. of New York City, who during the past number of years has also maintained a comprehensive list of Worldwide Agnostic AA Meetings.

I am most privileged to be a member of this board which is unanimous in its intention to function fully as an integral part of AA in accordance with our history, traditions, and concepts of service. Foremost in our minds is that AA be as inclusive as it possibly can be for any alcoholic, anywhere, who wants to stop drinking, regardless of what his religious beliefs are, to include no belief at all.

Since the summer of 2015 I arranged through the Corrections Desk of the AA General Service Office to correspond with an inmate in a Pennsylvania State Prison. Josh is serving a 35-years-to-life sentence for a murder he committed while blacked out during a bar fight. An agnostic/atheist, he has been very put off with the God-oriented AA meetings that are brought into the prison from the outside, including one speaker who reads from his Bible during a meeting. I've been able to get him secular AA literature and send him articles from secular AA websites. This has been one of the most rewarding AA service functions I've done throughout the long years of my recovery in AA. I've been able to provide Josh with support and information to help him understand that he can be a viable member of the AA Fellowship as an agnostic, that he does not have to drink the Christian-only Kool-Aid. I have helped him to understand that in AA our legacy of Unity does not mean uniformity to the predominate Christian beliefs of the majority of AA members.

Since Jill and I now live in the tiny farm town where she was raised in the middle of rural Illinois cornfields, we don't have anything like the vibrant and diverse secular AA communities that we enjoyed in Portland. We regularly attend the one weekly secular AA meeting available to us in the nearby small city of Bloomington-Normal. I volunteered recently to join our groups GSR at the local District Meeting where I was elected as Public Information Chairperson for the District.

Jill and I also choose to attend several traditional Christian-oriented meetings. There, when it is our time to share, we make sure to emphasize that we both have longterm recovery without specific religious beliefs, certainly not the predominant Christian beliefs of the majority of AA members in our community.

Jill leaves the meeting before the recitation of the Lord's Prayer, but I respectfully stay in the circle and scan for others who do not recite the prayer, attempting to connect with them after the meeting to introduce myself as a longterm sober member of AA without religious belief. I believe this is some of the most critically important General Service work in our AA community that we have ever done—we are living examples of agnostic freethinkers with longterm recovery, who are successfully practicing the AA program a day at a time, without following any religious orthodoxy. This, I believe, is in the finest spirit of AA's history, traditions and concepts of service.

Chapter 21: Deep Explorations of the Psyche

One of the articles that I published on *AA Agnostica,* which I most enjoyed researching and writing, was "Bill Wilson's Experience with LSD." In it, I reported how his life was significantly influenced for the better as a result of his use of LSD. Though at times normally depressed, he never again suffered from a debilitating episode of depression such as had dogged him throughout the first 20 years of his recovery. As I noted in the article, his creativity and writing after using LSD was prodigious. It included the following:

- *Alcoholics Anonymous Comes of Age* was published in 1957
- *The A.A. Service Manual Combined with Twelve Concepts for World Service* was published in 1962
- The Responsibility Statement was adopted in 1965
- The Declaration of Unity was adopted in 1970
- Over 50 articles were published in the *Grapevine,* including "The Next Frontier—Emotional Sobriety", "Our Critics Can Be Our Benefactors", "The Language of the Heart", and "God As we Understand Him: The Dilemma of No Faith".

I came of age during the heyday of my generation's extensive explorations of the psyche by using psychedelic drugs such as LSD, but I never took any psychedelic substances. I bought the negative hype about the potential dangers of LSD and other psychedelic drugs. Besides, my "crazy" experiences while being addicted to daily use of Colt .45, the liquid, legal drug of addiction, and the many times I used marijuana, led me to be most leery of using any psychedelic drugs. Nevertheless in recovery I found another way to deeply explore my psyche.

The First Holotropic Breathing Experience

During the 1980s and 1990s, I was an admirer and enthusiast of the work of Stan Grof, a Czech psychiatrist, and his wife, Christina, a recovering alcoholic. Stan had done extensive research using LSD and other psychedelics in mental health treatment.

After research was banned in the US, Stan and Christina developed a process of Holotropic Breathing, which was a process of deep, rhythmic breathing in a darkened room where loud, emotionally rousing music was played. Participants would be arranged in pairs, one who would breath and one who would sit to witness the session and attend to any needs of the breather. During the next session, after the initial session, participant roles would be reversed. At the end of each session, body work would be available to the breather, who then would draw a mandala, symbolizing the content of the breathing "trip".

This method was found to induce psychedelic-like states lasting two to three hours. During a Holotropic Breathing "trip," one would sometimes be able to uncover and explore traumatic events, including the process of birth. Though largely unconscious, these traumas could possibly persist to interfere with or prevent one from experiencing a satisfactory, fulfilling life, which would be difficult to achieve unless the hidden traumas were released.

I signed up for a two-day workshop, facilitated by Stan, in November of 1995. This was during a critical period of transition for me, a time of extended crisis. At the time, I was mostly estranged from my third wife, Sara. Largely due to unresolved issues I continued to experience problems with intimacy and rage, partially the result from being a Vietnam veteran. As a result for several months before I attended Stan's workshop we had been separated. She was also having an affair with Joe, an associate of hers from work.

The workshop took place in Wallace Hall of St. Ignatius Loyola Church in Manhattan at 84th Street and Park Avenue. Wallace hall was a cavernous basement room, catacomb-like, with huge stone columns and buttresses. Here is a journal entry I made prior to the start of the first session as a sitter for Elissa, a contemporary from Queens:

> *We gather, all ages, all pretensions, staking out our turf, our space, our spot, checking each other out with subtle sidewise glances, our old brain instincts on full alert, our ego-fears— Just mine? Do I project? – hyper vigilant, on guard; most of us, now in late middle-age, are grown up children of the sixties, still seeking, still searching for THE SELF, for meaning, for connection to both self and meaning, and so the beat goes on inexorably, following surely, but mysteriously, it's own daemonic spirit.*

> *So, here I am, manifesting another demonstration of the principle: visualize it, and it comes to be. Some 10 or so years after my first exposure to the writing and work of Stan Grof, I'm about to embark on a Holotropic journey into self led by the man himself. Am I too disappointed it's with breathing instead of LSD? No, not too disappointed, just is what it is !~!~!*

I don't recall that there was any bodywork offered. Maybe it was provided and I just wasn't aware of it. Nor do I recall today what I did on Friday evening. Probably I had a meal in one of my favorite restaurants in the City and then went to one of the AA meetings where I got sober in the 1970s.

The next Saturday morning I lay down on the mat with Elissa as the sitter, the lights darkened, I went through the guided relaxation phase, listening to the soothing, deep voice of Stan, following his instructions to start belly-breathing, deeply and slowly. The music began loudly to play, and WHOOOSSSSSSHHHHHH away I went for a two-and-a-half hour or so trip. It was as psychedelically experienced as any I could ever have hoped to have achieved by taking LSD. It was absolutely body-mind-emotion-and-spirit-blowing !~!~!

I traveled into myriad spaces and experiences throughout a multitude of realities, up, down and around all levels of existence. During this process, I had the full gamut of emotions from intense suffering to expanding ecstasy and hung-out in otherworldly regions deep within me with beneficent beings who were both separate and one with all of what ever I have always been. Here is the journal entry I made about the trip which includes the poem I wrote on the right-side of the mandala, as part of the experience:

A watcher
watching
I became aware
I was being watched

Through all
the pain
in spite of the
surrounding suffering
seemingly making
the error real

magnificent Being
bursts forth
in love
spiraling
through
an infinity
of Light

And what a sweet ride it was, spiraling through this infinity of light patterns and alternative universes, during which I experienced the void, the jungle, Cheetahness (my totem animal at the time), rageful gnashing of vicious teeth, skull-headed tarantula spiders, a huge two-handed broadsword, mauling in a blood-rage killing frenzy of Joe upon seeing the stark visual of him tongue-lapping Sara. This was eventually followed by a deep-hearted experience of compassionate love for his suffering and his missing of Sara that is exactly the same as mine. During the relaxation phase, which morphed into profound forgiveness for my manifestation of the OJ within, I was reborn into galaxies of love-spirals throughout infinities of light !~!~!

The Second Holotropic Breathing Experience

In October of 2009 I traveled to Pawlet, Vermont, for another Holographic Breathing Workshop, facilitated by Elizabeth and Lenny Gibson. My mat session took place on Sunday morning. In some ways it was almost identical to what I had experienced in 1995, especially in regard to my sense of being a watcher in the midst of other watchers and traveling through various levels of existence throughout multitudinous galaxies of time, space and light. It was also considerably different with several unexpected and startling occurrences. Let me relate the experience as I recall it. I again wrote a poem as part of the mandala:

Deep
within innerspace
I watch
the watchers
watching me
watch them
in the shadows
of the lightshow
as I shift
the Kosmos

*all around
US in the glory
of our connected
BEING*

During this part of my journey, as I focused on rhythmically deep breathing, my stomach roiled like I was experiencing birth contractions. I was acutely aware of being the center of a fantastical light show in which everything was connected with everything else in an eternal infinity of brilliantly cascading light, shapes, sounds and sensations. By shifting my inner vision, kaleidoscopes of emerging shapes, colors and sounds spiraled forth from my center, connecting with and connected by all existence throughout both inner and outer space. This was no doubt augmented by the throbbing music Lenny orchestrated throughout the session. I have no idea how long in "realtime" I stayed in this phase of the journey, but it seemed in an instant to last forever.

Next, similar to my first holotropic experience in 1995, I coursed up and down the chakras of reality, in and around all kinds of different states of being in an array of shifting and emerging crystalline shapes, ancient creatures swimming and morphing within an endless sea, rolling waves of first bright red hues and then brilliant green hues, continuous fields of yellow undulating grasses that stretched beyond all horizons … Again, I stayed in this state for an indeterminate period of real and/or inner time.

Suddenly I became acutely and painfully aware of incessant itches on the right side of my face, under my nose, up on the cheekbone, just beneath the ear lobe. Several times I violently scratched the itches, which randomly shifted from spot to spot along the right side of my face, with little relief. A close friend of mine believes that I experienced an overwhelming trauma very early in infancy, most likely preverbal. I have always sensed this, but despite years of various depth-psychology therapies, intense 12-step recovery work, imago relationship therapy and extensive self-analysis, I remain quite blocked from and unaware of whatever traumatic event may have occurred.

From my clinical training I chose to believe, particularly in the altered state of holotropic breathing, that the persistent emergence of the extreme itching was significant. I was, therefore, not too surprised when suddenly a sharp and most frightening image of grossly huge, bulging, bulbous, brightly-red-painted lips burst into consciousness, blotting out everything else. The image frightened me down beneath the marrow and I began to surrender myself to wherever it would take me. I began to emotionally sob with streaming tears, experiencing an overwhelming sadness, grief-stricken, deep within my core.

However, at this point one of the other breathers near me began mewing and whimpering like the tortured cries of babies and small children. This immediately catapulted me back into the very familiar and pervasive trauma from Vietnam, during which I experienced the brutal deaths and horrible wounding of several small children at the orphanage who were caught in a cross-fire during the Tet Offensive. I consciously tried to distract myself from the mewing and whimpering, not wanting to re-experience this old, too familiar ground from Vietnam. I wanted to get back to the Big-Lips experience, but I was unable to. The thought occurred to me that for years I have used the traumas I experienced from Vietnam to serve as a defensive mechanism to block myself from getting in touch with an older, more primal trauma I may have experienced from childhood or even infancy.

At first I was apoplectically angry and resentful that I had been distracted, indeed was distracting myself, from the Big-Lip image. For a long while I focused on my breath work, trying to sink again into the music so as to perhaps induce the re-emergence of the Big-Lip experience, but to no avail. I came to accept that it had passed and was not again forthcoming. For a long while I simply lay on the mat, resting, sinking into the music, experiencing a mellow state of total relaxation, as if I was floating on my back in a warm, soothing sea. I felt done, complete, and began gently contemplating what I wanted to express in the mandala, so I motioned to an assistant, telling him I felt done and wanted to go to the room where there were materials to create our mandalas.

He asked me about doing some bodywork. Although I really felt no need for it, since it was not a part of my first experience, I wanted to tell him no thank you. However, being a people-pleaser, I let him work on my lower, left back where I was experiencing some slight tension for a short while. Just as I was getting up to leave, the music shifted to Barber's "Adagio for Strings," which is the signature background music for the ending of Oliver Stone's movie about Vietnam, *Platoon*. It was like a sucker-punch to the solar plexus, and I was catapulted, supine on my face, in a prostrate position, back down on the mat, where I deeply sobbed once more in a seething rage about the never-ending meta-grief concerning the experience of my war and all war. After awhile, the sobs and raging subsided, and I recalled the final speech of *Platoon's* main character, Chris Taylor, played by Charlie Sheen:

> *The war is over for me now. But it will always be there for the rest of my days ... Those of us who did make it have an obligation to build again, to teach to others what we know, and to try with what's left of our lives to find a goodness or meaning for this life.*

Whoa !~!~! Here was the prime lesson from this mat-trip journey for me. Despite having in recent months ceased from most peace activism with veterans, while in the submissive position of lying prostrate, I surrendered to accept the reality that I am no less obligated to live the best life that I can possibly live, following Chris Taylor's directive. I recommitted my life to creating poetry and drama to convey not only the horror, but more important, the redemptive potential that veterans have to not only survive, but also to thrive through a fully lived life. I rededicated myself to extend help and comfort to all victims of any war, to continue to seek some meaning from the meaningless experience of my war by extending compassion and forgiveness through myself to all others. This, of necessity, includes an intention and willingness to continue to strive to forgive the unforgivable actions of the ubiquitous warmongers and elite manipulators of our most militaristic American society and culture. After the recent election of our Bully in Chief, President Donald Trump, this shall no doubt prove to be a most challenging endeavor, to extend AA's code of "love and tolerance," to which I add inclusivity, to him and his regressive administration.

Upon reflection it strikes me, as is so often typical of my nature, that in the mandala, I focused on the half-emptiness of the mat trip, expressing the rage and dismay at being catapulted back into the hellish experience of Vietnam. I neglected to convey on the mandala the half-fullness of my rededication to continue living up to the karmic (?) challenge of the Charlie Sheen character in his final speech. Oh well, I fully am aware and embrace it now ...

The Third Holotropic Breathing Experience

Several months later, Jill and I experienced a weekend with Elizabeth and Lenny in Pawlet together. Here is a journal entry I made while watching her draw her mandala.

> *I sit here in awe after sitting, witnessing, watching her process, trusting that what was happening for her was exactly as it needed to be. And oh, magnificently wow, as she manifests an incredible mandala, I bask in the gentle glory of*

> *being moved so completely by her, by us, by the process of opening our hearts up to the Kosmos.*

During her mat session, the lights were dimmed, the curtains pulled over the windows to block the bright winter sunlight reflecting off snow-covered hills, and the breathing began as Lenny, headphones intact, twisted knobs and dials as efficiently as any Oz behind the curtain, filling the room with cascades of rousing sound. The next couple of hours plus spun by with Jill breathing deeply, sobbing, contorting herself into incredibly complex full-body mudras, shifting her legs and torso into a rhythmic dance moving to the shifting music as intricate as that of any Balinese shadow puppet show. It was such an incredible privilege to sit with her, to witness her willingness to trust the process and do her sacred Holotropic Breathwork on the mat. She explained that she experienced a very deep healing from her traumatic childhood with a physically, emotionally and verbally abusive fundamentalist Christian Mother, who thwarted her childhood dream of becoming a ballerina. On the trip she moved from the darkness and blood-red terror of her childhood with the black face yelling in pain through a series of fantastic ballet leaps across healing waters to the light of the always sun within.

That afternoon I did my third Breathwork trip on the mat. This trip was extremely visual, filled with shifting amorphous shapes and flowing states of being through which I drifted for it seemed like an eternity or so. There was one rather ominous-looking but non-threatening mass of darkness on the left, balanced by flowing wings of purple on the right with a central core of bounteous life emerging from an all-seeing eye surrounded by both immense suffering and overflowing compassion within a brightly sunlit Kosmos. On the mandala I wrote the Sanskrit word, maitrī, which means loving kindness towards oneself and all others, as explained by one of my favorite Buddhist teachers, Pema Chodron. As well, I wrote the Buddhist chant, *Namo Guan Shi Yin Pusa*, which is dedicated to Kuan Yin, the female form of Buddha, who is prominent throughout Vietnam. The chant is translated as, "I call upon the bodhisattva who sees and hears the sufferings of the world."

To sum up the three Holotropic Breathing experiences I've had, both as a breather and as a witness/sitter, I can't imagine that I could have any more powerful or healing experiences under the influence of LSD or other psychedelic substances. Nevertheless, I did seek to experience a psychedelic plant medicine …

Ayahuasca

The vine of the soul, yagé, as South American natives call it, or Mother A, as it was referred to by Canadians and Americans in the two ceremonies I attended, is a combination of two Amazonian plants, one which contains a relatively high amount of the powerful hallucinogenic DMT. Ayahausca has been used by shamans in South American tribes for no one knows exactly how long, for many centuries most likely. The first recorded western contact was made in 1851 by Richard Spruce, the famous ethnobotanist from England.

During the last several years ceremonies have been increasing throughout metropolitan centers in North and South America and throughout Europe. Increasing interest has been devoted to Ayahuasca's potential benefits in healing depression and addiction. My interest in it was spurred by the work of Canadian psychiatrist, Gabor Maté. His book on addiction, *In the Realm of the Hungry Ghosts,* is perhaps the best I've ever read regarding our affliction. A central premise of Maté's work is that the root cause of addiction is due to some form of unresolved trauma.

Ayahuasca ceremonies consist of a four to six hour event starting around 9:00 p.m. after the community has shared a communal evening meal. The Ayahuasca is ingested by each participant under the careful guidance of a shaman accompanied by assistants. Throughout the long evening, the shaman and assistants pray, chant, burn sage and tobacco. For the majority of participants, the taste of Ayahuasca is awful and often is accompanied by violent purging, retching and vomiting, along with sobbing and screaming, sometimes giggling hilarity, as the hallucinogenic effects deepen.

After several hours the ceremony comes to a close when the shaman and his assistants light candles. The community then shares another communal meal and gets needed rest. Late the next morning, a brunch is shared and in the afternoon there is a sharing circle, during which each participant relates their experience, receiving feedback from the shaman, as appropriate.

I participated in two Mother A ceremonies when I lived in Oregon, one in September of 2015 and another in February of 2016. I have rarely been involved with a more loving and enlightened community of kindred spirits. Due to health issues, high blood pressure and Agent Orange-related coronary disease, I was only able to ingest tiny micro-doses of the plant medicine. Unlike most other participants, I absolutely loved the taste of Mother A. To me, it was sweet and tasted like the essence of plant life from Mother Earth. I didn't purge, nor did I have any significant hallucinogenic experiences, perhaps due to the small doses I was given. The only visuals I got were light patterns in the core of the Shaman as he chanted, sitting on pillows opposite from me across the darkened room.

The use of Ayahuasca is greatly influenced by the set and setting. In both ceremonies, the set and setting was most reverential and respectful, sacred even, of the plant medicine as well as the practitioners, both shamans, the assistants and each participant in the ceremony. How different this was from how psychedelics were used by my generation during the 60s, where it was experienced mostly for the drug-induced psychedelic highs, which occasionally morphed into bad trips with little support and no sense of community.

For several months, with a practitioner of herbal medicine, I explored coming off of the many allopathic medications I take daily from the Veterans Administration. I considered transitioning to treat my ailments mostly with diet and plant medicines. That way perhaps I would have been able to participate in other Mother A ceremonies with higher amounts of the plant medicine. Perhaps I would have discovered the trauma that I came close to experiencing during my second mat trip with the horrifying bright red, bulbous lips. However, after I suffered congestive heart failure, spending a week in the Manhattan VA hospital in 2015, I chose to continue my regimen of western medicine. Were I twenty years younger perhaps I would have made a different choice.

Nevertheless I am especially grateful for what I did experience in the Ayahuasca healing circles. They were as powerful for me as any experiences I've had with Holotropic Breathing or in the healing circles of AA meetings, where addicts share their experience, strength and hope.

Chapter 22: Why I am Mostly an Agnostic Nontheist—But Very Spiritual

> *This is the acknowledgement that not everything is knowable ... At it's best, however, agnosticism goes further: it takes a spirited delight in not knowing. And this delight is no boorish disdain for knowledge and intellect. Rather, it's a recognition that we need room for mystery, for the imagination, for things sensed but not proven, intuited but not defined—room in which to explore and entertain possibilities instead of heading straight for a safe seat at one end of the other of a created spectrum.*
>
> *Agnostic: A Spirited Manifesto by Lesley Hazelton*

Throughout my recovery in AA, I have evolved to currently consider myself as a Nontheist, one who does not believe in any form of a personal deity. I cannot believe in any kind of a personalized divine entity, a super-daddy, who watches over me, keeping score and checking it twice, to either reward or punish me in a mythical afterlife for what I do, or don't do, while on this earthly plane. It is incomprehensible for me to conceive of an all powerful male deity who is simultaneously all loving and wrathfully vengeful to sinners who violate his alleged commandments.

Were I to believe in any such anthropomorphic, interventionist entity, I would much prefer a super-mommy, a sensual, sensitive, anima-oriented goddess from my Scotch-Norman-Celtic heritage instead of a patriarchal, patronizing, testosterone-challenged god. No doubt, me being a Nontheist was likely influenced by my two experiences of vicious combat zones, Vietnam as a young man and Sri Lanka as an elder.

Even as a teenager in high school, soon after I had converted from a southern Baptist and Presbyterian protestant background to Catholicism, I had pressing doubts and questions concerning many tenets of Christian dogma. Whatever religious devotion I had was motivated more out of a terror of eternal damnation to the hellfire and brimstone than anything else. The doubts I conceived during high school were not alleviated when I obtained a Jesuit education at Xavier University in Cincinnati. In fact, two Jesuit mentors reinforced my agnostic tendencies. They taught me to question, if not actually doubt, most religious dogma.

Throughout the majority of my adult life following my return from Vietnam, I've been mostly a-religious. Rarely, if ever, have I gone into a traditional church, Catholic or Protestant. During my recovery, I've probably visited more Buddhist, Hindu temples and Moslem mosques, than I have Christian churches. An exception was the year when I was engaged to my second wife, Debbie. We would occasionally attend her home parish church, where we were married, mostly to please her mother. Another exception was on visits to my hometown of Jackson, MS, when I would sometimes accompany my mother to mass at my home parish, again mostly to please her. Other exceptions, of course, include when I would attend weddings, christenings, or funerals of Christian family and friends.

Nevertheless, despite being an agnostic nontheist, I consider myself to be quite spiritual. I have no qualms with living my life in AA recovery in accordance with generic humanistic, ethical and moral principles, which undergird the foundation of AA's 12 Steps, 12 Traditions and 12 Concepts of Service. These principles are common to the wisdom traditions of all peoples across the globe. Here is one listing of these principles: 1) Honesty, 2) Hope, 3) Faith, 4) Courage, 5) Willingness, 6) Humility, 7) Brotherly Love, 8) Discipline, 9) Perseverance, 10) Justice, 11) Spiritual Awareness, & 12) Service

The evolution of my spiritual consciousness as an agnostic nontheist, both before becoming a member of AA and throughout my 45 years of recovery, has been influenced by a number of poets, philosophers and theologians. Herein follow some of the more influential thinkers who have shaped my evolving beliefs:

ee cummings

This 20th century poet was one of my earliest influences. His poetry is iconic, most distinctive in style, characterized by a most eccentric use of grammar and punctuation, if any at all. It portrays the full gamut of human experience from idealistic, romantic love to raging, cynical despair. In Chapter 3, I described my experience with *an evening with ee cummings,* a theatrical presentation using only his published words. Though he often raged in despair, he ultimately came to accept life as being wonderfully worth it. Here is the closing speech from *an evening with ee cummings:*

> *you shall above all things be glad and young*
> *For if you're young,whatever life you wear*

it will become you; and if you are glad
whatever's living will yourself become.

I'd rather learn from one bird how to sing
than teach ten thousand stars how not to dance

As an old man today, over fifty years later, this passage still moves me to tears of gratitude. Other favorite poets include Allen Ginsberg, Jack Kerouac and Gary Snyder. In 1997, shortly after Allen Ginsberg died on April 5th, I organized and facilitated a memorial service for him in Huntington, NY, attended by many members of the Long Island poetry community.

Pierre Teilhard De Chardin

Another early influence were the writings of this Jesuit paleontologist who was involved in the discovery of the Peking Man, a protohuman ancestor of homo sapiens. De Chardin had radical theories about evolution for which he was censored by the Catholic Church while he was alive. He posited that humankind, along with the rest of the universe, is in a perpetual process of ever-evolving change over eons of time into ever higher realms of existence, both in material complexity and consciousness. He termed the ultimate result "the Omega Point," a state of divine unification of all being.

A central concept he derived in the 1930s was the concept of the noosphere, a sphere of thought that envelops the earth. He described it as "a living tissue of consciousness," which encloses the earth and grows ever more dense over time. Could he have imagined what we've come to know during the last 30 or so years as the Internet, which with each passing year becomes more complex, more dense, more deeply interconnected? A favorite quote of his that I became familiar with in early recovery is "We are not human beings having a spiritual experience. We are spiritual beings having a human experience."

Eric Butterworth

Eric Butterworth was the minister of the Unity Center of New York City for the last third of the 20th Century. As described in Chapter 11, I experienced just as astonishing a "white light" experience the first time I meditated at Unity, as Bill W. writes about happened to him at Towns Hospital.

During the 1970s, a large number of folks in 12-step recovery programs, several hundred at least, would attend his services every Sunday morning at Lincoln Center. Many of us would also attend his weekend retreats, one of which I described in Chapter 11 up in Greenwich, CT, and his week long retreats every summer at Cedar Crest College in Allentown, PA. For several years I was a small group leader at these retreats, as well as being employed transcribing Eric's weekly radio broadcasts.

Unity is part of the New Thought reform movement, which evolved throughout the US in the latter part of of the 19th Century in opposition to the proselytizing literal interpretation of biblical scriptures by evangelical Christianity. While being neither monolithic nor doctrinaire, New Thought stresses that there is an infinite intelligence throughout the whole of the Kosmos. Eric's primary message was one of unconditional love of self and for all of humanity. He also emphasized that the answers to problems and challenges one encounters throughout life can only be solved by discovering the hidden power that resides within each human being to evolve towards wholeness.

His teaching about Jesus was that he is one of many enlightened beings who manifest on earth as wayshowers to teach humans how to manifest the spark of divinity inherent within each person. Through Eric and Unity, I became acquainted with the spiritual paths of both Buddhism and Hinduism, including these two ubiquitous greetings: "Namaste," the divinity in me salutes the divinity in you, and "Tat Twam Asi," Thou art that.

Matthew Fox

During the 1980s, I became captivated by the New Age thought of this excommunicated Dominican priest, who asserts that the Christian doctrine of Original Sin is a mistranslation of the middle eastern Aramaic language of the Bible. Instead of Original Sin, Fox successfully demonstrated that the Aramaic phrase actually means Original Blessing. This radically upends the concept that as flawed human beings we can only be exempted from everlasting damnation through being baptized by the blood of Christ and absolved of any sin by the ministrations of a priest. Fox also strongly advocated for women to be an integral part of the Catholic liturgy. He was initially banned and eventually excommunicated by Mother Church.

Fox proposes, as an alternative to Christian orthodoxy, a Creation Spirituality, characterized by a reawakened mysticism whose primary objective is the protection of Mother Earth. He describes it as "a (r)evolutional movement based in the Judeo-Christian tradition but which is supported by leading-edge science, which bears witness for social, environmental and gender justice."

In the spring of 2001, I attended a weekend workshop he led on Creation Spirituality which was most inspirational. It was held in the Millenium Hilton, across from the World Trade Towers. When I was down at ground zero, serving as a Red Cross mental health volunteer, it was most surreal to realize that several months previously I had greatly enjoyed the Creation Spirituality workshop. Those were dark days indeed !~!~!

Thomas Merton

Another modern Catholic theologian and mystic, Thomas Merton, has also had a strong influence on me, primarily due to his avid writing about and work for peace with justice. He virulently opposed the Vietnam War and wrote pacifist screeds against nuclear weaponry, while strongly advocating for social justice during the civil rights movement of the 1960s. The most fascinating book of the several books of his I've read is *Learning to Love*, which is Volume six, 1966-1967, of the collected Journals of Thomas Merton.

He relates that during the holiday season of 1965, he participated in a retreat during which he implored the Virgin Mary to teach him how to love. The following March in a Louisville hospital for back surgery, he fell instantly and madly, head-over-heals in romantic love with a 19-year old student nurse by the name of Margie Smith. *Learning to Love* describes the torrid, secret affair they had for over a year until Merton breaks off the relationship and decides to return to his celibate life. I find this deliciously ironic.

Merton died of a freak accident In December of 1968, by electrocution from a faulty fan he grabbed as he exited a shower in Thailand, where he was attending an International Conference on Monasticism. The morning he died, he had delivered a talk to the ecumenical gathering of Hindu, Buddhist and Catholic monks entitled, "The Monastic Implications of Marcuse." In this talk he described Marcuse not only as a "very influential Neo-Marxist thinker" but also as a "kind of monastic thinker."

The strange circumstances of his death has spawned a plethora of conspiracy theories ranging from suicide to assassination, either by the CIA, because he was energizing the Catholic Peace Movement against the war in Vietnam and nuclear weaponry, or by ardent Catholics, who were afraid his affair with Margie Smith might bring scandal to the Church. He was also outwardly embracing Buddhist and Hindu philosophy and practices.

I've visited the Abbey of Gethsemane, where he lived most of his life, several times. Every time I visit I sit in reflection by his gravesite. On my first visit in 2002 while traveling about in the Rialta RV, I was able to sit in his hermitage deep within the wooded hills of Kentucky near Bardstown. On subsequent visits, however, it has now been cloistered, not available to the general public, which greatly disappoints me.

Dan Berrigan

Berrigan is another Jesuit priest whose writing and activism for peace with justice has been immensely influential to my thinking. With Thomas Merton and his brother, Philip Berrigan, a Josephite priest, he founded an interfaith coalition against the Vietnam war. Berrigan poured blood on draft records in Baltimore, MD, and achieved notoriety as a member of the Catonsville Nine for burning draft records with homemade napalm. During the 1980s he founded the Plowshares Movement, which took direct action against America's Nuclear weaponry, and spent the rest of his life resisting what he termed American military imperialism.

In 1987, shortly after I was released from the psyche ward that I described in Chapter 14, I participated in a very healing retreat with Fr. Berrigan and Thich Nhat Hanh, the Vietnamese Buddhist monk, who is also a noted activist in the peace with justice movement. I described to them how upsetting it was for me to hear the distinctive whomp-whomp-whomp of Huey helicopters which catapulted me back into intrusive recollections about the war I experienced in Vietnam. They suggested that, instead, I could choose to experience the disturbing sound as being like a meditation bell to remind me to be grateful that I survived. What a totally different concept !~!~!

I was most privileged to be present for a celebration of Dan Berrigan's 80th birthday in Manhattan. There I had a brief conversation with noted author, Kurt Vonnegut, in which I thanked him for his many novels, especially *Hocus Pocus*, whose central character is a former Vietnam veteran platoon leader. I told him that I really identified with his central character, because I had also been a platoon leader in Vietnam. Vonnegut took my hand, looking up at me with sad eyes, and said "I'm so sorry for that, Thomas." This moved me deeply, and I count it today as one of my most cherished memories.

Aldous Huxley & Ken Wilber

Besides writing the bleak, dystopian novel, *Brave New World,* Huxley is most known for *Perennial Philosophy,* his sweeping comparative study of Eastern and Western mysticism. Aldous Huxley and his friend Gerald Heard, an aesthetic mystic, were influential associates of Bill Wilson and introduced him to the use of LSD.

The life work of Ken Wilber has been the development of "Integral Theory," which expands Huxley's work exponentially. Wilber describes Integral as follows:

> *The word integral means comprehensive, inclusive, non-marginalizing, embracing. Integral approaches to any field attempt to be exactly that: to include as many perspectives, styles, and methodologies as possible within a coherent view of the topic. In a certain sense, integral approaches are 'meta-paradigms,' or ways to draw together an already existing number of separate paradigms into an interrelated network of approaches that are mutually enriching.*

I have borrowed his spelling of *Kosmos,* which for the Greeks, as he explains in his 2000 book, *Theory of Everything,* was considered:

> *...the patterned Whole of all existence, including the physical, emotional, mental, and spiritual realms. Ultimate reality was not merely the cosmos, or the physical dimension, but the Kosmos, or the physical and emotional and mental and spiritual dimensions altogether. Not just matter, lifeless and insentient, but the living Totality of matter, body, mind, soul and spirit.*

Frank Schaeffer

The past couple of years I have become an avid fan of Frank Schaeffer, who grew up in a fundamentalist, evangelical Christian commune in Switzerland, the son of a prominent Christian evangelist minister, who with his wife, Frank's mother, operated the commune and retreat center.

As a young man he and his family were instrumental in creating the radically Christian fundamentalist right wing of the Republican party, which brought Ronald Reagan to the presidency in 1980. However by the mid-80s, he had become an "atheist who prays." He describes this transformation most humorously in *Crazy for God: How I Grew Up As*

One Of The Elect, Helped Found The Religious Right, And Lived To Take All (Or Almost All Of It) Back.

Another favorite book of his is *Patience with God: Faith For People Who Don't Like Religion (Or Atheism)*. The first half of this book critiques both New Atheists and Christian Fundamentalists. His most recent book is *Why I am an Atheist Who Believes in God: How to Give Love, Create Beauty and Find Peace*. Caught between the beauty of his grandchildren and grieving the death of his father, he finds himself simultaneously believing and not believing. I deeply identify with this !~!~!

Buddhism and Hinduism

Since early in recovery I've been influenced by the eastern concepts of karma and incarnation. I've especially been drawn to the work of Thich Nhat Hanh, the Vietnamese Buddhist monk, and Pema Chodron, whose books I read as part of my daily spiritual practice for the two years I lived in Sri Lanka. One of the first books I bought and read in early sobriety was *Be Here Now* by Ram Dass. A prolific writer, formerly Dr. Richard Alpert, he was an associate of Dr. Timothy Leary, when they worked with psychedelics together at Harvard in the early 1960s. I've read most of his books and was particularly moved by his 1985 book, *How Can I Help: Stories and Reflections on Service,* in which he described how he was present in devoted service to both his mother and his father as they died.

It was my intention to be present for my father's death, but alas he suddenly died in July of 2001, several months before I was able to close out my life in New York and go on the road in an RV after my house on Long Island sold. For the last several years my mother was alive, even when Jill and I lived in Oregon, at least once every year I travelled to Louisville, KY, to bring my Aunt Mary, Mother's sister, down to visit her in Jackson. I also regularly called her at least once a week. These actions were making a living amends to Mother.

The first gift I bought myself in early recovery was a silver and black onyx Tao sign necklace. The Tao sign is an ancient Chinese symbol depicting a circle divided by an S-shaped line into a dark and a light segment. This represents respectively yin, the passive, negative force (dark), and yang, the active, positive force (light). Each contains a 'seed' of the other. For years I was fearful of losing this necklace, and eventually one day in 2007, as I was walking down 9th Avenue in New York City, I realized that I had lost it. Instead of being devastated, I accepted it as being in accord with Wu-Wei, the natural flow of life as it is. Several weeks later, I found another Tao sign that is even more appropriate for my evolving spiritual beliefs—instead of one "point of light," or seed of the other, there are a thousand shifting points of light in the colored cloisonné within the dark portion.

As another gift to myself, in the summer before I left Oregon to move to Illinois, I had the Tao sign tattooed on the back of my neck. I am, therefore, protected with a shield of yin-yang energy in front of me by the necklace, and a shield of yin-yang energy in back of me by the tattoo …

Native American Spirituality

I have read extensively about Native American spirituality which resonates with the indigenous roots from my Scotch-Norman Celtic heritage. I believe in the sacredness of Mother Earth and sacred energy places such as Stonehenge in England and Sedona in Arizona. To a great degree I am animistic, believing that everything in existence is sacred and imbued with spirit. On my visit to Great Britain in 2004, when I stood at the Scottish Border, I felt my corpuscles within me celebrating that they were once again home!

When I was a participant as a Vietnam Veteran in the Veterans Stand for Standing Rock in protest against the Dakota Access Pipeline during December of 2016, I was most honored to be inducted as a warrior in the Cheyenne River Tribe of the Sioux nation in Eagle Butte, SD, where I joined with them in prayerful protest for a week and plan to return during warmer weather. I have a Native American dreamcatcher in my car with totems from several tribes including an eagle feather from the Pascua Yaqui Tribe in Tucson, and the Red-tail Hawk feather I was given at the induction ceremony at Eagle Butte. I believe they help protect me when I am on my long drive-arounds.

Every morning I sit for a meditation time at the family altar Jill and I have created, which has many talismans from the earth, woods and seas of the many various places we've visited, around the US for Jill, around the world for me — rocks, crystals, sea shells, roots, an M-16 cartridge I found climbing up to the Qui Nhon Cham Towers on my first visit back to Vietnam in 2002, an antique bottle fragment I found in a former calvary fort in the New Mexico desert, statues of Buddha, Kwan Yin, Shiva and Ganesh, Tibetan prayer flags, and so on. All of these talismans are underneath a Bev Doolittle print, "Sacred Circle" depicting an Indian Warrior in the forest on his horse in the middle of a circle of animals, plants, rocks, and water within nature. Here's how Ms. Doolittle describes it:

> *The sacred circle is the circle of life; the delicate thread that unites all living things. Only man knowingly holds the thread. Of all the animals, only he has the intelligence to protect and preserve it. Only he can be the keeper of the sacred circle.*

I've always had an affinity for being in nature and though I've lived much of my life in cities and their suburbs, I've found deep peace while being out in nature. During my younger years it was through long-distance running. In my later years, it has been on daily walks and long distance drive-arounds, where I'm on the open road. I've found both running/walking and long-distance driving to be most contemplative.

Secular AA Literature

I am especially grateful for the growing literature of the secular AA movement during the past number of years. I wrote in Chapter 16 about how important it was to find Roger C.'s *AA Agnostica* in 2012, when Jill and I moved to Oregon. Through his website I was introduced to the wide range of books and authors who write about how we stay sober a day at a time in 12-step programs without belief in god, especially the Christian god as described in the Big Book, the Twelve and Twelve and other AA publications.

Books which have been especially helpful are those published by *AA Agnostica*, which include, *Don't Tell, Do Tell, The Little Book, Common Sense Recovery, Key Players In AA History* and *The Alternative 12 Steps: A Secular Guide to Recovery.* Other books include Marya Hornbacher's *Waiting*, John Lauristsen's *A Freethinker in AA, My Name Is Lilian and I'm an Alcoholic (and an Atheist): How I Got Sober in AA without All the God Stuff, The 12 Step Philosophy of Alcoholics Anonymous: An Interpretation by Steve K.* I eagerly look forward to reading Roger's latest book, *A History of Agnostics in AA.*

There are also a number of books printed in Great Britain including an excellent pamphlet, *"The 'God' Word – Agnostic and Atheist Members in AA"* published by the AA General Service Conference in Great Britain. Another wonderful British book with which I deeply resonated was *Christian Atheist* by Brian Mountford, which describes that though he has no belief in the dogma or concepts of a Christian God, he appreciates the cultural and artistic aspects of Christianity, especially the architectural splendor of Cathedrals with their stain-glass windows and the soaring music.

As an aging adult child of the 1960s, who has lived most of my adult life in or near New York City to include Woodstock and for the past seven years near Portland and Eugene, Oregon, I have retained many of the values of my hippy young adulthood. I have pursued many of the so-called "New Age" paths of spirituality, reading extensively, in addition to the ones enumerated above, such authors as Marianne Williamson, Deepak Chopra, Sam Keen, Frijoi Capra, John C. Lilly, Stan and Christina Grof, Rupert Sheldrake, Noah Levine and many others.

Thus, to conclude, I am mostly a rabidly agnostic nontheist. I believe in no deities conceived by any religious dogma. In my experience, I've observed that dogmatists of every religion, including militant atheists, create the deities and dogmas they worship in their own self-referential images. I'm pretty sure there is no way to definitely prove that there is a deity, but then again I'm equally fairly certain that there is no way one can prove for sure there is not. I guess one could define me as an agnostic atheist.

However I have a deeply spiritual understanding of the world and how I relate to my ever-evolving perception of the always-metamorphosing, ever-changing Kosmos. I sense there is some kind of providence, some kind of evolutionary force that operates throughout the Kosmos for survival, for progress, for expansion of consciousness. I can't know it, I can't prove it, but I can discern it in the ultimate mystery of being. This reminds me of one of my favorite quotes from Albert Einstein, written in 1930 in "The World As I See It":

> *The most beautiful experience we can have is the mysterious. It is the fundamental emotion that stands at the cradle of true art and true science. Whoever does not know it and can no longer wonder, no longer marvel, is as good as dead, and his eyes are dimmed."*

Like Frank Schaeffer, I am an agnostic who prays, sometimes ceaselessly, not because I believe there is some deity somewhere who will intervene and rescue me from whatever predicament I find myself facing, but to calm myself the fuck down !~!~!

One thing I can certainly discern is that I am radically different from the person I was when I attended my first AA meetings in October of 1972. I perceive that this process of change has continued throughout the past 45 years. Therefore, I follow this advice offered by Peter Russell, the British mystic: I pray to the Higher Self, the more enlightened person, into which I am in the process of evolving.

I meditate first thing in the morning, sitting before the family altar in candlelight with incense burning, during which I also read the daily reflection from Joe C.'s *Beyond Belief: Agnostic Musings for 12 Step Life,* and, the reflection from *365 Tao.* I also meditate as the last thing I do before falling asleep. If I wake up in the middle of the night, and can't get back to sleep, I'll put on a long meditation, focusing on listening to the words and deeply breathing. I've experienced that even if I don't fall fast asleep that I still feel alert and refreshed in the morning when I normally get up.

In the mystery of the Kosmos, I sense I still am able to commune with Peter my sponsor and dearly departed relatives and friends such as John Albert. Our physical elements become stardust. As well, I believe our memes become part of the noosphere. In other words, both our elements and our memes get reshuffled and reconstituted into new forms of physical matter and consciousness. Hey, I certainly can't know for sure, but it makes as much sense to me as any other theorem of higher mathematics and/or quantum physics, and certainly more sense than the vast majority of religious beliefs.

Regarding consciousness, I am not one who believes that only we humans possess it. When I observe my cats playing with each other or when my beloved Afghan Hound, Keira, leans into me and begs me with her eyes to pet her, I conclude they are demonstrating consciousness as non-human species. I hold that consciousness exists on a spectrum that is related to evolution throughout all living species. It's reasonable to me that the human species shall continue to evolve into higher states of consciousness as Pierre Teilhard De Chardin proclaims. A current author I'm reading, Yuval Noah Harari, predicts that homo sapiens shall continue to evolve until we are like gods in his provocative book, *Homo Deus: A Brief History of Tomorrow.*

The core of my spirituality occurs through the unfolding experiences of my day-at-a-time recovery in AA from addiction in the company of other alcoholics, primarily at AA meetings, but also when we connect outside of meetings whether face-to-face, on the phone or via the Internet. I derive much satisfaction from being actively involved with AA service work at the group, District and Area levels. The continuing evolution of my spiritual understanding is primarily manifested through the sharing of our stories in AA. These stories and communications recount our uniquely different, but commonly identified, anecdotes of experience, strength and hope. These deeply felt anecdotes often move me to tears of deep gratitude.

I've heard it said that the most perfect prayer is simply, "Thanks !~!~!"

Conclusion

Always the beautiful answer who asks a more beautiful question

ee cummings

So, is it done? Yes, the tome of my life's story is finally finished. It's an endeavor that has been some 20 years in the making. I am satisfied. I feel complete. No matter how it is received or viewed by others, I like it. I feel good about it. To me that's what mostly counts, that I am pleased with it.

A wave of thrilling sensation scurries up and down my chakras, bringing tears of gratitude to my eyes. I deeply smile, as I am reminded of one of my earliest vows to myself during my first year of recovery. See, when drinking, I was one who, especially as a callow youth, literally cried, quietly sobbed, in my beer, by myself, in some across-the-railroad-tracks, shit-kicking bar, alone, sitting in a darkened corner, listening to the oh-so-sad songs of unrequited and forever lost love.

When I was gifted with recovery, I vowed I would match tear for tear, every desperate tear I shed in alcoholic despair with tears of grateful joy that I survived very much despite myself. Remembering this arouses deep gratitude within me for the strange, long life I have been able to experience, the majority of it during the past 45 years, I truly believe, solely because I have been gifted a breath at a time with recovery in AA.

Sitting at my computer in the office space of my new home in Illinois, where most likely I'll spend the rest of my days, I look out the window upon the ancient red water pump in the front yard. A blustery March wind is blowing. The sun is brightly shining on fallow cornfields and leafless forest across the street as white clouds scuttle across a blue sky. I breathe a deep sigh of utter contentment. This is good. I am good. I am All Right. It just doesn't get any better than just this, right here, right now. My heart is filled with overflowing gratitude in wonder for the mere magnificent mystery of simple being !~!~!

I am most gratefully contented to be living the final years of my life with fourth wife, Jill. She takes such good loving care of me, in her childhood home in small town Wenona, Illinois, with our three animal friends, Elsa, Kiera and Savannah. Though I sometime miss the life that I had living for so many years in New York and the life that Jill and I experienced living for seven years in Oregon, I am most grateful to be two-thirds of the way back across the county from where we lived on the west coast. I can readily visit family and friends in Mississippi where I grew up, friends in Toronto and New York, my two daughters, one in Pennsylvania, the other in Maryland with my grandchildren. In fact, tomorrow morning, I do another drive-around to Pennsylvania and Maryland to visit my daughters and grandchildren.

While in Maryland, I'll go down to Washington, DC to march as a supporter of Native Nations Rise Up in Support of Standing Rock March on Washington. I'll march with other water protectors and rally in prayerful protest with them in Lafayette Park across from the White House. I am so privileged to be able to continue to do what so much of my life, especially in recovery, has been about, to nonviolently protest for peace with justice.

I am also most privileged to be an active participant in AA General Service work with secular AA. Our upcoming 3rd biennial conference in Toronto during August of 2018 shall continue the evolution of our growing secular AA movement fully as an integral part of traditional AA. We shall be rocketed into a secular 4th dimension for the evolving good not only of ourselves, but also, I fully believe, of AA as a whole. We shall live in accordance with our code of love, tolerance and inclusivity for all who desire to stop using.

Despite a dysfunctional childhood, surviving two combat zones, alcohol addiction and a slew of other mental health syndromes, I have been enabled, most gratefully, to live most fully a bounteously gratifying, a stupendously content, yea, even verily at times, a deliriously joyous life, as long and strange in many ways as it may have been, as it continues, in fact, to be. Each breath, indeed, has been a gift !~!~!

I most assuredly wish the same for each of you ……

Made in the USA
Columbia, SC
28 August 2017